On the Corps

A co-publication of the U.S. Naval Institute and the Marine Corps Association

On the Corps

USMC Wisdom from the pages of
Leatherneck, Marine Corps Gazette,
and *Proceedings*

Lt. Col. Charles P. Neimeyer, USMC (Ret.)

Editor

NAVAL INSTITUTE PRESS
Annapolis, Maryland

Naval Institute Press
291 Wood Road
Annapolis, MD 21402

Library of Congress Cataloging-in-Publication Data

On the Corps : USMC wisdom from the pages of Leathernecks, Marine Corps gazette, and Proceedings / edited by Lieutenant Colonel Charles Neimeyer, USMC (Ret.).
    p. cm.
  Includes index.
  ISBN 978-1-59114-591-2 (alk. paper)
  1. United States. Marine Corps—History. I. Neimeyer, Charles Patrick, 1954– II. Title: Leatherneck. III. Title: Marine Corps gazette. IV. Title: Proceedings of the United States Naval Institute.
  VE23.O64 2008
  359.9'60973—dc22

                                                                                    2008034604

Printed in the United States of America on acid-free paper ∞

14 13 12 11 10 09 08   9 8 7 6 5 4 3 2
First printing

CONTENTS

INTRODUCTION

This collection of "classic" articles derived solely from the archives of the *Marine Corps Gazette, Leatherneck,* and U.S. Naval Institute *Proceedings* captures the essence of what it means to be a U.S. Marine. As is the case with other anthologies, the purpose of this particular collection is to serve as a ready resource of material that defines the Marine Corps as an institution. Accordingly, the anthology is divided into four mutually supporting and component parts.

Part I focuses on being a Marine. The Marine Corps has been long renowned for its amazing esprit de corps. What are the essential qualities that combine in a person to create a Marine? Can it be defined? How does the Corps establish this set of intangibles and what is the true nature of the Marine Corps as a war-fighting institution?

Part II addresses USMC training, roles, and missions. How does the Corps go about creating Marines? What does the Corps do to ensure that they continue to maintain the highest standards of military excellence for which they are justifiably renowned? How are they organized for combat? What concerns do Marines traditionally have about their role and mission in the national security force structure?

Part III is about leadership and command. Throughout its illustrious history, the Corps has consistently produced very high quality combat leadership. Many of these leaders took the time to provide readers with some timeless advice on what it means to lead America's premier force in both combat and peacetime. Most of the authors in this section focus on preparing for the responsibility of command and provide advice that makes up a general and largely timeless philosophy of leadership.

Part IV describes the view of the Corps on warfare itself. How has warfare changed from the earlier days of a much smaller Marine Corps to that of today? What has remained the same? How does the Corps see itself engaging in warfare likely to be conducted in the future?

Taken together the four parts of this anthology reveal the essential quality of what it means to be a U.S. Marine. Reviewing and studying how the Corps saw itself in the past provides readers with an institutional road map to the present and even a look toward the future. In doing so, we can uncover the existential qualities of today's U.S. Marine Corps and how it sees itself in the larger national security framework that is charged with defending the nation against all enemies.

For readers who wish to delve further into the essential quality of the Marine Corps, Lt. Gen. Victor H. Krulak's book *First to Fight*, initially published by the Naval Institute Press in 1984, remains a timeless classic and even today is required reading for all Marines. Following in his father's footsteps, Lt. Gen. Krulak has penned recently several important articles, particularly one about the way the Corps will organize for future war for *Marines Magazine* in January 1999 when he was USMC commandant. Titled, "The Strategic Corporal: Leadership in the Three Block War," Krulak's article pointed to theories that were to prove prescient for current USMC operations in Iraq and Afghanistan. Another "must read" about USMC roles and missions is Lt. Col. Thomas C. Linn and Lt. Col. Charles P. Neimeyer's "Once and Future Marines." Published by *Joint Forces Quarterly*, in their Autumn/Winter 1994–95 edition, and written at the height of another attempt, this time by the U.S. Army during the mid-1990s roles and missions debate, to limit the USMC solely to amphibious operations, the authors argued that the true nature of the Marine Corps has always been expeditionary in nature and remains ideally suited and organized to respond to "varied and far-flung crises."

I would like to thank the editors of the *Marine Corps Gazette*, *Leatherneck*, and U.S. Naval Institute *Proceedings* for their cooperation and permission to reproduce these critical articles for this important anthology. Their continued and strong support of the Navy/Marine Corps team has further enhanced the illustrious combat histories of both services.

PART I

On Being a Marine

This section begins with an excellent summation by a contemporary author who successfully captures the innate quality of what makes a U.S. Marine. Lieutenant Colonel Alvarez asks whether Marines are "special" or a breed apart. If so, what is it that makes them so? Clearly, he believes that the Marine Corps style of leadership is what has traditionally done the trick for them.

This article is followed by two seminal works on the concepts of esprit and morale by Maj. Gen. John A. Lejeune and Brig. Gen. Robert H. Williams.

Next is an article by Lt. Cmdr. E. W. Broadbent, U.S. Navy, who provides a blue water point of view for why the nation needs a Marine Corps. Broadbent focuses on the requirement for the Marine Corps to maintain an expeditionary force in readiness supported by the fleet and on the integral nature of the Marine Corps to the Navy. Moreover, he goes to great lengths to demonstrate why the Marine Corps does not constitute a second land army. Broadbent believes that the Marine Corps could not operate for long without support from the Navy, and therefore the two remain necessary and co-equal brothers in arms during the course of landing force operations.

Broadbent is followed by Maj. Gen. John H. Russell. Here General Russell takes Broadbent's argument for an amphibious force in readiness one step further and argues strongly for a Marine Corps large enough to constitute a realistic striking arm of the fleet. He notes that, unlike the European powers, the United States largely lacks worldwide advanced bases, and a Fleet Marine Force is necessary to assist in forward naval operations. Russell successfully argues that "a fleet without [forward] bases is, axiomatically, a fleet limited to its home ports."

A brief but excellent article by Capt. John W. Thomason Jr. explains why the Marines were so successful during World War I. Perhaps no author better captures the spirit and essence of the "old Corps" than Thomason. While not denigrating the combat success of U.S. Army troops, Thomason is able to illustrate for readers the essential fighting quality of the Marine brigade in France, 1917–18.

Donald L. Dickson's article nicely complements that of Thomason, and he deftly captures the "disdain" that old Corps Marines usually held for newer enlistees. But Dickson goes a step further by describing how the character and quality of Marine recruits has changed over the years.

The Spirit of Marines

Lt. Col. Richard S. Alvarez, USMC

Marine Corps Gazette
February 1987

Shortly after I joined the Command and Staff College faculty in 1994, Headquarters Marine Corps asked for a summation of the College's Leadership Program. Apparently, an executive in industry was convinced that the Marine Corps was a champion at developing leaders and had asked the Commandant for some ideas that he could apply within the corporate world.

Marines, themselves, believe they have a special quality that puts them a cut above the ordinary, an edge that makes the difference in any mission undertaken. Yet we see evidence to the contrary when we consider specific individuals in leadership roles. We don't have to look far to conclude that not all our leaders are superior.

This paradox elicits a string of questions. Do we really have something special? If we do, what is it? Where does it come from? How do we perpetuate it? Could we lose it? After pondering the questions, and with the benefit of the perspective gained as head of the Leadership Program, I can postulate some answers.

Do we really have something special?

For an answer, I reviewed professional material from the business world and the Armed Forces. I considered the thoughts of field grade officers who have participated in the leadership seminars that were part of the college curriculum and studied critically their final leadership papers. (This last paper is each officer's "Concept of Command" and represents his or her leadership style and philosophy as an "officer of Marines.") Since the student body represents a cross section of successful midcareer field grade leaders from the Corps, I sought a common thread that would be germane. Unfortunately, no common thread appeared. I really uncovered nothing new from the students, business readings, or graduate-level texts on management and leadership.

The leadership styles and philosophies presented by the Command and Staff College students fell into four distinct categories. The first postulated that a good leader should be an expert at organizing, structuring, and controlling the organization through quick decisive actions; mission was the bottom line and there was little room for anyone who could not carry his or her fair share of the load. The second category centered around being competent, knowledgeable, and well read in every aspect of the organization or task; the proponents of the competent leader left little room for anyone deficient in knowledge. In the third category were the "people people." These officers stressed the need to take care of their people and to know all their needs and problems; if you did this your Marines would follow you anywhere. The last group favored a more charismatic style of leadership. This group could not care less about structure and control or paperwork; rather it emphasized the need to get out of the office, move around the organization, and find out what's going on in the pits. This category leaves the paperwork and the management chores to the staff. Although each student selected one of the four distinct areas to focus on as being most critical to leadership success, most students listed the other three as secondary attributes a good leader should also develop. They all agreed, however, that Marine Corps leaders should take risks—but that "risky" is getting "riskier" in today's zero defects Corps. Most agreed that integrity was important. But all had firsthand stories of present and past senior officers whose behavior or actions were not good examples of integrity.

My conclusion was that, depending upon the definition of success, anyone can pick any of the four styles of leadership as most important; however, successful leaders from the other three areas can be found also. In fact, the evidence showed that some were not truly proficient in any of these areas. In spite of a weakness in any or all of these four areas, leaders in the Corps, be they nasty, dumb, nice, or fidgety, do succeed. There was widespread agreement that Marine Corps leadership is good, "the best there is!"

So what makes Marine Corps leadership different?

General Robert H. Barrow, in his keynote address on leadership to the College in 1985, touched on these first two questions when he said, "One of the greatest dangers to the Corps is the leader who would destroy the spirit of our young Marines."

It seems to me that this is it. The *spirit* of the Marines we lead is the difference in Marine leadership. Marines don't create great leaders, they create great followers. As leaders we are no better or worse than those of any other organization. It is our followership and our spirit as Marines that makes the difference.

So, where does this spirit come from?

In my judgment, Marine spirit comes from our total commitment to being Marines. Our "always being" is that of always being Marines. Whether working, shopping, teaching Sunday School, or playing rugby, we do so as Marines. Most organizations are made up of people who are being engineers, welders, secretaries, lawyers, etc., while they are at work. When they are not at work their role shifts to being something else. A Marine may shift roles, but he or she never stops being a Marine. Leaders in business could rule their segment of industry if they could get the employees to be *their* company. Perhaps, only as Americans is there a greater sense of "always being" in spite of the role one is acting. "Once a Marine always a Marine" is more than a cliché. Any former Marine will tell you that the spirit of being a Marine lives forever. I am reminded of the story Maj. Gen. Robert E. Haebel used to tell about the bum who ran across a street in Cleveland once to greet him and tell of his life's greatest experience—being a Marine. During the course of the conversation, it became apparent that this individual was still a Marine in spirit; he would always be a Marine.

How do we perpetuate this difference?

Accomplishing this is a continuing challenge. Does it start in boot camp and Officer Candidate School (OCS)? Or is it the spirit passed down by those who served before us? I believe it is passed on in boot camp and OCS but it also comes from every Marine who went before us. Martin Russ, in his book *Line of Departure*, may have touched upon it when he said about Marines at Tarawa:

> It was the boot-camp training these volunteers endured at Parris Island that established the foundation of this proud military attitude. For eight to ten weeks the individual volunteer (boot) was hermetically sealed in a hostile environment, every moment calculated to prepare him to function smoothly on the edge of an abyss, subject to such harassment and confusion—very much like combat itself—that it spawned in his homesick heart a desperate yearning for order, and finally a love for that order and a clear understanding that in its symmetry lay his safety and survival.

In his address to the Army General Staff College on January 18, 1921, Maj. Gen. John A. Lejeune said:

> To be able to create and maintain this living thing which we call "esprit" in the hearts of his troops is to be a great leader. Whether he be a platoon, a company, battalion, regimental, division or army commander, the subject is worthy of his careful attention, and no officer should rest satisfied until he feels that he possesses that greatest of all assets—the ability to play upon the emotions of his men in such a manner as to produce that most wonderful of all harmonies—the music of the human heart attuned to great deeds and great achievements.

Every Marine feels a surge of excitement as the spirit of past Marines is renewed during General Lejeune's birthday message every November 10, at every boot camp or OCS graduation, and every time he stands at attention for the "Marines' Hymn."

In the text *Management* by Koontz, O'Donnell, and Weihrich, the definition of leadership is:

The art or process of influencing people so that they will strive willingly toward the achievement of group goals. The function of leadership is to . . . persuade all subordinates . . . to contribute willingly to organization goals in accordance with their maximum capability, zeal, and confidence.

Truly, leaders of Marines start out with a great advantage before they even start the process of learning to lead. The advantage is the already present followership of their Marines. I believe that great leaders, such as General Barrow, have a clear understanding of this point and use it as the basis of their leadership style. It is this distinction that allows them to bring out strengths in subordinates in a way that many of us fail to achieve.

Could we lose it?

This question is more complex than the others. Clearly, the issue of officer selection, screening, and training is crucial in Marine leaders. Earlier, I pointed out that there were four different leadership styles preferred by the students at Command and Staff College. A conviction that one of these styles is bad leads to the destructive kind of effect on subordinates that General Barrow alluded to in his address. We continually read articles that call for more organization, more structure, or more guidance. Some call for more competent leadership or for Marines more knowledgeable in their field. Others call for more concern for people and freedom to make mistakes. Still another group bids for more awareness of what our Marines are doing. In essence, the destructive approach would be to change everyone in the organization to conform to one style and to root out all contrary styles.

To state my position positively, we should not call for more organization, more structure or control, more knowledge or competence, more concern for people, or spending more time out of the office to make us better leaders, or more of anything. Rather, we should recognize and maximize file strengths in the individual Marine, just as we should recognize and minimize the individual weaknesses in ourselves.

Any of the four styles when carried to the extreme can be destructive. Most leaders have a preference or are stronger in one area, but they must recognize those stronger in the other areas and utilize their different leadership styles to strengthen their unit. It is logical that combining the styles will make the unit strong in all areas and will allow for the freedom to take risks and to make mistakes that is absent in the contemporary environment. The destructive leader punishes his subordinates who are different because he perceives them as being "weak" in the style or traits that he considers most important. Styles and traits do not measure performance or ability. Koontz, O'Donnell, and Weihrich again state that although theories on leadership differ there are three agreed upon ingredients in leadership skill: (1) the ability to comprehend that human beings have different motivating forces at varying times and in different situations; (2) the ability to inspire; (3) the ability to act in a way that will develop a climate for responding to and arousing motivations. In his 1921 address, Gen. Lejeune also said:

> The study of leadership involves, therefore, first of all a study of human nature. One must put himself in the place of those whom he would lead; he must have a full understanding of their thoughts, their attitudes, their emotions, their aspirations, and their ideals; and he must embody in his own character the virtues which he would instill into the hearts of his followers. True esprit de corps is founded on the great military virtues such as unselfishness, self-control, energy, honor, and courage.

Yes, I have concluded that our Marine Corps leadership is, indeed, special. But the key to our unique leadership is in our followership and not in any individual style. We must accept, develop, and use different styles and strengths in our subordinates, and in our superiors as well, if we are to enjoy the kind of leadership that has always given us the edge. The Marine spirit germinates, matures, and thrives under varied styles and qualities of leadership. We perpetuate our uniqueness by doing the things we have always done well—nourishing the spirit and pride of our young Marines and avoiding the destructive environment in which we are afraid to take risks or to make mistakes. Finally, so long as we all have intense pride in "always being" Marines we will not lose our special edge.

A Legacy of Esprit and Leadership

Maj. Gen. John A. Lejeune

Marine Corps Gazette
July 1979

"Combat leader, scholar, thinker, educator, innovator—all these describe the man who became the thirteenth Commandant of the Marine Corps and served as such for nine years during the 1920s." With these words Gen. Lemuel C. Shepherd Jr., 20th Commandant, describes Maj. Gen John A. Lejeune in the preface to the new edition of **Reminiscenses of a Marine**, *Lejeune's memoirs, republished this month by the Marine Corps Association.*

Over the years John A. Lejeune has become almost a legend in the Marine Corps. "Besides the many 'firsts' of his distinguished thirty-nine year career," General Shepherd goes on to say, "Lejeune can perhaps best be described as the man who charted the course of the Corps in the 20th century." And indeed he did, when he directed a study of amphibious warfare at Marine Corps Schools, Quantico from which the Corps' modern amphibious doctrine evolved. But above all else General Lejeune's legacy comes down strongest for his model leadership. He set forth the "teach-pupil" approach in the relationship between officer and enlisted which still provides the hallmark for Marine Corps leadership.

On January 18, 1921 he spoke to the Army General Staff College (forerunner of the Army War College), Washington, D.C., about esprit and leadership. He found the two inseparable. His message is timeless and proves that in leading men, leadership doesn't change much, only men do. On the 59th anniversary of General Lejeune's appointment as Commandant of the Marine Corps, we publish his talk on leadership as he gave it fifty-eight years ago:

When General Smith wrote to me and asked me to come down to the General Staff College and make a talk on the subject of esprit and leadership, I was very loathe to accept. In the first place, I had been at the school here for fourteen months and I felt like a fleet officer going back to the Naval Academy, getting up on the platform, and talking to the staff and students of the school. In the second place, I have been very busy. I could see ahead that I would be busy with that kind of work, which is very distracting; there are so many questions coming up all the time that it is very hard to concentrate on any one subject. In the third place, I did not think, and I do not think now, that I have any very important message, which would be of great value to the persons who were going to hear it. However, I wrote out a talk. Ordinarily I talk without notes, but I put them down because I might get a case of buck fever.

Esprit de corps and morale are kindred subjects; in fact, some writers consider them as synonymous. This, however, is not the case, as esprit de corps is only one of the factors which goes to constitute morale.

Morale is three-fold—physical, mental or professional, and spiritual. The physical condition of troops has a great influence on their morale. Men whose bodies are untrained physically, who are soft from leading sedentary lives, are unable to stand the strain and stress of long marches and active campaigning. Their morale is rapidly lowered, and they soon become demoralized.

The effect of physical training is exemplified in the case of Stonewall Jackson's division. In the fall campaign of '62, they made such long marches with so few stragglers that they were called the "Foot Cavalry." General Dick Taylor, who commanded one of the brigades, writes very interestingly in his book entitled *Destruction and Reconstruction*, telling how he trained his brigade to march. He said in '61 Jackson's division marched very poorly. It was composed largely of men who were brought up in the country and who were accustomed to ride on horseback, or were city men who were accustomed to riding in carriages. Taylor took his brigade and practiced it in marching during the winter of '61 and '62, so in the spring of '63 his brigade marched so well that it was adopted by Jackson as an example for the whole division. The whole division was practiced in marching with the wonderful results that history tells us about. The morale of that division as we know was very high; perhaps the physical condition of the men had a great effect on it.

Similarly, troops whose professional or military training has been neglected, and who are unskilled in the profession of arms, finding themselves unable to cope on equal terms with a highly trained enemy force of equal numbers, have their morale lowered, and it becomes increasingly difficult to obtain results with such troops until and unless they shall have received the careful training and instruction which all troops should have before being thrown into battle.

There are many instances in history of the failure of untrained troops. They are particularly liable to panic. I think in our own history the most notable example is the Battle of Bull Run, where the Union Army became panic-stricken in the afternoon of the battle and broke and fled to Washington. General Grant tells us in his memoirs of a regiment in Illinois, which was badly officered. Reports came into the governor's office of the depredations of the troops. They seem to have committed atrocities all around southern Illinois, murders, robberies, drunkenness, everything of that kind. The governor turned to General Grant, then Captain Grant, and said, "What are we going to do?" Grant said, "Give me command of the regiment and I can train them." He was appointed colonel and took command of this regiment, instructed the officers, trained the men, worked them about eight hours a day, and in a few months it was the best regiment of the Illinois troops.

Esprit de corps is the third factor in morale, affecting, as it does, the spirit of the troops. Like everything pertaining to the spirit, it is intangible, imponderable, and invisible. Esprit itself cannot be perceived by any of the five senses, but nevertheless, every leader of men knows that it does exist and that it is the most potent of the forces, which is necessary to utilize in order to achieve victory.

Napoleon has said that, of all the elements that go to make up battle efficiency, morale constitutes 75 percent, or that morale is to the material as three to one. Marshal Foch, I have read, has increased the value of morale over the material to four to one.

When we consider the meaning of these statements, we are at first amazed to find that these great masters of the art of war have apparently gone on record as believing that the element of morale in any organization or army is three of four times greater than the combination of all the material factors, such as the weapons of the infantry, artillery, and cavalry, and, in the case of Marshal Foch, of the air service as well. It is beyond the power of the average man's comprehension to fully visualize this. This version of their statements is, of course, an exaggeration, in that unarmed troops, no matter how high their spirit, could not overcome troops fully armed and equipped with modern weapons, unless they were absolutely lacking in morale, which is practically inconceivable, as even the most inferior troops have some spark of martial spirit and are not altogether cowards.

What I think was intended to be conveyed by the statement of Napoleon was, that an army with high morale, and necessarily high spirit, could defeat an army of low morale, and necessarily low spirit, which was three times as strong in numbers. A study of history shows that this has happened over and over again. In fact, small forces have defeated armies much greater than three times their size. The battles of the Greeks with the Asiatic armies alone are sufficient to establish the truth of this statement. For instance, Alexander's conquest of Asia; Xenophon's successful retreat with 10,000 men through the heart of Asia Minor although surrounded by hundreds of thousands of the enemy; the battles of Marathon, Thermopalae, and many others.

The Roman armies also overcame forces many times greater than they in numbers through their superiority in morale. A handful of Roman citizens ruled the world until the Roman Empire broke down through the loss of morale on the part of its people, when it then became an easy prey to the hordes of barbarians who had continually pressed against its outer circumference for centuries.

Napoleon verified the truth of his belief by winning many battles with forces inferior in numbers to those of his opponents.

If it be accepted then as true that the esprit de corps of any body of troops is of such tremendous value, evidently it is a most important subject for a military officer to study. To be able to create and maintain this living thing which we call "esprit" in the hearts of his troops is to be a great leader. Whether he be a platoon, a company, battalion, regimental, division, or army commander, the subject is worthy of his careful attention, and no officer should rest satisfied until he feels that he possesses that greatest of all assets—the ability to play upon the emotions of his men in such a manner as to produce that most wonderful of all harmonies—the music of the human heart attuned to great deeds and great achievements.

To be practical, then, how can we produce and cultivate morale, and particularly that important element of morale—esprit—in our troops? The physical and mental, or professional, phases of morale are well known to all of us. To acquire them it is simply a matter of applying practically and intelligently the rules laid down for physical training and military instruction. No proper excuse can be made for failure on the part of officers to bring their troops to the very finest physical condition and to so instruct them as to make them as skillful as the best in the profession of arms. These things are the manifest duty of every officer, including the subaltern, and any officer who fails in the performance of his duty in these respects is unworthy to hold a commission. They are the very "ABC" of his profession.

The third factor—the spirit—is a more or less unknown field to all of us and a field, which it is very difficult for us to comprehend by the exercise of our mental faculties. Logic and reasoning play but a small part of it. Education assists but little. It is a matter of dealing with the emotions, the spirit, the souls of the troops. A man successful in this realm is a great leader, and the qualities necessary to make him successful are known as the qualities of leadership. How, then, shall we inculcate and cultivate these qualities and become creators of esprit and, therefore, successful leaders of men?

Perhaps we can learn more on this subject, as on all military subjects, by a study of history than by any other method. By consulting history, let us determine who were some of the great leaders and then ascertain, if possible, the methods used by them.

All of us are familiar with the great Hebrew leader called Moses. All of us know, in a general way, that he reorganized his people and gave them a system of government, a body of laws, and a religion, but I do not believe that the average person quite comprehends the tremendous power of his leadership and the causes of his success.

Let us recall to our minds the old Bible story describing the history of the Jews in Egypt, their wanderings in the desert, and their entry into the Promised Land. These people, after several centuries devoted to carrying out the decree of Heaven to be fruitful and multiply, had become a numerous people, so numerous, in fact, as to make their masters, the Egyptians, fear that they might rise and overthrow them. In consequence, the ruler of the Egyptians enslaved them. He forced them to live in crowded ghettos, deprived them of the use of weapons, compelled them to do treadmill work, make bricks without straw, and did everything else in his power to abuse them physically, mentally, morally, and spiritually. In spite of this, the ruler of the Egyptians still feared these people, and in order to prevent their rapid increase in numbers, he issued an edict that the first-born male of each family must be slain at birth. The mother of Moses, in order to save his life, hid him in the bulrushes, and he was found and adopted by the daughter of Pharaoh. He was given the high degree of physical and mental training reserved for the ruling classes of Egypt.

Moses, upon attaining manhood, brooded over the condition of his people, and finally left the court of Egypt and went out into the desert, where he spent several years preparing himself for the great mission, which he had personally assumed—that of freeing his people and leading them into Palestine. During this time, he had opportunity to study the lore of the desert, to train himself in the profession of arms, and to sanctify his spirit to the unselfish service of his people and of his God.

This great leader, upon his return to Egypt, finally, after many vicissitudes, secured the permission of Pharaoh to remove the Hebrews and their belongings from Egypt, and actually succeeded in doing so. We know, at the present time, that the march from Egypt to Palestine is one of only a few weeks, although the Bible tells us that the Israelites were lost in the wilderness and wandered about, apparently in an aimless manner, for forty years.

It is inconceivable that Moses could have allowed this to be done without purpose. He had lived in the desert for several years; he knew where guides could be found; and he knew the routes across the desert himself. A careful study of the Biblical account shows clearly that the wanderings of the Israelites in the desert were carefully planned by Moses himself, and that he took advantage of this opportunity and of the time to build up the morale of his people. These poor and feeble ghetto dwellers either died from exposure or became hardy by their continued wanderings, their open-air life, and by the very difficulties, which they had to surmount. They were compelled to learn the use of weapons and the lore of the desert in order to live. Moses taught them how to get food by the chase, how to find water springs, and how to utilize the fruits of the ground, which they found from time to time. All of these things were so marvelous to them that they were called miracles.

Moses combined with this perfection of the physical instruction and training, the cultivation of the spirit of his people. He did everything in his power to cause them to lead virtuous and clean lives; he gave them the Ten Commandments, under circumstances which powerfully impressed the imagination of the ignorant Israelites, and these Commandments have come down to us unchanged and still constitute guides in the lives of all civilized people. He drew up and enforced a body of wise and salutary laws. He organized them by tribes into twelve fighting units. He insisted upon their adoption of the worship of the only true God.

Finally, after they had lived for forty years in the wilderness, during which time every man, woman, and child who had left Egypt—with the exception of Moses, the civil ruler, and Joshua, the military leader—had died, Moses was able to look upon his people and see, in place of the weak and feeble race he had led from Egypt, a warlike host of 600,000, every member of which had been born, raised, and developed in the desert, who were inured to hardship, were vigorous physically and alert mentally, trained in the use of warlike weapons, organized into a fighting force, filled with a religious enthusiasm that amounted to controlled fanaticism, and determined to re-conquer the land which they had been constantly taught had been promised their forefather Abraham by God himself. Moses and Joshua therefore concluded that the time to enter Palestine had come. Moses himself, having completed his work, turned over the control of this warlike host to Joshua, and climbing to the top of a mountain, saw the Promised Land in the distance and was gathered to his Fathers.

Joshua led the troops into the Promised Land, easily overran the country, conquered and destroyed the tribes occupying it, and his people took it for their own.

This constitutes, I believe, the greatest example in history of the upbuilding of the morale of a whole people, and the changing of a race of slaves into a nation of mighty warriors.

There are other similar examples in history, although not quite so striking. Hannibal after the First Punic War prepared himself and the Carthaginians, a commercial tradespeople, for the great war with Rome, which he saw could not be avoided. The history of the early years of the Second Punic War tells us of his marvelous success. Cromwell led a religious rebellion against the king, carrying the Puritans to victory. George Washington for eight years led the revolutionary armies of our own country and kept up the spirit of his faltering compatriots. Napoleon seized the opportunity of a regenerated France, whose people were fired with an enthusiasm for liberty and freedom, to lead her armies into the path of military glory and conquest. Finally, in World War I we have the example of our own country—a peaceful nation—suddenly becoming filled with military ardor and the fighting spirit.

In nearly all of these great historical examples, we find a great leader who, in his own character, was the incarnation of the aspirations of his people and who, in his turn, built up their morale and esprit and led them to their goal.

Human nature is much the same as it has always been, although it has evolved with its environment, and the first essential of a successful military leader is to be able to understand and comprehend the emotions and the spirit, which lives in the hearts and souls of the men he commands.

The study of leadership involves, therefore, first of all a study of human nature. One must put himself in the place of those whom he would lead; he must have a full understanding of their thoughts, their attitude, their emotions, their aspirations, and their ideals; and he must embody in his own character the virtues which he would instill into the hearts of his followers. True esprit de corps is founded on the great military virtues such as unselfishness, self control, energy, honor, and courage.

In time of peace, the cultivation of esprit is much more difficult than in time of war. The men have no great mission before them, and it is hard to convince them that it is necessary to train arduously and to prepare themselves for an eventuality which does not appear to be imminent. Careful instruction in the history and traditions of their organization is very helpful in peace times, and the stirring up of a spirit of competition between organizations is of the utmost importance.

The United States Marine Corps has always been noted for its esprit de corps. This has been largely due to the fact that it has always been in competition with some other arm of the service. It habitually serves side by side with the Navy, and every officer who is worth his salt feels impelled to have his detachment, company, or other organization, win out in every competition, whether it be baseball, football, or other athletic activities, target practice, drills, discipline, appearance, conduct, military etiquette, or any of the other many things which go to make for efficiency. This competitive spirit is constantly drilled into the men, and as a result, every good Marine is ever on the qui vive to find some way to "put it over" the Navy. The same spirit exists when the Marines are detached for service with the Army, and an appeal to it always receives a response. The esprit of the Marines is that of the Corps, and while there is always a regimental and company esprit, the esprit of the Corps predominates.

In peacetimes, too, creature comforts have a great effect in keeping up the morale of the men. The officers must see to it that the men are properly housed, clothed, and fed and that their time is taken up in useful and interesting instruction and entertainment. Idleness is the curse of the military life, but any treadmill instruction is a poor substitute. Officers must use ingenuity and initiative and must have their own minds trained and developed so that they can properly train their men. Discipline, in its true sense, should never be neglected. The men should be made to realize its great importance, but in enforcing it, officers should never be harsh or arrogant in their dealings with their men, but always kind, humane, and just.

In time of war, the leader must keep in touch with the current of thought of his men. He must find out what their grievances are, if any, and not only endeavor to correct the faulty conditions, but also to eradicate any feeling of discontent from their minds. He should mingle freely with his men and let them understand that he takes a personal interest in the welfare of every one of them. It is not necessary for him to isolate himself in order to retain their respect. On the contrary, he should go among them frequently, so that every man in his organization may know him and feel that he knows them. This should be especially the case before battle.

He should watch carefully the training and instruction of the troops, and let them see that he is determined that they shall be fully prepared for battle. And if there be no liability of the information reaching the enemy, he should take his entire organization into his confidence and inform them of the great events that are taking place in other theatres of operations, the part being played by other units, and by their allies, if any; and give them full information on the eve of battle as to the plan of operations and the part to be played by each unit of the organization. Of course, that depends entirely on whether or not the information can be kept from the enemy, if you are in reserve position, for instance.

It is especially advisable, whenever it can be done, for the commander to assemble his troops by battalions and address them, telling them of the great traditions and history of their organization and appealing to their patriotism and their esprit de corps. No stone should be left unturned to fill their hearts and minds with a determination to conquer, no matter what difficulties are to be overcome, and what losses they may be called on to suffer. The commander himself should be the symbol of the fighting spirit, which he endeavors to foster and should show in himself a good example of patriotism, honor, and courage.

The first words of the Articles of Government of the Navy, which correspond to the Articles of War, require that the commander of every vessel should show in himself an example of virtue, honor, patriotism, and subordination. That is the preamble for the Articles of Government of the Navy.

In the larger units, it is frequently impossible for the commander to address all of the men or to come in personal contact with them. In this case, battle orders should be issued. These orders should be based on a careful study of the problems involved and an intimate knowledge of the thoughts of his men. Following the battle, it is well, too, to issue an order recounting the exploits of the troops and telling them of the effects of their efforts. At this time the men are exhausted in mind and body, and even though they may have been victorious, they are depressed in spirit on account of the many losses they have suffered—their comrades have been killed and wounded, they have witnessed many terrible scenes,—and every effort should be made to cheer and raise their spirits. Praise and commendation should be given freely. Decorations should be promptly awarded and delivered immediately after withdrawal from the front lines. Addresses to organizations that have distinguished themselves should be made. Replacements should be furnished promptly, if practicable, and the thoughts of the men immediately turned to building up their shattered organizations and preparing again to strike the enemy. Skulkers and cowards should be promptly and publicly punished so that all may see the great gulf which separates them from the gallant men who have served faithfully and courageously.

One is just as important as the other. The way it appealed to me overseas is that there were three classes of men. The first class, [were] the gallant, courageous fellows who did not require any urging or any leadership practically, but who from a sense of duty, loyalty, and patriotism would stay up in the front lines and fight until all hell froze over. And the third class, [were] the skulkers, the white-livered fellows whom you could not expect anything of at all. Then there was a great middle class who could be swayed either way, and that was the class you had to deal with. If the services of the men who fought bravely were not promptly and properly recognized on the one hand, and if the skulkers and cowards were not punished on the other, the sentiment might grow that it was just as well to skulk. You got nothing for doing your duty and you got nothing for not doing your duty. The two go hand in hand, and punishments should be prompt and merciless to a real coward. On the other hand, praise, commendation, and rewards should be freely given and promptly given. The French, I think, understood the psychology of their people from the way they lined up their troops and decorated them immediately after they came out of the fight.

Finally, the most vital thing is to make the men feel that they are invincible, that no power can defeat them, and that the success of their country's cause depends on the victory of their organization.

I mentioned in reading this about informing the men beforehand what they were going to do. That policy was exemplified before the 2nd Division went into the battle of the Meuse-Argonne. We moved up in the reserve of the Fifth Corps. We had the general officers and the chief of staff, who was Colonel Ray, at several conferences at Fifth Corps headquarters, in which General Summerall explained in the greatest detail just what each division of the corps and the whole army was to do on November 1st. I took this back to division headquarters and had the senior officers of the division together, and Colonel Ray and myself explained everything to them. We were then in reserve with no opportunity for information to seep through the lines. It was directed that every officer and every man in the division be informed of the part we were going to play and what the object of the battle was, and what would be accomplished if victory was achieved. A map was drawn and given to every platoon, and each platoon leader had his men up and instructed every one down to and including the privates of just what his platoon was going to do in the battle. There was plenty of time and opportunity to have it all worked out in advance and the consequence was that the whole division felt absolutely certain what it was going through on that day and it did go through.

> *"Esprit itself cannot be perceived . . . but nevertheless every leader of men knows that it does exist and that it is . . . necessary to . . . achieve victory."*

Morale and Esprit de Corps

Brig. Gen. Robert H. Willliams, USMC

U.S. Naval Institute *Proceedings*
January 1961

Morale and esprit de corps are intangibles with which naval and military commanders everywhere are concerned. While the former is an individual attribute, the latter pertains to a group, and can be instilled in the individual only insofar as he identifies himself with a group, such as a ship's company or a regiment, that possesses it.

The essence of high morale in a group is simply the consciousness of well-being in the individuals. Its requirements in a military organization appear to be these:

1. The individual must feel that he is reasonably well fed, clothed, sheltered, and paid—very nearly as well as circumstances permit. Circumstances, of course, vary in peace and war, ashore or onboard ship.
2. His social, religious, and recreational needs must be reasonably well provided for.
3. He must be assigned a task within his capabilities, trained to perform it well, kept occupied with it, and afforded an opportunity to qualify for promotion.
4. He must believe that his superiors will take note of a job well done, that effort and high performance are related to selection for promotion.
5. He must regard his assigned task as a necessary and useful one.

The collective morale of the individuals who compose a group will be in direct proportion to the success achieved by those in charge in meeting these requirements, or so it would seem. Yet this is not quite so. In some measure it is not the facts with respect to the fulfillment of these requirements, but what the individuals *believe* to be the facts. That the officers in charge are competent and are doing their best within the limitations imposed by factors beyond their control are not enough. The men must believe it. The inculcation of this belief is not a matter of direct communication, of simply asserting it is so. Men observe their leaders and judge them by the competence and sense of purpose they display. Their opportunities for observation are limited. They can reach wrong conclusions.

Many tend to think of esprit de corps as simply the collective morale (high) of the group. I do not agree. No attempt will be made here to list the factors that, if operating, will create esprit de corps. There are too many variables and imponderables. An individual, although he reflects it if he belongs to a group which possesses it, can never create esprit de corps by himself. He can only contribute to its development in proportion to the forcefulness of his own personality and the extent that it is drawn into the magnetic field of the group.

Pride is its essence, the collective pride of individuals in being members of a group which has, or which they believe has, a special competence surpassing that of other similar groups. This pride is born of a deep conviction, dimly comprehended and seldom articulated, which grows in the hearts of men who comprise a ship's company or a squadron. This is that the whole is greater—much greater—than merely the sum of all its parts. A realization emerges, accompanied by a mighty sense of belonging, that the group can perform functions far beyond the aggregate of the individual capacities of its members. They know that their separate skills have been integrated and coordinated by their leaders, who themselves are of the group, to create a new coherent unity to which all are fiercely loyal.

If the group is unique, the first of its type as to equipment or function, the feeling of pride is more intense. If, in addition, the duty performed is dangerous, even in peace time, the intensity of esprit de corps that can develop is almost unbelievable. Examples of this category are the first squadron or group to be equipped with jets, the crew of the first nuclear-powered submarine, and a unit with which I was familiar personally before World War II, the first Marine parachute battalion.

This is how esprit de corps is generated in newly organized units, such as a recently commissioned ship or a wartime regiment. In established groups other factors operate to preserve and intensify it. When valid traditions are fostered and handed down within an established group, their impact on the newly joined individual, whether commander or recent recruit, is immediate and forceful. His heart swells at the realization that he now belongs to a group apart. A man in a ship named for a former famous warship is conscious of a challenge to perform his duty in a manner worthy of that former ship's company with whom he is now identified, however tenuously, by the magic name. This can be observed in certain regiments of the Marine Corps. Although the Corps as a whole has always been noted for its esprit, it is probably highest in the 5th and 6th Regiments, which gained a special fame in World War I.

Esprit de corps is dynamic. It thrives on the desire to excel, on the determination that the group shall have no peer in the performance of its special function. It is reflected in a general smartness of behavior and turnout, outward signs of the harmony, good discipline, efficient organization, and pride in craft that prevail within. It reveals its presence in other ways. Members of the group are apt to affect a certain condescension toward outsiders. They incline to mannerisms in speech and dress that enable them to be readily recognized. Many successful commanders have exploited these tendencies.

Clearly esprit de corps and morale are separate entities. Either can exist independently of the other. It is obvious that morale is always a positive or negative factor in
all groups, military or civilian. The term esprit de corps is usually used only in connection with the armed services, and within them, generally only with reference to combat
units. It appears to exist only in groups which are intended to engage directly in battle.

Service elements and base personnel are frequently dedicated to their tasks and
imbued with a great sense of purpose. In a crisis they can rise to prodigious efforts,
provided their morale is high. They do not, however, have esprit de corps. On the
other hand, the latter, once firmly established, can sometimes persist even when
prolonged hardship, poor leadership, or defeat have reduced morale to a negative factor,
provided the group survives and believes in its own integrity. If the group will still fight,
though the individuals who compose it are in a state of hopeless despair, it still has esprit
de corps.

What then is the relationship between morale and esprit de corps? I suggest that
they are not complementary. A newly organized unit will never develop esprit de corps
without first achieving good morale. Good morale, we may infer, provides the necessary
climate for the birth of esprit de corps, and the best climate for its mysterious growth
and preservation.

The competent commander is therefore extremely sensitive to morale. He is as
conscious of its variations as he is of changes in weather. What should he do if the
morale of the command dips and continues on an alarming downward trend? It will
soon become obvious in a lowering of effective performance on the part of the group,
and a reluctance to give of their best on the part of individuals. The trouble will almost
invariably be found in the leadership. If the cause of bad morale is difficult to detect, I
suggest, this analysis:

1. Examine the morale of the command in the light of the requirements stated
   above. Identify the deficiencies.
2. Cast the deficiencies found against the performance of subordinate leaders *at all
   levels* in their assigned responsibilities with respect to the requirements.
3. Identify those whose leadership and supervisory performance are marginal or
   unsatisfactory.

There are then some steps to be taken with respect to those subordinate leaders.
Before taking action it will be necessary to decide into which of three categories each
falls. This is fairly simple. For each there is a specific corrective action.

1. The capable, but lazy: Tell them to pull their socks up, and see that they do.
2. The well intentioned, but inexperienced: Hold school for them.
3. The stupid and incompetent: Get rid of them.

The Fleet and the Marines

Lt. Cmdr. E. W. Broadbent, USN

U.S. Naval Institute *Proceedings*
March 1931

Two armies: One under the War Department, the other under the Navy Department. One, the United States Army, the other the United States Marine Corps. The former numbers about 130,000, in peace time, the latter numbers about 18,000.

At first glance this seems to be an anomalous condition, a duplication of effort. Why should the Navy maintain its own army? What does it do with this army? The answer to these questions lies almost entirely in the one word "bases." Naval bases constitute the sources of supplies, the ports of refuge for repairs, overhaul, and maintenance, to which a fleet may retire for recuperation and refitting. Lying on the edge of hostile zones, perhaps thousands of miles from the homeland, the naval bases constitute a vital, indispensable link in the chain of maintenance of the fleet at sea.

Diplomacy and ancient campaigns have provided some navies with far-flung bases circling the globe. Ours is not one of those fortunate navies. During the World War, our naval forces abroad used the naval bases of our allies. May we always have such complacent and well-situated allies!

But suppose we haven't! The only answer is, we must seize our bases. To seize bases, we must have suitably organized expeditionary forces. Hence the Marine Corps. Our fundamental naval policy includes that we "maintain a Marine Corps of such strength that it will be able adequately to support the Navy by: (a) furnishing detachments to vessels of the fleet in full commission; (b) guards for shore stations; (c) garrisons for outlying positions; (d) by the maintenance in readiness of an expeditionary force."

But, one may ask, why should not this expeditionary force come from the Army? Our fundamental naval policy requires that we "develop and organize the Navy for operations in any part of either ocean." Time is an essential element in all military operations; so is mobility. But mobility is not only essential to a fleet, it is also vital and indispensable. Experience has shown that when mixed military and naval forces are engaged in a joint operation, unity of the highest command is essential to success. Admiral Nelson experienced difficulties in his landing operations due to lack of direct command over the military as well as the naval forces. These same difficulties were repeated as recently as the World War at Gallipoli. The subject is hoary with age. But the net result is that dual command of mixed forces does not work. The law of the land does not permit an Army officer to exercise command of naval forces, nor a Navy officer to exercise command of Army forces. The obvious solution is to provide the Navy with its own landing force, and as we said before, hence the Marine Corps.

Now that we have the Marine Corps, what shall be done with it? Major General John A. Lejeune, USMC (Ret.), said, "From its very establishment, the Marine Corps has constituted an integral part of the Navy. It has played its part with the Navy in all its achievements, both ashore and afloat." (Foreword; U.S. Naval Institute *Proceedings*, U.S. Naval Institute, November, 1928). More recently, the late Maj. Gen. Eli K. Cole, USMC, said, in part, "The major war mission of the Marine Corps is to support the fleet by supplying it with a highly trained, fully equipped expeditionary force for the minor shore operations which are necessary for the effective prosecution by the fleet of its major mission, which is to gain control of the sea and thereby open the sea lanes for the Army overseas." (U.S. Naval Institute *Proceedings*, U.S. Naval Institute, November, 1929). Although the latter quotation is somewhat involved, its import is clear, namely that the primary mission of the Marine Corps in time of war is to conduct minor land operations for the support of the fleet.

A recent publication, *Joint Action of the Army and Navy*, approved by the secretary of war and the secretary of the navy in April, 1927, and issued by them to the two services "for information and guidance" states the following functions of the Marine Corps, as "adjunct of the Navy".

To provide and maintain forces:
a. For land operations in support of the fleet for the initial seizure and defense of advanced bases and for such limited auxiliary land operations as are essential to the prosecution of the naval campaign.
b. For emergency service in time of peace for the protection of the interests of the United States in foreign countries.
c. For marine detachments on vessels of the fleet and for interior protection of naval shore stations.

The wartime mission of the Marine Corps will be found clearly stated in the first section above, namely, "to support the fleet by conducting land operations for the initial seizure and defense of advanced bases and by such limited auxiliary land operations as are essential to the prosecution of the naval campaign." To quote again from the Navy's fundamental policy: "To make war efficiency the object of all training, and to maintain that efficiency during the entire period of peace," and again, "to maintain a

Marine Corps of such strength that it will be able adequately to support the Navy by the maintenance in readiness of an expeditionary force." "Readiness" for what? From the foregoing it would seem that the Navy Department expects the Marine Corps to be at all times organized and trained to fulfill its primary war mission, that is, the seizure and defense of advanced bases. Is the Marine Corps so organized and trained? Later on, we shall have occasion to ask a similar question of the Navy.

Four years ago, in 1925, an extensive joint exercise was held in Hawaiian waters. The fleet, assisted by the Marine Corps as the landing force, attacked and attempted to establish an advanced base in Hawaiian waters. The islands were defended by the Army garrison and the local naval-defense forces. This exercise was the most elaborate joint Navy–Marine Corps operation ever planned and executed. The lessons learned from the operation emphasized the need for extensive study of the whole subject of forced landings. Previous landing exercises had been conducted on a small scale, and valuable lessons learned, but the broad importance of this type of operation had never been clearly demonstrated as in the exercise of 1925.

Two years later the study of landing operations was taken up at the Naval War College and at the Marine Corps schools at Quantico, Virginia. Some effort had been made by the Army previously to investigate the subject, inspired by the Army's task of defending our shores from attack. At Quantico an extensive course in joint overseas operations was introduced into the curriculum, and a naval officer was detailed to the staff of the schools to assist in the presentation of such features of the subject as were purely naval.

There can be no more appropriate place for the study of this subject, from the standpoint of the land operations, than in the Marine Corps school. For years the Marines have recognized the fact that reading, study, and instruction in all the branches of the military profession are essential to efficiency in their role. The corps has maintained four schools in which their officers receive their fundamental training in tactics. These schools are the Basic School for all newly commissioned second lieutenants; the Company Officers' and Field Officers' Schools, and the correspondence schools for all officers, including reserves. But lack of time and facilities have limited the work covered in these schools to bare necessities. To amplify their training, and to produce the group of specialists necessary to thorough development of all branches of their service, officers of the Marine Corps have been detailed to courses of instruction in many of the schools of the Army and the Navy. Included in these schools are:

Army: Infantry, Field Artillery, Cavalry, Aviation, Motor Transport, Chemical Warfare, Signal, Subsistence, Industrial, Command and General Staff, L'Ecole de Guerre (France), Army War College.

Navy: Communications (radio), Naval War College.

This is a most impressive list of institutions of learning, and it must be admitted that the Marine Corps has at its disposal a military school system unequalled anywhere else in the world. To this must be added the school of experience, which has been available to the Marines to an extent that must satisfy the cravings of the most ardent seeker after the practical training of active service.

But schooling and policing Central American countries do not necessarily produce an organization adequately prepared and designed to meet the requirements of the war-time mission. For this purpose, one must have training of and with the forces involved, and an organization suited to the probable employment. The Marine Corps is organized, broadly speaking, into two expeditionary forces: the East Coast, based at Quantico, Virginia, and the West Coast, based at San Diego, California. These two forces, when not occupied by emergency peacetime operations beyond our continental boundaries, are engaged to a limited extent in the training such forces require for their specialty, the seizure and defense of advance bases.

Let us turn now to the other side of the picture, the naval. In war, the Navy's great task is to gain and exercise command of the sea in the theater of operations. Underlying all of the operations of the fleet in the execution of this task is the question of bases: gaining and holding our own bases, and denying bases to the enemy. When the theater of operations lies beyond the usable range of our prepared bases, the seizure of new bases becomes an unavoidable preliminary to the fleet battle by which alone command of the sea may be assured. Further, in major base-seizure operations, there may be necessary the preliminary gaining of a succession of small bases, advanced bases, from which the fleet or portions of it may operate in furtherance of the larger mission. In short, where a maritime nation goes to war without prepared bases, the seizure of advanced fleet bases becomes immediately of pressing importance. Is the Navy organized, trained, and prepared for the difficult task of seizing bases for its own use?

It will be interesting to examine certain of the naval aspects of base seizure. Experience has shown that the first essential to successful base-seizure operations is local command of the sea. Without such command, the operations against the intended land area cannot be successful. It was lack of this local command that resulted in the Battle of Lissa, important because it was the first battle between fleets of armored vessels. It was to gain this command that the Battle of Tsushima was fought. It was loss of this command of the local seas that forced the British out of the Mediterranean, leaving their Neapolitan allies to face Napoleon on shore, unsupported by the British fleet.

One cannot state in general terms what may be required to meet all situations under this preliminary condition. The operations required may be against submarines, air forces operating from floating or shore bases, and surface craft. It is a task, however, for which the Navy must be prepared. One German submarine reported to be in the vicinity of the Gallipoli peninsula during the Gallipoli campaign drove all the large British ships to cover for days, and left the British Army without naval support. Had the situation on shore been critical at that time, the whole campaign might have ended disastrously then.

The Navy's next big task is to land the assaulting force, the Marines. The picture that comes to mind is a fleet of boats making rapidly for a beach, the water cut on all sides by zipping bullets, the air filled with flying fragments of shell, and clouds of deadly gases, some of the latter perhaps invisible. But this is not all. There are guns to be landed, ammunition, tanks, radio sets, food, and innumerable articles of supply. And there may be surf to be passed, and long stretches of shallow water, and submerged wire entangle-ments. In short, mere boats will not suffice; yet the Navy must land the troops and their paraphernalia.

When the troops reach dry land, their work has just begun. Now they must advance and secure the beach, penetrate inland, gain a beach head, spread farther and farther, until the offshore waters are made secure and space is gained for consolidation of forces and their organization for the main attack. Every foot of this advance must be fought for, and the indispensable adjunct to the advance of infantry is the artillery. The Navy must be the Marines' artillery until such time as the Marines' own artillery can be landed and brought into action. The attack is now in the stage which inspired the late General Cole's motto in his article in the November 1929 issue of the U.S. Naval Institute *Proceedings Aut vincere aut mori*, either conquer or die. And the deciding factor may be the Navy's artillery fire.

What is needed for this supporting fire? Guns that will deliver a hail of bursting shell on the heads of defending troops; guns that can blast out and destroy shore batteries; guns that can reach far inland and destroy lines of communication; guns that can drop their shells almost vertically behind protecting rises of ground; high-explosive shells; shells with supersensitive fuses; bombs with similar characteristics that can be dropped from aircraft; and with it all, a sureness and accuracy of control and facility of commu-nication that will give to the Marines the assurance of support when and where the lack of support means disaster.

Naval vessels are not designed for this type of action, nor are naval guns and ammu-nition. The British found it necessary to build special types and to rebuild other vessels to meet their needs. What better use could be made of vessels no longer able to keep their place in, or in support of, the battle line than to reserve them for such use, equip them for experimentation? Never since the beginning of naval history has a naval commander had so many vessels at his disposal that he could afford to detach as many as he desired from his fleet for such secondary purposes. Always concessions have been made to necessity, makeshifts have been resorted to, and operations against shore bases have proved costly and frequently disastrous. If the same thought, care, and degree of preparation were devoted to the operations for the seizure of a base that are devoted to the preparation of a fleet for battle, the base operations would not fail, and time and lives would be saved.

One more major task remains for the Navy. It must serve as a floating base for the troops ashore. It must provide supplies of men and material, food, water, fuel, ammunition, and the thousand and one items that will be required. Everything must be transported ashore, landing places constructed, and shelter provided for. The needs of even a small army that is self-supporting are staggering, and the water transportation involved in the constant flow of supplies ashore is no mean problem. Ships carry boats, but these boats, in fact all the small boats in the Navy, would be only a "drop in the bucket," compared to our needs.

Last comes the care of the wounded. Hospital ships are not built overnight, and the need will be great. Oddly enough, hospitalization afloat is something which was either overlooked or disregarded when forces were assembled for the first attack on Gallipoli. In a very short time every vessel offshore was loaded to capacity with wounded, and men lay for hours on deck without the necessary medical care and attention.

It is the mission of the Marine Corps to "support the fleet." But likewise it will be the mission of some part of the fleet to support the Marine Corps landing force. When two forces of different arms have a mutual task, there must be mutual understanding, common thought, study, preparation, and training. With these, if the time ever comes when the Navy needs more and better bases the Navy and the Marines can take and hold them.

The Fleet Marine Force

Maj. Gen. John H. Russell, USMC

U.S. Naval Institute *Proceedings*
October 1936

The fleet marine force is a unit of the United States Fleet, and serves under the orders of the commander in chief. It was authorized by the secretary of the navy in General Order No. 241, dated December 7, 1933. It consists of such units as may be designated by the major general commandant of Marines, and it is maintained at such strength as is warranted by the general personnel situation of the corps. It is available to the commander in chief for fleet operations, and for exercises in connection with fleet problems, either afloat or ashore. The commanding general of the Fleet Marine Force, and his staff, are detailed by the major general commandant. In matters pertaining to the employment of the force, its general communicates directly with the commander in chief of the fleet and makes routine reports to that officer on the strength and dispositions of his several units. The major general commandant, naturally, is kept informed of the requirements and employment of the force; takes the necessary steps for its maintenance and general administration; and supervises matters of armament and equipment.

The headquarters of the Fleet Marine Force are now established at San Diego, under Brig. Gen. Douglas C. McDougal, USMC. The personnel are divided between San Diego, California, and Quantico, Virginia. Tactically, it corresponds to an infantry division, containing infantry, artillery, aircraft, the special weapons, and the maintenance units necessary to make it tactically independent.

Owing to the fact that the supply of marines is exceeded by the demand for them, the Force is substantially below strength. In case of emergency, it would be forced to exceedingly rapid expansion, and this circumstance receives the scrupulous attention of the responsible officers in the Marine Corps.

Navy General Order No. 241 is less than three years old, but the employment of armed men in the manner it specifies is as old as maritime warfare. In Mediterranean fleets of antiquity, the Greeks had their *Epibadai*, the Romans their *Classiarii*, who served in ships of war. The medieval fleets embarked soldiers for their operations, and a company of soldiers was a unit of the man-of-war complement in the Tudor period. The

English Marine Corps, which is the direct ancestor of our own, dates from 1664, when they raised "The Duke of York and Alban Regiment of Foot," "land soldiers prepared for sea service." The United States Marine Corps was authorized by act of the First Continental Congress, in November, 1775, although there had been several colonial marine formations prior to the American Revolution.

All naval experience has indicated value of such a corps, habituated to customs and at home aboard ship, and trained and equipped for those amphibious operations which have always been inseparable from naval warfare. History is rich in examples: the British seized Gibraltar in 1704 with an amphibious force, and hold it to this day. Our own marines have performed important duties in every war of this republic. The Civil War offers numerous cases of the joint simultaneous employment of land and forces. The Gallipoli episode in the World War is still fresh in mind.

Such attempts-at-arms have been successful, or unsuccessful, in exact ratio to the degree of co-operation obtaining [sic] between the military and naval elements involved. The passionate recriminations between McClellan and Goldsborough come to mind; they gravely compromised the issues of the Peninsular Campaign against Richmond in 1862. It is hard to say a charge against the British soldiers and sailors of the Gallipoli adventure, because they appear generally to have done as best they could and, except Sir Roger Keyes, to have kept quiet about it since. But a fleet marine contingent landed early in 1915, when Sir John de Robeck first attempted the entrance of the Dardanelles, would have been able to seize and, in all probability, to hold the salient features of that hard littoral which later cost the British Empire 120,000 fruitless casualties.

In the plans for the employment of the naval forces, the Marine Corps has certain definite missions. It furnishes detachments to serve on board cruisers and capital ships; it provides guards for naval shore stations; it maintains garrisons in certain outlying possessions and embassies; and it holds forces in readiness for such expeditionary duty as may be indicated.

The first three assignments are normal in peacetime and wartime alike. The Marine Corps has been called upon to perform the fourth in every war this country has waged, and on many occasions other than in formal war, the Marine Corps has dispatched expeditions for duty beyond the seas. As a war mission, the last is of the highest importance.

The United States naval establishment, potentially at least, is as strong as any in the world. But the geographical situation of the United States is such as to impose unusual strains upon the Navy. We lack naval bases. England, for example, has a chain of these right around the world. Outside the Caribbean, there are Panama, Honolulu, and Manila, and no other naval stations in the world where an American man-of-war can refuel and refit.

A fleet without bases is, axiomatically, a fleet limited to its home ports and the waters immediately adjacent. It is not a blue-water outfit. Weighing and providing for the possibilities of war—as it is the duty of responsible officials to do—it is obvious that, should we become embroiled with any people whose political and economic requirements clash with ours, the first phase of such a conflict would be naval. Our fleet, or parts of it, would at once become involved in situations a long way from our coasts. Lacking bases for distant operations, the fleet would have to seize them. It is for this purpose that the Marine Corps Expeditionary Forces have been held in readiness in the past; and to meet such an emergency in the most efficient manner possible, the present Fleet Marine Force has been developed from the former expeditionary forces. In composition there is little new, but the placing of the force under the orders of the commander in chief, U.S. Fleet, is a long step forward. The Fleet Marine Force is now an integral unit of the combatant sea establishment.

There has always been something like it in the Marine Corps: a permanent nucleus from which the required organizations could be developed. For many years the old First Company, called the Advanced Base Force, was maintained at the Philadelphia Navy Yard. In those days Marine Corps expeditions were formed around the relatively few officers and men of the Advanced Base detachment, by transferring individuals from wherever they could be spared, throwing them aboard a transport or battleship, and organizing them during the voyage to the objective. Such measures were adequate in the innocent days before the World War, but military operations have now grown vastly more complicated. You can no longer hit the beach with some navy landing guns, some pushcarts, and your rifles and bayonets. Infantry, artillery, the special weapons, the communication details, air forces, chemical warfare experts, in addition to the sanitary, supply, and recreational units, are all features of the modern expeditionary forces. Automatic riflemen, machine gunners, artillerymen, radio operators, aviation pilots and observers, the smoke and gas people, and the mechanics for tanks, armored cars, and tractors, are specialists whose individual training is a matter not of months, but of years. They can neither be improvised overnight from the recruit depots nor called up on short notice from the reserves. Furthermore, the efficiency of every military force depends upon the coordination of its parts; each element must be trained in conjunction with the other elements. Finally, naval plans envisage the possibility of immediate action upon the development of emergency. In the event of naval war, it is not likely that time will be granted for the assembly and training of a fleet unit.

Marine officers, and not a few naval officers, have been thinking along these lines for a long time. In 1933 there were drawn up, and presented for the consideration of the major general commandant, plans calling for the actual organization of a staff, whose duties would be the perfection of the arrangements for Marine Corps emergency mobilization. Plans already existed for the creation of such a staff, to be brought into being at the time of mobilization, and the units composing our East Coast and West Coast expeditionary forces, maintained at Quantico and San Diego, had been earmarked for emergency employment in the same manner. The plans were approved, and the proposed staff was assembled at the Marine barracks, Quantico, Virginia.

Proceeding along the logical lines of development, it was recommended that, in order to achieve a more satisfactory state of readiness, the Marine Corps Expeditionary Forces, then in being, be included in the Fleet organization as a unit of the sea establishment, subject to the orders, for tactical employment, of the commander in chief.

Study by the Office of the Chief of Naval Operations, and by the commander in chief, resulted in their endorsement of these conclusions and recommendations, which had, moreover, the cordial support of all informed Marine officers. It was further decided that the term "Expeditionary Force" was not exactly applicable to fleet unit, and the term "Fleet Marine Force" was adopted as more specifically describing the unit and its functions. Mutual study by the Marine officers and the naval officers involved clarified the matters of maintenance and supply. In due course, there was issued the administrative order set forth in the opening paragraph of this paper and the Fleet Marine Force came into being.

Its progress, so far, has been highly satisfactory to all concerned. The Marine Corps has been gratified by the expression of approval proceeding from the naval officers under whom the force has operated and for their helpful and constructive criticisms. The drills and training schedules of the force are carried out with scrupulous adherence to its wartime mission, and every maneuver has been subjected to careful and critical scrutiny, in order that the fullest advantage may be taken of every phase of its experience and the lessons learned usefully applied to the future. Under energetic commanders and skillful staffs, the Fleet Marine Force has consistently maintained the Marine Corps tradition of efficiency and resourcefulness. It is the Marine Corps' most important contribution to the great cause of national security.

The Marine Brigade

Capt. John W. Thomason Jr.

U.S. Naval Institute *Proceedings*
November 1928

The war with Germany was an anonymous sort of war, fought obscurely by unnamed battalions behind a veil of censorship. In other wars, the patriotic citizenry back home, eating corn bread and enduring meatless days, might find spice for such unexciting rations in the dispatches from the front. In Rome, the plebs around the bulletin boards learned with cheers of the smart conduct of the 10th Legion, which, taken in a narrow place by swarming Gauls, rallied to the personal appeal of Caesar, broke the enemy and drove him. Paris of the Consulate was informed by the fastest post of the fortitude of the 52nd Demi-Brigade (Seine-et-Marne); it formed front to a flank under Austrian fire, and struck terribly across the bridge at Lodi; General Bonaparte considered that the 52nd Demi-Brigade (Seine-et-Marne) deserved well of the Fatherland. Englishmen drank themselves blind to the Foot Guards who held Hugomont against the battering of Ney on the flank at Waterloo, and to the 92nd Highlanders who charged, clinging to the stirrups of the Scots Greys, until the Cuirassiers of Milhaud and Löbau cut them down. There are men alive today who read the flashes from Gettysburg, of the Iron Brigade of Wisconsin at Culp's Hill by Gettysburg, and of Pickett's Division that attacked on the third day in the center. Most of us remember headlines: the Rough Riders at San Juan Hill. But in our last war, the hands of the correspondents were held where their eyes were not hooded. Mr. Forbes would never have gotten the story of Balaklava past the censors, nor would Alfred, Lord Tennyson have been allowed to publish "The Charge of the Light Brigade."

In the American Expeditionary Forces (AEF) there was one unit, and only one, while the Germans still held out, whose name got through the fog. This was the Brigade of Marines in the 2nd Division, U.S. Regular. The story involves certain war correspondents, so charged with suppressed news that they were near to bursting, and a chief of censors, honest and able and anxious to accommodate, but perhaps a little clouded in his mind as to what Marines were, and why—a condition not ever uncommon in the Army; and for two thrilling days the press of the nation clanged with the doings of 7,500 leathernecks at a place called Belleau Wood, while numerous infantry brigades, earnest and meritorious, sweated in silence, and continued so to toil. A little later, when calmness descended, and the instructed press was making what it could out of such sterile items as, "Yesterday the American 1st Army Corps made some progress towards the Vesle," people asked: How come these Marines, anyway? We thought the Army fought on land—it did, and does. But about that Marine Brigade. . . .

Major General George Barnett was commandant of the Marine Corps. Stirred by small enterprises at Vera Cruz, in Santo Domingo, and in Haiti, the Marine recruiting service had evolved the slogan, "First to Fight." Headquarters read the writing on the wall, and Headquarters realized that the Marines must get into the German War or become quite ridiculous—all this aside from the sound necessity of giving Marine officers experience in large operations ashore. Very early in 1917, the major general commandant had a concentration of veteran Marines at Philadelphia, and others within reach. When the United States declared war against the Germans, General Barnett was able, with the fullest cooperation from Mr. Secretary Daniels, to offer to the President for service with the Army, a war-strength regiment of Marines, assembled and drilling in battalions, and ready to go.

At that time, the Army was hard put to it for trained soldiers. The old regular regiments were being split into three; you had one old regiment, much diluted, and two new ones. The draft was in the air and the National Guard was recruiting up to strength. The secretary of war was pleased to accept the proffered regiment of Marines: he promised that it would sail with the very first Army contingent.

But when that contingent was made up—the infantry units which became the American 1st Division—in June 1917, the Navy was advised that, most unfortunately, no transportation for Marines existed. They would surely go in the next convoy sailing. The commandant of Marines had this in a personal note from Mr. Secretary Baker, and he took it to Mr. Secretary Daniels. And General Barnett relates that it was the proudest moment in all his long career, when he informed the secretary of war that the Army need give itself no distress about sailing accommodations for Marines: he had the *Henderson*, and the *De Kalb*, and the *Von Steuben*—ex-German liners, the last two—and the Navy would see its own Marines to France.

So the 5th Regiment of Marines, Colonel Doyen, sailed in the first convoy, trained for a while in France with the 1st Division, General Sibert, and was then split up variously on military police and construction details, laying the ground work for the AEF.

In the meantime, on September 20, 1917, the War Department approved the organization of a unit to be designated as the American 2nd Division, U.S. Regular. To it were posted the 2nd Field Artillery Brigade, the 2nd Engineers, various auxiliaries, and the 3rd Brigade of Infantry, which last was made up of the 9th and 23rd Infantry Regiments. The other infantry brigade would be formed by the major general commandant of Marines, and would be known as the 4th Brigade. General Barnett had his second regiment of Marines ready: it was formed at Quantico. The 5th Regiment had been largely veteran; old-timers with all the campaign ribbons and rows of hashmarks. The new regiment, the 6th, had a seasoning of trained men, but its ranks were filled with volunteers, from college graduates to ditch-diggers. In the fall and winter of 1917 it crossed to France, and with it the nucleus of the 6th Machine Gun Battalion, Colonel Catlin commanding the 6th Marines, and Major Cole, the machine guns.

In October, 1917, the 2nd Division was directed to its designated training area in France. All its regiments were much scattered, and although General Bundy of the Army had been detailed to command, its first orders were signed by Brigadier General Doyen, of the Marines, newly promoted, and senior officer present. Through the winter of 1917–18, the division assembled, coming in by battalions and companies from the jobs on which it had been dispersed. A detachment of the 5th Regiment went as far afield as Southampton, England, policing Army rest camps in that vicinity. It was February, 1918, before all the infantry of the division was together; it was March before the artillery joined, and not until May were all its elements brought under the division command. About the middle of March the 2nd Division went up to the front, taking over sectors of the Toulon-Rupt-Troyon line, between Verdun and St. Mihiel. Two American divisions, the 1st and the 26th, were on the front before it. Of all the American regular divisions, the training of the 2nd was the most haphazard and sketchy, and its assembly the most delayed. It got many of its officers and some of its "non-coms" to the service schools before it went into the line, but actually, it learned its business under fire.

From the point where the division entered the line, in that bleak, wet March 1918, to the day in August of the next year when the Marines took train for Quantico, after the parade in New York, it is very hard to set forth a separate history of the Marine Brigade, which was the 5th Regiment and the 6th Regiment and the 6th Machine Gun Battalion, and officers and men of the Navy medical corps. Its first commanding officer was General Doyen of the Marine Corps; his health failing, General Doyen was relieved by General Harbord. After June, 1918, it had a marine brigadier, General Neville; after Soissons, in July, the 2nd Division was commanded by a Marine, General Lejeune. But its history is the history of the American 2nd Division, and they all—four regiments of infantry, three machine gun battalions, three regiments of artillery, the engineers, the signal troops, and the trains—write the same names on their battle flags.

Divisions, like regiments and companies and ships and persons, have individuality. The 1st Division, for example, the most thoroughly trained and the oldest of the A.E.F. units, was methodical, tenacious, and steady in all its fighting. It did not move quickly; its blows were calculated and powerful and sustained. The 2nd Division was character- ized by the quality of dash. No troops in any war ever reorganized more quickly, given a breathing space, than the Germans. If you stopped to bring up your services and to adjust your communications, Heinie was at you with a counterattack. But if you hit him and kept on hitting, he tended to disintegrate. There are three great attacks in the annals of the 2nd Division: the attack of July 18, that broke through the Forest de Retz, rolled over Chaudun and Vierzy, and stopped within rifle shot of the vital Soissons-Château-Thierry road; the attack of October 3, that overwhelmed Blanc Mont Ridge in the Champagne so swiftly that German observers were captured in their towers, and all the German defense system to right and left paralyzed until too late to recover anything; and the strange thrust of the night of November 4, when the 3rd Brigade seized a narrow bit of German front and marched in column by a wood road, through the rainy dark, from La Nouart to Tuillerie Farm, disrupting a German corps and seizing the Beaumont ridge, so that the German organization crumbled on the whole corps front, and the Germans fled across the Meuse. All these had a terrifying swiftness about them. And I think that the secret lies in the mixed character of the 2nd Division. United against everything outside the division, there was within it a fierce rivalry between the Marines and the infantry. Looking over to the left, where the Marine battalions also lay under hells of shelling, the doughboys of the 3rd Brigade considered that they could stand anything them dam' leathernecks could. Working forward under the scourge of machine-gun fire, Marines of all ranks were goaded by the fear that them Army files might get ahead of them—Come on, you birds! And the careful records of German divisions attest the savage energy of these attacks; as attest also the battle maps that show advances day by day and the casualty lists. The 2nd Division had more casualties than any other American division; in captures of prisoners and guns only the 1st Division approached it.

Napoleon rated high among the military qualities essential to success, luck. The Marine Brigade was lucky. The pure chance of battle brought it the opportunity which lifted it briefly from the anonymity of this war. Luck can do no more for any man or any brigade than bring opportunity; after that it is a matter of training, of discipline, of skill. I do not think these facts have been before set down.

At the end of May, 1918, the 2nd Division lay in the area Chaumont-en-Vexin, which is north and a little west of Paris, as you go towards Rouen, and more than a hundred kilometers from Château-Thierry. The division was to go to the area Beauvais, behind Cantigny, where the 1st Division had had an adventure, taken some mauling, and captured a town, and was due for a relief. The drive of the German 7th Army, down from the Chemin des Dames, between Reims and Soissons, to the Marne at Château-Thierry, upset these plans. The 2nd Division was ordered to the French 6th Army, then broken into pieces by the impact of von Boehn's shock divisions, and fighting desperately in the Château-Thierry area to restore the front. The division was moved by camions on the last day of May to the area Montreuil, as you go to Château-Thierry from Meaux; the infantry regiments debussed during the afternoon and night of May 31, near the town May-en-Multien, and marched towards the front. The fog of war existed very terribly on this front, that day. The French 21st Corps, General Degoutte, did not know where the front was, for the front was moving very fast, or where its own divisions were, for they were fighting bitter rear-guard actions, by companies and battalions, and being destroyed; and the German 4th Reserve Corps, having taken Château-Thierry, was swinging westward in an orderly advance, rolling up the broken French elements. Consequently, between four o'clock in the afternoon of May 31 and midnight, May 31/ June 1, the 2nd Division received four sets of orders from the French corps and army command, each set locating it in a different area, as the situation changed in the eyes of French Headquarters. The last order deployed it in the area Montreuil, between that place and Château-Thierry, astride the great Paris-Metz highway. The 2nd Divison issued its own orders on this basis, locating the 3rd Brigade of Infantry to the north of the road, where it would have faced the Bois de Belleau and Hill 142 and Bouresches, and the 4th Brigade of Marines to the south, in front of Hill 204 and Vaux.

Meantime, the 9th Infantry, having marched all night with its colonel on foot at its head, came upon the Paris-Metz road soon after sunrise, June 1. The Germans were then mounting Hill 204, and to the French corps command the more immediate menace seemed from the east, from the direction of the hill. The 9th Infantry was deployed to meet it, and formed line south of the highway. The next regiment to arrive was the 6th Marines, in the afternoon. The Germans were appearing on the high ground north of the road, and the Marines went into line behind the French then fighting in that direction. On these two movements, dictated by the emergency of the moment, the division line built up during the succeeding days, the 5th Marines going in on the left of the 6th Marines, and the 23rd Infantry with the 9th. Later, when the situation began to stabilize, the French corps commander considered it necessary to improve his left front, and this called for the reduction of the towns of Veuilly and Bussiares and Bouresches, and the Bois de Belleau, the last two points named being on the front of the Marine Brigade. The Marines and the French 167th Division, on their left, were at this task for the rest of June, and accomplished it. The regulars of the 3rd Brigade did not have their opportunity until July 1. Then they stamped Vaux flat.

As for the German contribution to the reputation of the Marine Brigade, the Germans had seen a great deal of fighting, and they did not get excited about Belleau Woods. The mission of the German 4th Reserve Corps was to form a defensive flank for the line along the Marne, and to cover the left of a push westward toward the Ourcq. The valley of the Clignon Brook, which runs a few kilometers north of, and roughly parallel to, the Paris-Metz road, offered a suitable site for their main line, as well as a convenient covered area for the assembly of troops in the event of a decision to drive farther down the Marne. This line had certain natural exits: the depression leading south from Bussiares, and the Bois de Belleau, and the point Hill 142. The Germans included these places in their outpost zone, when, in the first two days of June, they drove the French across the Clignon. The Bois de Belleau they organized and held in force. Then they sensed a stiffening in the enemy on their front, and presently identified the corpse of a 6th Marine, and on June 6, got a few prisoners from the 23rd Infantry and the Marine Brigade. Finding Americans on their front—American regulars—they considered it desirable to thrash, thoroughly, this new opponent; to assert a moral superiority at the outset of his entry upon the war. Bussiares—Torcy—Bouresches—the Bois de Belleau, even they were not particularly important. But it was important to beat the Americans, and German division commanders so advised their troops. It followed that for a little space the attention of the world was centered on a few square kilometers of blood-soaked woodland, and it was the fortune of the Marine Brigade to answer the question: Will these Yankees fight? And it is recorded that they answered it.

Thereafter, the Marine Brigade did not emerge from the dispatches as a unit. The 2nd Division continued to have opportunities. It was one of the three divisions—the others were the American 1st Division and the Moroccan 1st Division—that attacked south of Soissons on July 18; and that day the war was lost to the Central Empires. It went to Gouraud in the Champagne, at the end of September, where the Germans held firm in the massif Notre Dame des Champs, and pierced that place in one of the great, clean-cut assaults of the war. It drove up from the Argonne to the Meuse in November with the Americans; the last night of the war the Marine Brigade got men perilously across the Meuse and was attacking when the Armistice fell. It marched to Germany, and it came home in August of the next year and disbanded. It so fell out that all its opportunities were conspicuous. It came upon the front at critical times. Great events hinged upon its attacks. Much of that was chance; the AEF had several divisions that would have done well anywhere. But there was nothing of luck—there was cold, hard discipline, and much war-wisdom, learned under the guns, and sheer, clean skill, in the fighting which made these opportunities good.

These things came at a price. Statistics are not interesting; the butcher's bill of the American 2nd Division will compare cruelly and honorably, for the five months it was engaged, with that of any division in any Army in the war. The casualties of the Marine Brigade were nearer two hundred than one hundred percent. Such things carry little meaning except to men who can remember the dreadful wheat field to the west of Belleau Woods, and shrapnel-flailed slopes betweeen Blanc Mont and St. Étienne, and the line of dead engineers on the path between the heights of the Meuse near Pouilly and the place where the bridge was, that last night of the war.

For the rest, there is transmitted a certain old blood-stained glory, peculiarly of the Marines and of the United States naval service. That was the Marine Brigade.

Since '17

Donald L. Dickson

Leatherneck
November 1967

In the past 50 years there have been many changes in the Marine Corps' rank structure, uniforms, weapons, and equipment—even in the caliber of men.

"For the luv'a Mike, are they robbing the cradle to build up the Marine Corps?"

It was a question undoubtedly asked many times before and it would be asked many times in the future.

This time it was 1917 and new recruits were "flocking to the standard to make the world safe for democracy."

The "old breed" Marine viewed the newcomers with less than enthusiasm, for it threatened his way of life.

He was, as Col. John Thomason was later to describe him, "the old breed of American regular, regarding the service as home and war an occupation."

Stripes were not as common as hashmarks to the old regular. He knew every officer and senior NCO in the Marine Corps and had served with most of them, in one corner of the world or another. He had his favorites among them and referred to them (behind their backs) as Hiking Hiram or Old Gimlet Eye or Terrible Terry. He had other names for those upon whom his wrath fell.

Within this tight organization he lived, trying to steer clear of "Rocks and Shoals" (Navy Regulations). And he didn't always succeed. Whether compounded by beer in Boston or tequila in Tampico, he often ran afoul of rules, and when he did, he expected and received quick judgment and quick punishment.

"Lock him up!"

There was no UCM then. He could be awarded anything from office hours through Deck, Summary, or General Court Martial.

He might get any punishment from so many hours EPD through fines, brig time, days of bread and water to "20 and a kick," and "Portsmouth" (Naval Prison) was something to be feared.

He was salty and tough physically. He looked down on the "sick-bay soldiers," and unless he couldn't move, he refused to take advantage of the sick bay for which twenty cents per month was deducted from his meager pay.

He very carefully signed the "no erasure" payroll once a month for his "thirty bucks and a horse blanket." And then, unless he had the duty, he went on liberty—probably to make a "speed run." Or the cards and dice came out. Acey-deucy was one of his favorite games.

Sometimes he had a little trouble signing his name exactly as spelled.

America was less distant from the melting pot in those days, and the old Marine Corps echoed to various accents. There were Germans, Irish, Scots, Poles, and many other nationalities represented. Most of them were professional soldiers who had received their initial training in the army of their native country. At one time it was half seriously believed that you couldn't become a gunnery sergeant unless your name ended in "ski."

But above all, these were fighting men who had drawn a bead along the sights of a Lee Straight pull, a Krag, or a Springfield in any part of the world where American interests were threatened. These were the men behind the almost monotonous announcement that "the Marines have landed and the situation is well in hand."

Now there was a war on—not just another war, but a big one.

The "old breed" took the new recruits in hand. They taught the new Marines how to shave, brush teeth, take a bath, and swab down the decks—all with a half-bucket of water. They taught them the finer points of being a good Marine in salty, seagoing terms, trimmed with exotic words from faraway places. They showed them how to roll "heavies" and adjust pack straps and, above all, they taught them the care and use of weapons. The new men learned how to "hold 'em and squeeze 'em" until they could plug the 20-inch bull at a thousand yards. They learned musketry and fire distribution. They learned to field strip their weapons blindfolded. And, through it all, they continued "squads right—squads left; and right-front-into-line" close order drill until each corporal's eight-man squad was a machine of oiled precision.

The new men were quick learners. They were a cross section of young America. Fighting was not their business, but they intended to make it their business until the war was won. In return for what they learned from the "old breed," they taught the "old breed" a few things. They asked questions which needed to be asked. They brought new efficiencies to the old-timers when, because of the expansion to 30,000, many of them made stripes or bars. When they returned to civilian life at war's end, they left their mark on the Corps.

Many of them didn't return to civilian life but chose to "go for 30," and make the Corps a career.

These men had seen many changes in warfare. They had experienced the introduction of the airplane, poison gas, tanks, artillery preparation, rolling barrages, the automatic rifle, the resurgent use of grenades, and the folly of close-packed frontal charges against well-emplaced machine guns.

They knew that new techniques would be required and that a good leader would need more than an iron fist and an iron jaw.

The new "old breed" placed heavier emphasis on a good mind as well as a strong right arm. A good warrior needed brains as well as brawn.

The Marine Corps Institute was formed to teach Marines a wide variety of subjects by mail. The School of Application for officers evolved into the Marine Corps School at Quantico. Education was encouraged. It was no longer uncommon to find a private first class or corporal who could intelligently discuss current events, literature, or art.

Despite the rise in educational levels, the Marine was primarily a fighting man, and he was employed fully in the Banana Wars and in guarding American interests wherever they might be.

The green uniform, developed during the WWI period as a field uniform, became his winter service, with "blues" reserved for ceremonies and liberty. Khaki was worn most because the Marine so often found himself in the tropics. The old wool shirt was being phased out and the cotton shirt was seen everywhere. The "field scarf" was not yet called by the civilian name of "necktie," and it was of cotton with square ends and required good judgment to "two-block" it, or make the ends even. The everyday headgear was the campaign or field hat, which was worn by the Army, as well. Trousers were long and all hands were delighted when the Marines were away from the Army supply system in France and its issue of tight-knee pegged breeches with their wrap leggings. The Marine legging was side laced. A good Marine could slip on a pair of starched khaki trousers, lace up his leggings, and never show a wrinkle—for a few minutes, or so.

The Marine of the '20s still wore his Munson-last, high-laced shoes of brown (not cordovan yet). His socks were white, whether of cotton or wool, and, as time went by, he began to wear "low cuts" on liberty.

His weapons had changed, too. Now he had the BAR and the Tommy gun. But his basic weapon was still the tried-and-true, bolt operated 03 Springfield with its 18-inch bladed bayonet. He depended on his 30-cal. heavy Browning machine gun and moved it around when not in action on hand drawn machine gun carts. His artillery was getting more sophisticated. He still had his 75 pack howitzers and his little 35mm, but he also had French 75's. His transportation improved, too. He now had liberty Quad trucks, and some of them lasted into the early '30s.

In the air he saw a variety of planes carrying the globe and anchor.

All these new weapons required an increase in skills and, one by one, the "professional privates" began to disappear. It was still not uncommon for a man to be given his first stripe as a come-on to ship over. Promotions were not automatic or even reasonably rapid. It was a small Marine Corps, smaller at times than the Police Force in New York City. Its detachments, less than a regiment in size, were scattered from China to Nicaragua.

New ideas were being generated topside, and Marines began to practice a great deal more landing exercises.

Amphibious Warfare, they called it.

The Great Depression of the early '30s was becoming history, and finally the detachments assigned to ride the mail trains were returned to the Marine Corps. There was talk of pulling out of Haiti after all the years of helping to stabilize that country. Almost everyone who had served a cruise in the Corps had pulled duty in Haiti. Sandino was no longer a will-o'-the-wisp in Nicaragua. As a matter of fact, chasing him and his guerrillas had taught the Marines a great deal about laying and avoiding an ambush. It had also taught the Marine a good deal about something that was later called close air support and about something called dive bombing. The Germans were fascinated by the Marines' development of this tactic.

The men of the Fourth Marines learned some things, too. They had watched while the Japanese forces took on China in a highly professional manner. Clouds were gathering over Europe and bomb blasts in Ethiopia stirred men's minds everywhere.

With one eye on the headlines, the Marine of the late '30s redoubled his training. He went over the side oftener and in greater numbers into a new craft called a Higgins boat. He sweated over boat tables, boat divisions, and new lines of departure. He spent more time on hastily rigged transports. As likely as not, his bunk would be in what was once the ship's swimming pool. And he got a little tired of the old refrain, "a clean sweep down fore and aft!"

But he was learning, refining, and applying new lessons learned every day.

He was still wearing his campaign hat with an emblem turned green by sea spray. And he wore blue denim overalls and jumper. While he now had field radios with a hand-turned generator, he still used wig wag and semaphore flags for short distance communications or in lieu of still faulty field telephones.

Suddenly the "old breed" were startled by an influx of new recruits and reservists—battalions of them. A First Division was formed, then another. . . .

The old-timers again felt themselves threatened. Some of them said the same thing about the new that had been said of them in 1917. It was a time of reorganization and of a proliferation of new weapons and gear. There was this little auto called a Jeep that could go almost everywhere. There was a new rifle being tested called a Garand. It was semiautomatic and its magazine held eight cartridges. The old Marine regarded it with open doubt.

"It'll jam!"

Then the old pack was redesigned, and at Guantanamo, everyone blossomed out in "elephant hats." New field shoes with the rough side of the leather outside were issued. They were called "boondockers" and, with a remembrance of peacetime spit and polish, some old-timers shined them up.

Changes were swift and often.

The old "wash basin" helmet of World War I was withdrawn and new "coal scuttle" helmets with liners were issued. A new, green, herring-bone utility uniform was introduced, but the old-timers didn't take too kindly to it at first, preferring good old khaki—except when it was required in formation.

The new recruits and reservists took to these changes more readily since the older gear had never become a "habit" with them.

But, again, the "old breed" took the new in hand.

This time there was a difference.

The Reserve battalions were integrated into mixed units. Regular and Reserve looked alike, spoke alike, and except for experience, operated alike. As a matter of fact, many of the reservists were former regulars.

After a minimum grinding of gears it was difficult to tell regular from reservist.

The Japanese attack on Pearl Harbor didn't overly surprise the Marine. He had known for some time that trouble was brewing.

The First Marine Division by now was the "old breed" and as such was selected for the first U.S. offensive at Guadalcanal. Many of its blooded veterans provided experience for newly formed divisions and it speaks highly for the old-timers that no Marine division was ever a failure. The First made all Marines part of the "old breed" with its professionalism and esprit de corps.

Again times changed and with them weapons changed.

The basic Marine didn't change; he just had to study harder to keep up with the new, sophisticated weaponry and gear.

There was no rest for him after the war. He had to consolidate the knowledge he had gained in combat, and further refine the new gear and its employment.

He had learned the value of his Reserve and he knew better how to get the best use out of it.

Nuclear warfare posed a tremendous problem, but the individual Marine learned that he could take cover relatively near a nuclear blast and still survive. It was said by the eggheads that there would never be another amphibious operation.

If the individual Marine climbing the sea wall at Inchon had remembered that prophesy, he must have laughed, however hollowly.

There were still a few, very few, of the old, "old breed"—all very senior NCOs or officers. Again they had to adjust to new weapons and gear—and fighting in sub-zero cold.

But, as always, they did adjust.

Vertical envelopment was the new word.

Helicopters.

After Korea, the boot camps didn't quite get back to full peacetime operations. Overall strength remained high in comparison to previous "peace" eras. But the boot camps were changing, too. Some of the old-timers grumbled that recruit training was getting soft. As a matter of fact, it was getting tougher but in a different way. Differences of opinion between D. I. and recruit were settled more judiciously than they had been when the verdict was reached behind the barracks. There was still plenty of "troop and stomp" but as much strain was placed on a boot's brains as on his muscles. The boot camps were turning out more fighting Marines and smarter Marines.

Language began to change subtly as "slop chutes" changed to "gedunks," "field scarfs" to "neckties," and "flat-hatting" and "gun-decking" became known as "direct disobedience of orders."

The aura of the tropics and the Orient had to make room for Mediterranean expressions and Marine blues could be seen at our embassies around the world.

There were changes in the blues. The blue cap cover was gone, and the white cover served all year, but with a new, wider grommet. The coat had four pockets and the old fair leather belt was gone. The old ranks of gunnery sergeant and lance corporal returned and crossed rifles appeared on nearly all stripes.

Combat gear was refined rather than changed and World War II boondockers were exchanged for combat boots.

The combat gear was in the unlock position in places like Lebanon, Cuba, and the Dominican Republic.

Many were new weapons. There were missiles of all sizes. There was an exchange of M1's for M14's and refinements in all the lethal tools of the Marine with the possible exception of the .45 cal. pistol. It was almost the same as the day it was introduced in 1911. There was new electronic gear and the Marine of the early '60s had to spend hour on hour schooling himself in its use and maintenance.

When he fanned out from Da Nang, the new Marine as well as the old one found himself calling upon historic memory of guerrilla fighting during the Banana Wars, and doing again what he had always done in previous wars. Except now it had a name—Civic Action.

Marines, whether "new breed" or "old breed," always loved kids.

So, here is the Marine of today fifty years after *Leatherneck* began describing him.

He's in better health; he's better trained and he's a lot smarter than he used to be—and that's saying a lot! Fighting is his business and there's no one better at it. He has the habit of winning and he intends to keep the habit.

He's today's Leatherneck!

PART II

Training, Roles, and Missions of the Corps

Throughout its history, the U.S. Marine Corps, being the smallest of all the armed services, has had to fight for its organizational existence. In the first article in this portion of the anthology, Lt. Col. Robert D. Heinl Jr. wrote about the past historical attempts to eliminate, reduce, amalgamate, or change the essential role and mission of the U.S. Marine Corps. With "one foot in the sea, one foot on land, and its head perpetually under the sword of Damocles," Heinl noted that the Marine Corps had been consistently able to fend off past attempts by outsiders to get rid of it or substantially change its core mission largely thanks to its consistently superb combat performance.

One of the earliest roles and missions for the Marine Corps was to provide shipboard detachments for naval vessels, man secondary ship's batteries, and to provide the Core of any landing parties that might be deemed necessary. But service afloat was not the primary mission that Marines envisioned for themselves. An important article by future Commandant John H. Russell forcefully argued for a more-defined USMC mission and doctrine. Russell noted that while the "general mission" of the Marine Corps remained firmly wedded to working with the Navy in expeditionary operations, the Corps would likely be tasked with numerous "special missions" that could give an outsider the impression that the Corps would do more work away from the Navy than in cooperation with it.

By the early twentieth century, leading Marine Corps thinkers like Maj. Gen. Commandant John A. Lejeune and amphibious visionary Maj. Earl "Pete" Ellis saw the need for the creation of doctrine for a robust Marine landing force well above any that had been used by the Corps in the past. Colonel E. B. Miller, USMC, wrote in the 1930s in this same vein and neatly laid out the requirements for a naval expedition that involved the landing of a Marine expeditionary force. In extraordinary detail Miller's work provided a valuable reference to better understand how the Marine Corps amphibious doctrine evolved during this formative period in its history and saw the Corps put these tenets to practical use with great success in World War II.

One of the greatest lessons learned by the Corps during many a bloody World War II campaign was the efficacy of the Marine Air/Ground Combat Team or MAGTF. An early pioneer and advocate of Marine Corps aviation was the Corps' first commissioned aviator, Maj. Alfred A. Cunningham, USMC. Cunningham strongly argued that aviation, while distrusted in its early stages by many USMC combat commanders, would soon prove invaluable to Marine operating units on the ground. Cunningham hinted that in the future, the Marine Corps would find that its air wing was not only useful but indispensable as well.

Thanks to the development and refinement of USMC amphibious doctrine during the 1920s, 1930s, and throughout World War II, Headquarters Marine Corps commissioned a trilogy of articles to be published in the *Marine Corps Gazette* from April through June 1957. The intention of the Corps was to capture and publicize the findings of a path-breaking board assembled at the direction of the Commandant of the Marine Corps and headed up by World War II veteran Lt. Gen. Robert Hogaboom. Later known as the Hogaboom Report, these three articles gave readers a comprehensive account of the new organization and structure of the Fleet Marine Force (FMF).

Moving into the present era, two short articles by Larry James and Chris Lawson respectively described the new post-Vietnam Marine Corps and the changes in training that revolutionized the way the Marine Corps operated. Lawson pointed out that despite the amazing advances in technology the infantry still played a crucial role on the modern battlefield.

Three final articles—two of them by Gen. Charles C. Krulak—summed up how the Corps intended to prepare for the modern battlefield. One of Krulak's most important innovations as commandant was the establishment of a "capstone" exercise at Marine Corps basic training depots called "the Crucible." He boldly stated that the intention of the Crucible was not to fix anything about basic Marine recruit training—that it was still as effective as ever in creating new Marines. Rather, due to the changing environment of the modern battlefield, Marines would need better skills to be good decision-makers. The Crucible was designed to do just that and in the process also be a transformative event for all who underwent its rigors. And by all accounts it has met with tremendous success. His final article, written halfway into his term as commandant, reviewed the Corps' progress to date and delineated what tasks he believed remained ahead.

The Cat with More than Nine Lives

Lt. Col. Robert D. Heinl Jr., USMC

U.S. Naval Institute *Proceedings*
June 1954

On a rough average of once every eleven years since 1829, the U.S. Marine Corps has found itself compelled to fight for existence—not against enemies of the United States, but against enemies of the Marine Corps.

These attacks have come equally from all quarters, from War Department, Navy Department, White House; from efficiency experts, budgeteers, brass-hats, and presidents. Habitually, every attack has been justified as a move to get rid of "needless duplication." No attempt has ever succeeded, and several have touched off legislative action which further strengthened the Marine Corps. The rock on which all but one of these proposals foundered has been Congress in other words, the will of the people.

If ever an organization has thrived on attempts to abolish it, it is this small Corps with one foot in the sea, one foot on land, and its head perpetually under the sword of Damocles. The battlefield and beachhead victories of the Marine Corps need no advertisement. Not so well known, on the other hand, is the Corps' durability in the face of ten successive attempts (all launched from within the U.S. Government) to legislate, administer, or remodel the U.S. Marine Corps out of existence.

Like a cat with more than nine lives, however, the Marine Corps has emerged safe and sound from each ordeal, and, if anything, it has prospered on opposition.

Andrew Jackson's Waterloo

On December 8, 1829, President Andrew Jackson, himself a fighting general of no mean standing, struck consternation throughout the Marine Corps by a passage in his first annual message to Congress:

"I would also recommend that the Marine Corps be merged in the artillery or infantry, as the best mode of curing the many defects in its organization. But little exceeding in number any of the regiments of infantry, that corps has, besides its Lieutenant-Colonel Commandant, five brevet lieutenant-colonels, who receive the full pay and emoluments of their brevet rank, without rendering proportionate service.

Details for Marine service could well be made from the artillery or infantry, there being no peculiar training requisite for it."

The Marine Corps had been in existence fifty-four years. Its Commandant, Lt. Col. Archibald Henderson (who was destined, before retirement, to outlast ten presidential administrations), had already had his worries in keeping the tiny Corps (1,800 strong) a going concern. In 1821, less than a year after he had taken office on the heels of a ne'er-do-well predecessor deposed by general court martial, the secretary of the navy had tried to abolish the offices of Commandant and Quartermaster of the Corps and to replace the two key Marine officers by civil servants. In 1824, things were still far from rosy, as witness Henderson's prophetic plaint to the secretary of the navy:

"Our isolated Corps, with the Army on one side and the Navy on the other (neither friendly), has been struggling ever since its establishment for its very existence. We have deserved hostility from neither, especially the Navy."

To make matters worse, real doubt existed as to the legal and administrative status of the Corps. Some believed the Marines to be part of the Army; others, part of the Naval Establishment; and still a third faction held the Corps to be autonomous. These administrative headaches had begun to throb in the late 1820s, and it is hardly a surprise to find the incumbent secretary of the navy, John Branch, firmly aligned with the president on the Marine Corps problem. Said Branch, in effect, to Congress, "Either settle the status of the Corps or get rid of it."

So, in early 1830, the survival of the Marine Corps was squarely up to Congress. "On this point," to quote Secretary Branch, "the opinions of many of the superior officers of the Navy were called for, and presented to the honorable Chairman of the Committee on Naval Affairs by the Senate, during the last session of Congress. These, it appeared, were by no means in accordance with each other; and this diversity of sentiment amongst persons best qualified to determine the question has induced the Department to withhold any recommendation on the subject."

Andrew Jackson, Army man by long experience and predilection with his conviction that the Marines needlessly duplicated the Infantry and Artillery of the Army, had also, however, steered his recommendation into the House Committee on Military Affairs. That committee, turgidly reported the Hon. William Drayton, its chairman, "took cognizance of the Marine Corps, in consequence of the expediency of merging it in the Army" (whatever that meant), and finally did not "think proper to interfere with" the status of the Marine Corps, but rather to pass the buck back to the Committee on Naval Affairs, where the president's proposals were put to sleep and died.

Meanwhile, Colonel Henderson, quick and prompt in legislative matters as he was in combat, had laid down an aggressive defense with both the Naval and Military Affairs Committees, whom he bombarded with statistics and arguments regarding continuation of the Marine Corps. Equally to the point, when a new secretary of the navy, Levi

Woodbury, succeeded Branch, Henderson undertook his education as well, in a characteristic letter:

> Sir—The Corps of Marines is one of the oldest in the service. As the exigencies of the Country required, it has served in time of War both the Navy and Army. No want of military efficiency nor of honorable performance of duty was then heard of. In peace no dereliction of duty has ever been more than once charged upon it, at least as far as I have heard. The propriety of any change in the organization of such a Corps is at the least questionable. As the Commandant of the Corps, if I thought such change necessary for the public interests, I should be among the first to recommend it. It is my fixed opinion that no such change will eventuate in the promotion of either economy or utility.

Further Congressional action was definitely aborted, confessed Congressman Drayton to Henderson—President Jackson or no Jackson. The public, setting a pattern which still holds, had jumped into the foray with both feet, and the press (notably in New England) rallied to support the Marines.

The time now seemed ripe for counteroffensive, and Colonel Henderson pressed for Congressional action to protect the Corps and to remedy the organizational weaknesses which the controversy had uncovered. The result was that, on June 30, 1834, Congress passed "An Act for the better Organization of the Marine Corps." This statute (spurred by Henderson and even by petitions from all the Marine officers on duty at Headquarters) firmly constituted the Marine Corps as a part of the Naval Establishment (although not a part of the U.S. Navy), directly under the secretary of the navy, and gave Archibald Henderson a substantially increased Corps to lead toward new laurels.

Andrew Jackson, having been afforded a good look at the back of Archibald Henderson's hand, let go of the Marines in favor of more digestible game and signed the bill. The Marines, able at length to abandon the foxholes of Capitol Hill, returned with a single mind to normality—which then consisted of swamp and jungle fighting against insurgent Indians in the Creek and Seminole Wars.

Because the Jackson foray was the first of many to come and because it foreshadowed, crudely perhaps and in miniature, basic elements to be found in subsequent anti-Marine proposals, it might be well to examine it on the post-mortem slab.

Woven through the 1829 controversy ran threads of thinking that were destined to become deadly familiar to Marines during the next 120 years. Those propositions ran as follows:

a. The Marine Corps must be eliminated as a unit because it duplicated someone else (the Army, said General Jackson), and because it was administratively troublesome.

b. On the other hand, there never arose any question but that the functions or duties being performed by Marines had to be done by someone (the Army again, said General Jackson).

c. The proponents of the measure could never show that, even if someone else took over essential Marine functions, the latter would be any better performed.

d. Perceiving the closed-circle character of the foregoing propositions and realizing that this was manifestly an attack on the entity of the Marine Corps and not on its functions, Congress acted with logic and soundness on the side of the Marines.

This was a pattern destined to appear and reappear whenever opponents of the Marine Corps plotted its downfall.

Saved by the Admirals

It never took a house to fall on Archibald Henderson where matters concerning the security or improvement of the Marine Corps were concerned, and, by 1852 (six presidents after Andrew Jackson), the venerable but vigorous colonel-commandant had amassed a special file of testimonials from the flag officers of the Navy regarding the usefulness and need of Marines in any well-run Naval Establishment: "All urge in the strongest terms," it was stated, "an increase in the Marine Corps, basing their view on the specific necessity of Marines for duty on board ship, owing to their usefulness and efficiency."

In 1859 (as if this were not enough) in his Annual Report of December 2, the current secretary of the navy brought a reminiscent smile to brave old Colonel Henderson, by his comment: "The Marine Corps is an indispensable branch of the naval service. . . . It is a gallant little band upon which rests the most widely extended duties at home and in every sea and clime, without sufficient numbers to perform them."

Only six years later, incredibly, after Archibald Henderson had finally sheathed his sword, the Marine Corps found itself at low ebb.

Most Marine fighting in the Civil War had taken place on shore, under the Army, and only one successful amphibious assault—that by Major Reynolds's battalion against the Hilton Head forts—marked the Leathernecks' record. True, Marines had fought and died on Henry House Hill at the first Bull Run (where, as a later Commandant, Maj. Gen. Ben H. Fuller, observed, "Surely they were among the last to run"); they had soldiered at Island No. 10 and with Grant at Vicksburg. It was not surprising, therefore, in 1864, to see a Congressional resolution introduced with the aim of transferring the Corps intact to the Army.

Colonel Commandant Jacob Zeilin, newly appointed, heavily bearded, much shot-at since entering the Corps in 1831, and already famous as the first Marine officer to land on Japanese soil, moved aggressively in this crisis. Having learned his techniques as Henderson's aide and protege, Zeilin without hesitation canvassed the senior flag officers of the Navy for their ideas on the status of Marines. The admirals' response was unanimous. With David G. Farragut, David D. Porter, and Samuel DuPont heading the list, the naval hierarchy opposed any such change, and Congress, wisely respectful of such authority, tabled the resolution.

Encore for the Admirals

On February 21, 1867, Colonel Zeilin—now, it might be said, a veteran of such affairs—was notified that a resolution had just been introduced in the House of Representatives, not merely to transfer the Marine Corps to the Army, but to abolish it entirely, after detaching its members to the latter service. The resolution, he noted, was being referred to the House Naval Affairs Committee, then headed by the Hon. Alexander Rice, a salty and conservative member from Massachusetts. In the course of hearings on the proposal, Zeilin again produced the sheaf of testimonials which he had employed with such success in 1864, together with new ones as well, and the Committee elected to concur with the views of Farragut, Porter, DuPont, Wilkes, Stribling & Co. The resolution was reported out adversely and died still-born, on the floor of the House of Representatives.

The Sailors Object

The early 1890s marked the end of the doldrums in which the Naval Establishment had drifted since the Civil War. The Marine Corps, under efficient command of its 8th commandant, Charles Grymes McCawley, seemed never safer. In 1890, the admiral of the navy, David D. Porter, had written:

> I have had the Marines under my observation since the year 1824, since I first joined an American man-of-war, a period of 66 years, and during that time I have never known a case where the Marines could not be depended on for any service. Without that well drilled force on shipboard, an American man-of-war could not be depended on to maintain discipline and perform the arduous duties assigned her. There is not an intelligent officer of the Navy who can speak anything but praise of the Marine Corps, or, if there are any, I cannot conceive upon what they can ground their opposition.

If Admiral Porter had only known it, his closing sentence, quoted above, had a prophetic ring.

Within four years, in 1894, a determined minority group of younger Navy officers, spark-plugged by Lt. William F. Fullam, U.S. Navy, had launched a full-fledged attempt to force Marines off the ships of the Navy and, ultimately, into the Army.

Fullam's initial test case (there were destined to be several during the succeeding fifteen years) had to do with USS *Raleigh,* whose Marine detachment, it was proposed, should be radically pared in strength and duties. This the Navy Department, after weighing pro's and con's, disapproved in favor of the Marines. What followed can be described in a subsequent letter from Maj. Gen. George F. Elliott, 10th Commandant, to the secretary of the navy:

> The wishes of the movers of this proposition being thus frustrated by the Department, petitions were circulated for signature among the crews of the vessels of the Navy addressed to the Congress of the United States, asking for withdrawal of Marines on board ship. The attention of the Department being called to said petitions, the Secretary deemed it his duty to issue a Special Order reprobating this procedure on the part of the enlisted men, which was nurtured by the few officers previously referred to.[1]

Although the sailors' complaint undoubtedly had sub-structure in the occasional bad feeling, which arose in those days between bluejackets and Marines (who were unaffectionately termed "policemen"), such an agitation could not have lasted five minutes without countenance by ships' commanding officers.

Be that as it may, on July 31, 1894, Vice President Adlai E. Stevenson, presiding over the Senate, read into the Record the sailors' petition, and, less than a month later on August 24, Sen. Charles F. Manderson of Nebraska (a land-locked state in which almost half the counties are named for Army generals) introduced on behalf of Sen. John Sherman (brother of Army General William T. Sherman) Senate Bill 2324, designed to consolidate five artillery regiments of the Army with the Marine Corps; to redesignate this body as a Corps of Marine Artillery; and then to transfer the whole Corps to the Army. This approach, novel to American ideas on the subject of Marines, followed closely the prevailing European fad which considered Marines primarily as coast-defense and fortress-artillery troops.

At this juncture, the sailors' petition went to the Senate Naval Affairs Committee, which pigeonholed it promptly, on the very same day that Secretary of the Navy Hilary A. Herbert issued official reprimands to certain officers whom he believed responsible for instigating the petition and went further by promulgating Navy Department Special Order 16 (previously mentioned by General Elliott), in which the Department stated:

Advantage is taken of this opportunity to state that the Department, after maturely considering the subject, and particularly in view of the honorable record made by the Marine Corps . . . is convinced of the usefulness of the Corps, both ashore and afloat, and of the propriety of continuing it in service on shipboard.

Senator Manderson's bill was referred to the Senate Military Affairs Committee, where it collided head-on, as in 1864 and 1867, with the disapproval not only of the secretary of the navy just expressed, but that of senior admirals of the Service. Following precedent, the senators concurred in expert opinion and decided in favor of the Marine Corps as it was.

Fighting Bob Fights the Leathernecks

Captain Robley D. Evans, U.S. Navy, carried throughout his service career the well-deserved nickname of "Fighting Bob." He had begun earning it on the fire-swept beaches short of Fort Fisher, North Carolina, on January 15, 1864, by holding a pistol to the head of a surgeon who had announced intention of amputating his wounded leg. On this occasion—"about as bloody a place as a lot of men ever got into," Admiral Evans later mused—he had observed the relative inefficiency of ships' landing forces (including Marines) in the assault of a defended beach.

Almost thirty years later, still fighting and quite evidently undaunted by the secretary of the navy's expressed views on Marines afloat, Captain Evans, now prospective commanding officer of the new huge (10,288-ton) battleship *Indiana*, asked that the customary Marine detachment be left off the complement of the ship, inasmuch as her demands in the way of a working crew left neither accommodations for Marines, nor billets, he felt, in which they could economically be employed.

On November 1, 1895, Secretary Herbert replied to "Fighting Bob." First, to make matters clear, the basic request was disapproved. Second, for the record, it was prescribed that *Indiana*'s Marine detachment would be composed of "One Captain, one subaltern and 60 noncommissioned officers, privates and musics." These Marines were to be considered part of the working force of the ship; they would man certain guns of her battery, wherever possible under command of their own officers; and they would assist in all-hands evolutions such as provisioning, coaling, ammunitioning, and the like. To the present day, in fact, this letter sets a pattern of duties and responsibilities for Marines on board ship.

As if to set the seal on the matter and to follow up his repeated expressions during the past two years, the secretary embodied in his annual report for 1895 a rationale of his views on Marines afloat. The modern ships of the "New Navy," he pointed out, were complicated pieces of machinery, in which the crews had of necessity to be much more concerned with precise evolutions, drills, and weapons than in the days of sail. Following this generalization on the modern warship came his clinching particularization about Marines:

> It is precisely in infantry and gun drills that the Marine is, or may be, an expert. It would therefore seem that there is far more propriety in having the ship's crew composed in part of Marines now than could have been in the days of the sailing ship. The having on board of two organizations, if a proper spirit of rivalry between the two is encouraged, ought to be considered another advantage.

As far as Secretary Herbert was concerned, therefore, Marines were here to stay.

"The Marines Has No Place . . ."

Stubborn and combative as Marines themselves, the Navy opponents of the Corps were still bound to have their way. Evidence of their determination, and of the headway that their views had gained, may be found in the first 1896 issue of the U.S. Naval Institute *Proceedings*. This issue contained the Institute's annual Prize Essays; the Honorable Mention paper, submitted by Lieutenant Fullam, was entitled, "Organization, Training, and Discipline of Navy Personnel as Viewed from the Ship." Under this full-rigged title, Fullam moved swiftly to his ancient quarry, the Marine Corps. His essay contains such gems as, "The Marine officer has no *raison d'etre*. . . ." It is followed by a printed "Discussion" which is extraordinarily revealing, not only because of the intense anti-Marine feeling made manifest, but because it identifies many officers, destined for naval renown, who overtly espoused Fullam's views. Extracts from this discussion follow:

Captain Robley D. Evans: "That I am opposed to Marines on board ship is pretty well known. . . . The more Marines we have, the lower the intelligence of the crew."

Lieutenant H. S. Knapp: "As regards the Marines, every day's experience strengthens my conviction that they detract from rather than add to the discipline of ship life, and that they are room-takers and 'idlers.'"

Lieutenant Harry P. Huse: "The Marine has no place . . ."

Lieutenant Bradley A. Fiske: "I am strongly in favor of withdrawal of Marines from our modern ships. My reasons are exactly those stated by Lieutenant Fullam."

Lieutenant A. P. Niblack: "It would seem the part of real wisdom to draw on the artillery of the Army for marine duty on board ship, if we are to have the present system."

Lieutenant C. E. Colahan: "They have no place on board ship."

Commander J. N. Hemphill: "Regarding the Marines, I think they should be turned over bodily to the Army."

The foregoing statements have little significance unless we realize that those who made them (together with many others not quoted here) were largely destined to hold flag rank in subsequent years and would represent a definite hurdle for the Marine Corps to cross in the future. It must have heartened the Marine of 1896, however, to find such Navy men as Luce, Wainwright, and Ellicott supporting him and to read the spirited, closely reasoned papers submitted for the defense by Lieutenants Lauchheimer and Doyen, two young Marine officers destined to go far.

The spatter of this bitter eruption was not long in coming to earth. A new presidential administration was in office, and with it a new assistant secretary of the navy; the impetuous New York gentleman-politician and naval historian, Mr. Theodore Roosevelt, a "mover and shaker." Under his chairmanship, in the all-powerful Bureau of Navigation, a Departmental board was soon convened in 1897 with the mission of studying and recommending measures for reorganization of the personnel of the Navy (Fullam's project). Before the board had been long underway, one of its members arose with the resolution, "It is desirable that Marines be not embarked as a part of the complement of sea-going ships." After heated discussion, a majority of the board disapproved, and the motion, like the sailors' petitions, died on the table.

For the time being, the status of Marines afloat was safe if shaky. The Fullam wing was still a minority, though an increasingly influential one. Their cause, originally baldly aimed at getting rid of the Marine Corps, was now much strengthened by a refinement in tactics; the Marines made available by disbandment and withdrawal of ships' detachments, urged Fullam, should be formed into shore-based battalions for employment with the Fleet. Had this proposal been wholly candid, rather than a stalking-horse to get the Marines ashore, and thence out of the Naval Establishment, it might have anticipated by a third of a century the formation of the Fleet Marine Force.

Nor should the involvement of Assistant Secretary Theodore Roosevelt be overlooked. A radical reorganizer by temperament and intellectual bias, Roosevelt had, at the outset of his naval association, fallen in with a keenly ambitious, articulate group of "radicals," so pro-Navy (as they would have described themselves) that they were apparently eager to maim the Naval Service by amputation of a trusted member.

"... the Marines Should Be Incorporated in the Army"

On November 10, 1906 (the 131st Birthday of the Marine Corps), Rear Admiral G. A. Converse, chief of the Bureau of Navigation, testified before the House Naval Affairs Committee that Marines should be taken off sea duty and should be grouped ashore for expeditionary service and to safeguard Navy property. Less than four months later, Fullam, now a commander, was back in the ring, breaking his (official) silence of ten years by a letter to the secretary of the navy, Victor H. Metcalf, in which he reiterated his own and Admiral Converse's proposals, now emphasizing the expeditionary battalions which might result. As endorsed by the major general commandant, Elliott, the Marine Corps views indicate a sense of weariness after more than a decade of nagging by Fullam & Co.:

> In view of the fact that this is simply a suggestion of Commander Fullam, and as it is not believed that the Department will consider such suggestion seriously, it is not deemed necessary on the part of the undersigned to enter into a lengthy argument to show that neither the Navy nor the Marine Corps will be benefited by said suggestion, but that on the contrary the efficiency of both services would be impaired.

The continued desultory agitation of this subject simply tends to injure the efficiency of both the Navy and Marine Corps, and causes dissension amongst its various officers, which cannot but be injurious to the service as a whole.[2]

If General Elliott really believed that Fullam's proposal was unworthy of comment or concern, he was whistling in the dark, for he had already received intimations in early 1907 from Secretary Metcalf and from the attorney general that trouble was brewing for the Marines.

Although Metcalf inclined toward the Corps as an essential part of the Naval Establishment, he in turn was well aware of the president's feeling, which has been summed up by an eminent Roosevelt scholar in these words:

> Roosevelt considered that the Marine Corps' major function was to act as an overseas garrison and police force. He believed that it could carry out this function more effectively as part of the Army. . . .[3]

While Metcalf remained in office, however, the line held, despite a proposal advanced in 1908 by the Army chief of staff that the Marine Corps be absorbed into the Coast Artillery. Fullam's letter was consigned to the waste-basket, and his idea was shelved for the time being.

On October 16, 1908, Rear Admiral J. E. Pillsbury, still another chief of the Bureau of Navigation, as a final act prior to retirement from the Navy, addressed to a new secretary of the navy, Truman H. Newberry, an old suggestion:

> SIR: The Bureau is of the opinion that the time has arrived when all Marine detachments should be removed from United States naval vessels, substituting bluejackets instead. . . .

The Bureau of Navigation, long a center of anti-Marine feeling (and perhaps somewhat nettled by the Corps' traditional autonomy directly under the secretary), was now in the position of urging a proposal very near to President Theodore Roosevelt's heart. He too, it seemed, wished not only to get the Marines on shore, but, moreover, to transfer the Corps, as he possessed Executive authority to do, to service under the Army.

> They have augmented to themselves (wrote Roosevelt) such importance, and their influence has given them such an abnormal position for the size of their Corps that they have simply invited their own destruction. . . . They cannot get along with the Navy.[4]

On October 23, 1908, therefore, over the vehement protest of General Elliott, the secretary, acting on presidential mandate, approved Admiral Pillsbury's suggestion, and directed progressive withdrawal of the Marine detachments serving afloat.

In reply to Elliott's agonized reclama, Secretary Newberry merely quoted President Roosevelt: "I know all about it—*take them off!*"

On November 9, 1908, eve of a Corps birthday which many Marines feared might be its last, General Elliott made his final plea, in person, to the president. "T. R." was obdurate in his reply: "I believe in their removal."

As Elliott subsequently testified before the Senate Naval Affairs Committee, this interview coincided closely with a proposal in the *Washington Post* (never a friend of the Marine Corps) that a force of infantry, artillery, and cavalry forthwith replace the Marines stationed at Pearl Harbor Navy Yard. In Elliott's subsequent words,

> Indeed, the Marines had reached the vanishing point. There was not a duty left. About three days after the President's order, a general officer of the Army expressed a strong desire to embrace the Corps into the Army as infantry. While we had been quietly following our duties, elimination and absorption were casting, unknown to us, their shadows at our heels.[5]

"The vanishing point" seemed at hand indeed when, on November 12, 1908, President Roosevelt signed Executive Order 969. This order restated the roles and missions of the Marine Corps, omitting conspicuously the time-honored function of service at sea.

To intimates, the president added that this was the first step toward transferring the Corps to the Army. In this inner circle, which included T. R.'s great and good friend, Gen. Leonard Wood, chief of staff of the Army, Roosevelt's views were not exactly secret, but Wood, nonetheless, sought a green light before openly proceeding for all-out annexation of the Marines. On November 28, 1908, the president wrote Wood:

Dear Leonard:

I have your letter of the 26th. You are quite welcome to quote me publicly in the matter. I think the marines should be incorporated in the Army. It is an excellent corps and it would be of great benefit to both services that the incorporation should take place.[6]

During the winter of 1908–09, Marines were removed, by orders of Secretary Newberry, from thirteen major combatant ships, namely, the USS *California, Idaho, Montana, South Dakota, Washington, Tennessee, New Hampshire, Mississippi, Connecticut, Maine, North Carolina, Vermont,* and *Charleston.*

Congress, traditional preserver of the Marine Corps, was not so ready to swallow all this. On January 7, 1909, the House Naval Affairs Committee summoned before it Newberry, the secretary of the navy; Pillsbury, the offending chief of the Bureau of Navigation; the major general commandant, Elliott; and a full panel of lesser advocates on both sides, including Fullam and Evans. For the next week, the fur flew. As the testimony unfolded, it became clear that Congress, in its own fashion, was conducting not merely an inquiry into a matter of ships' detachments, but into the justification for the Marine Corps; and that Congress was using the hearings as a means of driving home to the executive branch (just as it would on many future occasions) the legislature's conception of what the Marine Corps should be and do.

Foremost among those who testified in support of the executive order were: Fullam, Pillsbury, Helm, Winslow, Sims, Rodgers, Ingersoll, Evans, and Taussig. On the other hand, the Marines, outside their own ranks, could claim generous support from such naval officers as Schley, Goodrich, Brownson, and Badger. Within the Corps, the witnesses in support of General Elliott read like a Marine Corps roll of fame: Littleton Waller Tazewell Waller; Lauchheimer, father of Marine Corps marksmanship; Feland and Dunlap, already marked as leaders and thinkers; "Whispering Buck" Neville, destined to serve as commandant; Mahoney, Doyen, Denny, and Murphy.

The Naval Appropriations Act of 1910 returned the verdict. Passed by Congress on March 3, 1909, hours before the sands of T. R.'s administration ran out, that act included the following unequivocal proviso:

Provided that no part of the appropriations herein made for the Marine Corps shall be expended for the purposes for which said appropriations are made unless officers and enlisted men shall serve as heretofore on board all battleships and armored cruisers and also upon such other vessels of the Navy as the President may direct, in detachments of not less than eight per centum of the strength of the enlisted men of the Navy on said vessels.

And with that Congressional thunderclap, the issue of the ships' detachments closed forevermore.

The affair of 1909 brought to a rousing finish the fifteen-year cycle of opposition to the Marine Corps within the Navy. To students of these matters, these attempts to do away with the Marine Corps brought in real innovations in technique. Item one was the device not of attacking the entity of the Corps by all-out demand for its abolition, but of urging curtailment of the roles and missions which gave it vitality and raison d'etre. By depriving the Marine Corps of its then primary shipboard role, its ill-wishers reasoned that they would soon see the Corps withering on the vine, just as, under similar enforced constriction of roles and missions, the Royal Marines of Britain were shortly destined to fade into desuetude. The device was subtle and destined to reappear less than half a century later.

Item two in the innovations of 1909 was the bold use of presidential executive powers to constrict the Marine Corps. Prior to the day of Theodore Roosevelt, executive steamroller par excellence, none had questioned the prerogative of Congress to arrive at all major decisions regarding the status of the Marine Corps. From that time on, however, the possibility of unexpected executive action, without recourse to Congress, remained a threat to the Corps.

Then as later, however, Congress possessed the insight to protect its Marines, and neither the attempted surgical removal of Marine Corps missions nor the danger of conference-table knifing by executive fiat met with any more success than the frontal attacks of years gone by.

Quiet Interlude, 1909–1932

The Corps was now destined for an interlude of quiet—one of the longest in the history of the Corps, at least as far as its domestic tranquility was concerned.

Even during this period, however, two attempted incursions deserve mention, although neither could be fairly described as endangering the existence of the Marine Corps as a whole.

The first of these forays was a seemingly obscure piece of legislation (drafted and proposed by the still new War Department general staff) which essayed to regularize inter-Service command relationships. When mixed forces of the Army and Navy (including Marines) served together ashore, read this War Department bill, the senior Army officer present was to exercise command, regardless of the relative seniority of Marine or Navy officers with the force. This bill was actually passed by the Senate in 1912, but was stopped dead in the House of Representatives as its implications became clear. Colonel John A. Lejeune, subsequently to become 13th commandant of the

Marine Corps, had an active part in exposing the fallacy of this proposal insofar as the capability of Marine officers to command joint forces (which was at the heart of the matter) was concerned.

The second foray against the Corps marked the valedictory effort of the tenacious Fullam, now a captain.

By 1912, the Marine Corps Advanced Base Force (precursor of the Fleet Marine Force) had become a reality. It was to be tested in the Atlantic Fleet Maneuvers of January 1913, by an exercise involving the seizure and defense of the island of Culebra, Puerto Rico, a spot destined to hear the tread of many a Marine field-shoe in years to come.

Without the knowledge of Marines, Captain Fullam secured audience with the secretary of the navy's "Aide for Operations" (as CNO was then known) and demanded that he—Fullam, a Navy officer—be detailed by the secretary to command the new Marine Advanced Base Force. Fullam's argument at that crucial conference speaks volumes for the mentality of those who had worked so unceasingly against the Corps: ". . . the Marine Corps would never successfully accomplish the very difficult task assigned to it, of its own volition, *but would have to be driven to do it.*" (Italics supplied.)

Fortunately for the future of the FMF, Admiral Badger was then commander-in-chief of the Atlantic Fleet, and was present at Fullam's conference. Badger had been one of the few Navy witnesses to take the part of the Marines in the Naval Affairs Committee hearings of 1909. If Fullam epitomized the Navy officer in opposition to the Marine, then surely Badger spoke for the long tradition, past and future, of admirals who have resolutely defended the Corps against intrigue and vendetta. Replied Badger to Fullam, ". . . he had never known the Corps to fail in any duty which it undertook, and that it would be an uncalled-for humiliation of its officers and men to accede to Captain Fullam and that he would not stand for it."[7]

It was to be almost twenty years before the Marine Corps again found itself in jeopardy.

Trouble in the Thirties

In the two decades between 1909 and 1932, both the nation and the Marine Corps had changed perceptibly. The Corps had come through World War I with a sterling combat record, and, fully as important, it had gotten well launched in its systematic rationalization of the tremendous problem of amphibious warfare. Ships' detachments were no longer the principal characteristic organization of the Corps, and, in the lean years of the pacifist, anti-military 1920s, the appropriations and troop strength of the Corps, frugal though they were, attracted wishful attention from without.

At the turn of the 1930s, the president of the United States was Herbert Hoover and the Army chief of staff was Douglas MacArthur. Neither had particular reason to be counted among the many friends of the Marine Corps. From where General MacArthur then sat, the Marines represented competition and diversion of funds and manpower, which the attenuated Army wanted badly.

The 1931 strength of the Corps was 18,000. In 1932, the Bureau of the Budget recommended appropriations for 15,343 Marines. And for 1933, President Hoover, whose controversy with Maj. Gen. Smedley Butler had made headlines in 1931, recommended a further cut in Marine Corps strength to 13,600. As a yardstick for comparison, the total proposed reductions in the armed forces strength, 1931–33, were: Army, none; Navy, 5.6 percent reductions; and the Marines, urged the president, were to receive a 24.4 percent cut.

Shortly after Mr. Hoover's economy message hit Congress, it was widely rumored that the president had on his desk an executive order which would transfer the Marine Corps (as the president legally could) to service under the War Department. This order, it was said, had been drafted in the War Department for or by General MacArthur.

At the same time, the War Department set on foot a project to convert the 29th Infantry, then stationed at Fort Benning, Georgia, into a sort of expeditionary regiment that might attempt to carry out the type of expeditionary-force, readiness missions traditional to the Marine Corps.

Between the known fact of the ruthless budgetary mauling and the less known information as to the projected executive order, a public-opinion shock wave developed. Press and public rallied to defend the Corps Major General Harbord, U.S. Army (now retired and chairman of the board, Radio Corporation of America), went on the air over a national hook-up to defend the Corps whose 4th Brigade he had so dauntlessly led at Belleau Wood. Congress, ever quick to champion the Marine Corps, was johnny-on-the-spot in the persons of two outspoken members, Representatives Fiorello H. LaGuardia and Melvin J. Maas. Very little behind were the Naval Affairs Chairmen of the two Houses of Congress, Representative Vinson (long a Marine friend) and Senator Hale.

After a heated conference at the White House, the draft executive order disappeared from sight. A steady fire of statements and testimony from the Navy supported the hardpressed Marines, as elder statemen of seapower, like Admirals Hugh Rodman and Pratt and Secretary Adams, rallied to the cause. In January 1933, the House Naval Affairs Committee, piloted by Vinson, voted down the proposed cut, restored the 18,000 strength, and, once again, Congress had proved to be the Marines' champion. It would be fourteen years, with nothing intervening more eventful than a world war, before the Marine Corps would again fight for existence.

Merged, but Not Submerged

The conclusion of World War II, like the end of every other major war in American history, brought to the United States a mood of profound self-examination in military matters. True, we had just won victory in a herculean contest, unequalled in the world's history. But was this enough? Couldn't we have done it better? Would not "a proper organization" have achieved miracles—and achieved them sooner and more miraculously than the undoubted miracles of 1941–45?

In such a mood as this, in the spring of 1946, the joint chiefs of staff began a searching enquiry and debate into the proper future roles and missions for the U.S. Armed Forces. In the course of this great debate (whose proceedings, because of their national interest and implications, were ultimately made public by Congress), it became clear that the War Department (more particularly, its general staff), abetted by the all-but-autonomous Army Air Forces, favored reduction of the Marine Corps to military non-entity. The missions of the Marine Corps, proposed the War Department, should in future be as follows:

1. Security forces at Navy Yards and aboard ship.
2. Maintenance of "lightly armed forces no larger than the regiment" for minor police actions.
3. The "*waterborne* aspects of amphibious operations" (e.g., shore party, landing craft crews, amphibious communications personnel, and such-like miscellaneous jobs).

To effectuate such roles for a Corps which had lately fielded six elite divisions and spearheaded the greatest amphibious campaign in history, the Army and Air Force chiefs proposed:

1. That the Marine Corps be limited permanently to a ceiling of 50,000, with no expansion in wartime or on mobilization.
2. That the Corps not be permitted to conduct combined-arms operations (with the unspoken but evident corollary that the Marine Corps should not be permitted use of the combined arms). Also that any amphibious operation requiring the combining of arms be commanded by the Army.
3. That Marine Corps aviation be ceded to the Air Force.

Despite the candid and direct manner in which these recommendations were urged, they were anything but palatable to the 18th commandant, Gen. A. A. Vandegrift, victor of Guadalcanal. On May 6, 1946, General Vandegrift appeared before the Senate Naval Affairs Committee and presented the facts in a public statement, which awakened

Congress to the peril in which the Marine Corps stood. The following passage indicates the tenor of Vandegrift's forthright testimony:

> In its capacity as a balance wheel, the Congress has on five (sic) occasions since 1829 reflected the voice of the people in examining and casting aside a motion which would damage or destroy the United States Marine Corps. In each instance, on the basis of its demonstrated value and usefulness alone, Congress has perpetuated the Marine Corps as a purely American investment in continued security. Now I believe that the cycle has again repeated itself, and that the fate of the Marine Corps lies solely and entirely with the Congress.

How accurately and forcefully General Vandegrift had estimated the situation can be demonstrated by the ultimate Congressional reaction to his testimony, when, more than a year later, in passing the National Security Act of 1947, the Congress laid down in Section 206(c) what is now the charter of the modern Marine Corps:

> (c) The United States Marine Corps, within the Department of the Navy, shall include land combat and service forces and such aviation as may be organic therein. The Marine Corps shall be organized, trained, and equipped to provide fleet marine forces of combined arms, together with supporting air components, for service with the fleet in the seizure or defense of advanced naval bases and for the conduct of such land operations as may be essential to the prosecution of a naval campaign. It shall be the duty of the Marine Corps to develop, in coordination with the Army and the Air Force, those phases of amphibious operations which pertain to the tactics, technique, and equipment employed by landing forces. In addition, the Marine Corps shall provide detachments and organizations for service on armed vessels of the Navy, shall provide security detachments for the protection of naval property at naval stations and bases, and shall perform such other duties as the President may direct: Provided, that such additional duties shall not detract from or interfere with the operations for which the Marine Corps is primarily organized. The Marine Corps shall be responsible, in accordance with integrated joint mobilization plans, for the expansion of peace-time components of the Marine Corps to meet the needs of war.

Crisis in 1949

The feeling of surcease and security which descended on the Marine Corps after passage of the National Security Act of 1947 was relatively short-lived. By 1948 it was apparent that forces hostile to the Corps still enjoyed audience. The operation of these forces was made manifest by such gestures as the point-blank refusal of Secretary of Defense Louis Johnson to allow the marine commandant to attend joint chiefs of staff meetings, even on an informal basis, when Marine Corps matters were under discussion, and by evidence that, in lieu of the proven Marine division, some personnel planners of the Pentagon favored the Marine battalion landing team as the largest organized tactical unit which the Corps should have—a direct echo of 1946's proposals.

Still more alarming was the Senate testimony in April 1949, of Army Secretary Kenneth C. Royall that the president should, in the former's picturesque verbal counterpoint, "make the Marines part of the Army, or the Army part of the Marines." When asked by Sen. Leverett Saltonstall if he were advocating that the secretary of defense "abolish the Marine Corps and make it part of the Army," Royall shot back, "That is exactly what I am proposing."

The Marine Corps had cause for further apprehension, as Gen. C. B. Cates, 19th commandant, testified before the House Armed Services Committee in 1949, when it was learned in the nick of time that unpublicized Defense Department plans were all but signed to transfer Marine Corps aviation to the Air Force. This transaction was aborted by Chairman Carl Vinson of the House Armed Forces Committee, who presented the entire question directly to the then secretary of defense, Mr. Louis Johnson, and secured the latter's assurance that any such policy actions would be referred to the Congressional committee involved.

And here again the Congress had thrown decisive weight toward preservation of the anomalous but effective entity in which the Corps of Marines had won its great victories.

Korea would demonstrate soon enough that the Marine Corps was still fit, ready, and worthy of preservation to fight another day.

Epilogue, 1951–52

In 1951 and 1952, the 82d Congress, its members seemingly hoped, brought the 120-year Marine Corps cycle of unrest to full stop by passage of the Douglas-Mansfield Bill, sometimes called "The Marine Corps Bill." This bill affords the commandant place among the joint chiefs of staff on Marine matters and provides the Corps with a legally stable division and air wing organization.

This notable legislation passed in final form only after lengthy hearings before the Armed Services Committees of both the Senate and the House, unanimously by the Senate and after a floor debate in the House of Representatives in which the 8-to-1 pro-Marines majority swept away the few arguments that the bitter-end opposition attempted to raise.

In the Douglas-Mansfield Bill, students of Marine Corps history could see strong similarities to the 1834 legislation with which this article opened. As in 1834, Congress had acted once again to clear up misunderstanding as to the status and organization of the Corps and to guarantee it an effective strength. The Congressional method of approaching the question was definitely reminiscent of 1909, and much of the quality and reasoning of the opposition was similar—strikingly so. Students of Marine Corps history could say truthfully that not since 1909 had the Corps been the subject of so-single-minded, detailed Congressional examination—an examination which, like that in 1909, found the Corps no whit wanting.

Thus it may be, if history is any guide, that, just as after the 1834 and 1909 Congressional debates, the Marine Corps may look forward to a long period of tranquility, at least as far as its domestic opponents are concerned.

After 1834, it was thirty years before trouble brewed again; after 1909, it was more than twenty. Today's Marines hope that history may, at least on this score, repeat itself.

★ ★ ★

Down through the twelve decades from 1829 to 1949, a historical pattern stands clear. Most striking in that pattern is the fact that the proposals to eliminate or hamstring the Marine Corps originated, very nearly fifty-fifty, from both sides of the State, War, and Navy Building.

Six of these jihads (1829, 1864, 1867, 1932, 1946, and 1949) took form, in greater or less degree, as attempts to amalgamate the Marine Corps with the Army (or latterly, the Air Force). Four, however (1894, 1895, 1896–97, and 1907–9), had their origin within the Navy. Thus it is a fair conclusion that the Marine Corps, in its day, has withstood storms from every quarter. Conversely, no one (except Congress) has been the Marines' consistent protector.

A second rather striking observation is that, regardless of origin, every proposal to modify or abolish the Marine Corps has been justified at some point by its proponents as a move to eliminate duplications of one kind or another within the armed forces. In 1829, 1864, 1867, 1932, 1946, and 1949, the Corps was stated to be in duplication of the Army. In 1894, 1895, 1897, and 1909, it was maintained that Marine detachments aboard ship needlessly duplicated the functions of seamen. Curiously enough, however, it appeared that, whatever these duplicating functions were, they had to be performed by someone. For example, in 1908, when Secretary Newberry finally acceded to removing the Marines from onboard ship, he was forced to direct a *gradual* withdrawal—for the simple reason that the departing Marines would have to train equivalent bodies of sailors to perform distinctive duties hitherto assigned to Marines. Conversely, as early as

1829, Andrew Jackson's proposal stipulated that "details for the Marine service" would, upon abolition of the Corps, be made from the Army. Ninety-eight years later, in 1932, a necessary preliminary to disbandment of the Marine Corps was the projected conversion of the 29th Infantry into a sort of miniature Fleet Marine Force.

In other words, it may well be observed that all these proposals, each directed toward getting rid of a supposed (or claimed) duplication, have been aimed, not as might appear, at the functions of the Corps, but rather *at the existence of the Corps as a separate entity.* Superficial similarities between the Marine Corps and the Navy (in some respects), or between the Marine Corps and the Army (in other respects), or between the Marine Corps and the Air Force (in still other respects), have thus repeatedly bemused outsiders into accepting as real, rather than apparent, "duplications" which functionally do not exist.

What perpetually laid the Marine Corps open to attack, at least prior to the 1920s, was its anomalous character, not a body of seamen, and yet by no means conventional shore-going soldiers. In theology this indefinable status would be called a "mystery," and, in the case of the Marine Corps, it was disastrously easy to oversimplify.

Commencing in the twentieth century, the Marine Corps mounted a full-dress attack upon the reputedly insoluble problems of amphibious warfare, particularly that of the opposed landing. History records how well the Corps succeeded, and how, prior to 1941, it had not only evolved the doctrines for, but had actually organized the only amphibious striking force of, the United States. This development demolished the factual groundwork of any claimed duplications of function leveled against the Marine Corps, which had, in effect, invented and then executed in the best style a new military function of crucial importance. And this unique role of the Corps has now been recognized in law.

★ ★ ★

With all said and done, why—we may still ask—have the American people (through Congress) sided unanimously with the Marines?

There are a multitude of well-reasoned, logical answers, and it is on these that Congress has so often reached conclusions in favor of the Corps. But it is not enough to say that Marines have pioneered where military orthodoxy has lagged; that the readiness of the Marine Corps is a national insurance policy; that dollar for dollar, man for man, the Marine Corps represents economy and efficiency unsurpassed.

Perhaps, on the whole, it is not too much to conclude that the Corps is just a little more than a mere "component" in our Armed Forces. The U.S. Marines have become, a unique, vital, and colorful part of the American scene. Perhaps, indeed, the Corps has matured into a national institution.

---

1. As to the admitted identity of the ringleaders, the following quotation from hearings before the Senate Naval Affairs Committee on January 9, 1909, is illuminating:

   Gen. ELLIOTT: Were you not aboard the *Chicago* when the crew of that ship circulated petitions to come to Congress to have the Marines withdrawn from ships?

   Cdr. FULLAM: Yes, sir.

   Gen. ELLIOTT: And did not the Secretary of the Navy, Mr. Herbert, get out a general order that really referred to you?

   Cdr. FULLAM: I do not know whether it referred to me or not, but I will say that if it did, I am willing to take the responsibility.

2. Endorsement by MGC to SecNav on Fullam letter, February 26, 1907.

3. Letter from Alfred D. Chandler, Jr., Assistant Editor, *The Letters of Theodore Roosevelt,* December 5, 1951.

4. Letter quoted in "'The Marines' First Spy," by John L. Zimmerman, *Saturday Evening Post,* November 23, 1946.

5. "Hearings Before the Committee on Naval Affairs, House of Representatives, on 'The Status of the U.S. Marine Corps," Government Printing Office, 1909, pp. 216–220.

6. Letter made available through the kindness of Mr. A. D. Chandler Jr., Theodore Roosevelt Research Project, Massachusetts Institute of Technology.

7. *The Reminiscences of a Marine,* by Maj. Gen. John R. Lejeune, Philadelphia, 1930, 202.

A Plea for a Mission and Doctrine

Maj. John H. Russell, USMC

Marine Corps Gazette
June 1916

As information from war-torn Europe gradually drifts across the Atlantic, we learn of the use of new implements of war and the consequent changes to modern tactics. In all of this intelligence the one point that stands out clearly is the high degree of "efficiency" of the opposing armies of Germany and France. These forces serve as a "standard of efficiency" to which military organizations can and should be trained.

It is therefore but natural that we, of the Marine Corps, should turn to our own organization and compare its "efficiency," as we know or believe it to be, with the standard set for us. Such a comparison shows that, while in recent years great strides have been made in improving the efficiency of the Corps, there are some factors that go to make efficiency that have been overlooked, or a sufficient amount of stress not laid on them. It is for the purpose of succinctly pointing out these deficiencies and suggesting remedies that this article has been undertaken.

Efficiency

Efficiency is often defined as "the quality of producing results." It is of high or low standard according to the results produced. To reach its maximum all the factors that enter into it must be developed to their maximum and thoroughly harmonized. Then, and only then, can an organization, either public or private, be said to be efficient.

While the necessity for a high degree of efficiency in a private organization is great and is usually stimulated by competition and money greed, in a public organization, especially in a military or naval organization, the necessity for the maximum efficiency becomes peremptory, while the suscitating influences that assist the private concern are lost.

To be truly efficient a military or naval organization must be prepared to place at the command of its government and in the shortest possible time, all its power.

The governing factors of such efficiency may be stated as follows:

(a) Organization

(b) Materiél

(c) Personnel

(d) Policy

(e) Leadership

(f) Discipline

(g) Morale

(h) Doctrine

The value of some of these factors is not as great as the value of others, but each and every factor is important. Lacking any one, the maximum degree of efficiency can never be attained.

It is, accordingly, of the utmost consequence that every military organization carefully develop each factor and include the coordination of all. Such an organization then would become a multiple of the factors, or an organic mass. A healthy, sound organization that is capable, in the shortest possible time, of placing all its power behind its blow.

Organization

To accomplish the exchange of commodities private business organizations are necessary. The transfer of goods from producer to consumer is thus effected. Formerly, it was the custom for business to create the demand for goods, but a scientific investigation of the subject induced, in part, by numerous failures soon established the general principle that the demand or necessity creates business. This is the only logical assumption and, at the present time, no great business is undertaken without a careful and exhaustive study that clearly demonstrates the necessity for its establishment. Such an investigation conducted along modern lines insures, as well as can be insured, a lucrative profit that is the final object of all private enterprises. In other words, it may be said that "business, like government, is an evolution and grows out of general economic conditions."

The necessity for a certain undertaking having once been shown, the next step is to outline, in general terms, the "task" to be accomplished. For example, wheat raised in the middle west may ultimately be destined for England or some other non-wheat producing area, but the definite task of the farmer is to raise the largest possible amount of wheat in the most economical manner. His work is then accomplished. The transporting to the mill, the milling, the storing in elevators, and the final shipment form separate and complete tasks with which the farmer is only indirectly concerned. The above principle of the division of labor applies, equally well, to nearly every form of human activity.

Public or government business, like private business, is created by demand. It is a fact that the final object is not the same, for while in private business it is financial gain, in public business it is social betterment. The underlying principles, however, are the same and the analogy may be carried to many points of similarity in both organization and methods.

As already stated, the determination of the "task" or "mission" is the second step. What is to be accomplished must be clearly and definitely understood by everyone charged with the direction of a business, either public or private. In many cases, especially in public undertakings, the "mission" can only be stated in very general terms, and in the accomplishment of it many "special" or "sub-missions" may be found necessary, but the "general mission" will always be found to stand out clearly above them all. It represents the purpose for which the organization was created and exists and never, for a moment, must it be permitted to become smothered by the introduction of "minor missions." The trail once lost is hard to regain.

Organization may be defined as the act of bringing together related or interdependent parts into one organic whole so that each part is, at once, end and means. In other words, the cooperation between the various units must be perfect.

It is generally asserted that the success of certain private undertakings, over others, is due to their more efficient organization. The fact that German business firms have been successful competitors with those of other nations, in all parts of the world, has been stated to be due to their more perfect organization.

The analogy between a great business and a military organization is especially close. Each has its mission; each is divided into various branches or units that must be separately officered and united into a perfectly disciplined, controlled, and efficient organization. In each case the organization must be such as will best suit the fulfillment of the "general mission." This is the prime factor of organization for which all others must be laid aside. Furthermore, it is a fact that a military organization must be perfected in time of "peace," for after "war" has been decided on it will be too late.

The writer believes that the "general mission" of the Marine Corps is to cooperate with the Navy, in peace and war, to the end that in the event of a war the Marine Corps could be of greatest value to the Navy.

But is this the "general mission?" How many officers of the Marine Corps, if interrogated separately, would give the same answer? What then is our "great work?" No matter how well an organization is organized, if it does not know its "mission" how can it reach the highest degree of efficiency? It must necessarily lack a concerted action to accomplish its work.

In performing its "task" the Marine Corps will, naturally, have many "special missions" presented to it; in fact, in years of peace, they are apt to become so numerous that the impression is likely to prevail that such subsidiary work is not at all subsidiary but is, in reality, the master work of the Marine Corps. Such an impression is worse than misleading; it is dangerously false, and if allowed to permeate the service would result in its failure to properly prepare itself for the real issue and cause it to fight at an enormous and perhaps decisive disadvantage.

It is believed that the "general mission" of the Marine Corps should be drawn up by a board of Marine officers appointed for that purpose. The result of this board's work to be submitted to a conference of the field officers of the Corps, or as many as might be available, for discussion, amendment, if necessary, and ratification. The conference to be presided over by the major general commandant of the Marine Corps. Every officer on entering the Corps would be at once instructed in the mission of the Marine Corps and commanding officers would preach it to all their subordinates.

Materiél

This factor depends, to a large extent, on the organization and personnel. If the organization is excellent and the personnel alert to its necessities, the materiél should, in a well governed nation, be brought to a standard equal to or better than a similar organization belonging to any other power.

If, on the other hand, the organization is defective and the personnel of poor quality, the materiél is certain to be correspondingly in poor condition and obsolete.

Personnel

The importance of this factor is paramount. With poor personnel, no matter how well organized and equipped, an organization will, in short order, deteriorate. In fact, in general terms, the efficiency of an organization may be gauged by its personnel.

Policy

After the organization of a public or private undertaking has been perfected, management begins.

The "policy" of an organization may be defined as the system of management necessary to accomplish the "mission." It is the conduct of the affairs of the organization. For governmental organizations, to a great extent, policy is governed by regulations but nevertheless a great deal is left and must necessarily be left to commanding officers, permitting them to initiate a policy of their own covering their particular commands.

Leadership

The qualities that go to make a leader of a military organization are will power, intelligence, resourcefulness, health, and last, but not least, professional knowledge and training.

It is a mistaken idea that leaders are born and not made. It is true that a certain amount of personal magnetism may be of assistance in the making of a leader, but if an officer cultivates and develops the factors enumerated above, he will necessarily develop into a leader. Of prime importance is a study of psychology and its relation to discipline and morale.

Leadership may be either actual or directive. Actual in the lower grades of the commissioned personnel of a military organization and directive in the higher commands. It is, however, just as important in the one case as the other, and the same factors are applicable in each.

While the preparation for "leadership" must be left to the individual, the Marine Corps could materially assist its officers by pointing out the road and by establishing and maintaining schools where officers could receive the best theoretical and practical training.

Discipline

Years ago Kempenfelt wrote, "The men who are the best disciplined, of whatever country they are, will always fight the best."

In some countries the form of government naturally tends to promote discipline among all classes and the recruit, when called to the "colors," enters the service already more or less inculcated with the habit of subordination. In other countries, however, where the method of living is more free, the recruit is not as susceptible to discipline and it is for this very reason that discipline in the military and naval organizations of such a nation assumes great importance.

It may be said that the laxer the rule, order, method of action, or living in a country the stricter should be the discipline in the military and naval organizations of such a country.

A study of the best method to be employed in obtaining excellent military discipline implies a study of the psychology of suggestion and its application to military life.

The recruit who has matured under certain free conditions of city or country life is suddenly placed in an entirely new atmosphere, and it is to overcome the perhaps bad impressions of such a sudden change of environment and to direct the mental attitude of the recruit along proper lines that psychology must be employed.

The study of this important subject by all commissioned officers of the Marine Corps should be made imperative, a proper course of study being outlined in general orders.

Morale

The necessity for maintaining the "morale" of an organization at a high pitch, during both peace and war, is now recognized. This subject has been dealt with most thoroughly, in recent years, by students of psychology, and in the present European war great attention is being devoted, on all sides, to this important factor.

It would therefore seem proper that special attention should be given by the Marine Corps to this subject, such, for example, as the appointing of a board of officers to study the subject and draw up a concise manual outlining a method, applicable to the Marine Corps, for increasing the morale of this organization and maintaining it at its maximum during peace and war. Such a method if properly enforced would result in the study of this important subject by all officers and tend to greatly strengthen the organization as a whole.

Doctrine

During the past few years a number of articles that have become classics have been published on the subject of doctrine and its relation to war. The writer, therefore, feels a decided hesitancy in even touching on this subject, but he believes its importance to the Marine Corps to be so vital that he cannot refrain from a general discussion of it in the hope that the seed once sown will quickly germinate and develop into the strong branch of action, and that the day is at hand when the Marine Corps will be indoctrinated.

It is well understood by military men of the present time that the art of war has its theories and its principles, otherwise it would not be an art. It follows that it also has the application of its principles, or doctrine.

The common acceptation of the word "doctrine" makes it synonymous with "principle." This is not true. A principle is a fundamental truth. A military principle is a fundamental truth arrived at by a study of the military history of wars and adapted to the circumstances and characteristics not only of the military organization but also of the nation it represents. Napoleon has aptly said, "The principles of war are those which have directed the great leaders and of which history has transmitted to us the main facts."

The word "doctrine," as applied to military life, means a teaching that provides for a "mutual understanding" among the commissioned personnel of a military organization. In plain words, "team work."

Military doctrine is born of military principle. It is the application of principle. A principle cannot be wrong; it is a fact. A doctrine, on the other hand, may be wrong. As it becomes ripened by experience or to suit new conditions, it is altered. It is thus, at first, tentative and gradually built up by a process of evolution.

The historical study from which we derive certain principles is nothing more or less than an estimate of the situation. The principles deduced represent our decision. Having once made a decision it becomes necessary to put it into execution; in other words, to apply the principles. This is true military doctrine.

In the preparation of a doctrine the "general mission" of the organization must never be lost sight of. Let the doctrine be clear, concise, and founded on the accomplishment of the general mission in the shortest possible time. With doctrines covering "sub-missions" confusion is certain to arise, and we would have some officers indoctrinated for one situation and some for another—a grave error.

Such a work as the formulation of a doctrine, however, is not the task for one man but is rather a labor for a general staff, or lacking a general staff, for a conference, a reflective body.

All the great powers of the world, except the United States, have instilled into their armies and navies doctrines of war which have inspired them with new life.

Without a doctrine all the drill regulations, all the field service regulations, all the textbooks are, as one writer puts it, "But dead bones and dry rust."

General Langlois, one of France's most astute generals and foremost military writers, has well said, "Eans doctrine, les textes ne sont rien: a des textes sans doctrine, serait beaucoup preferable unf: doctrine sans textes, ce qui etait le cas a l'epoque napoleonierne."

General Kuropatkin, in his book on the Russian campaign in Manchuria, tells us, "Although the same drill books and manuals are used by the whole army, there is considerable variety in the way the tactical instruction is imparted, owing to the diverse views held by the District Commanders."

The first phase of the British campaign in South Africa resulted, as a clever British writer puts it, in "the unforseen spectacle of a highly trained and well disciplined regular army, whose armament and equipment were abreast of the requirements of modern war, checked at all points by the levies of two insignificant Republics whose forces were but loose gatherings of armed farmers."

During the period of Frederick the Great, military forces were maintained in mass formations and maneuvered in combat by commands.

During the Napoleonic age conditions changed; the rigidity of the mass formation was replaced by open and flexible formations, resulting in a consequent separation of units. This pin in flexibility and ability to maneuver was obtained only by a corresponding loss of control or command. No longer could one man directly control the entire force. For example, Napoleon had to depend on the ability of his subordinates to interpret the meaning of his orders and instructions. But few of these had been trained in the same school of thought. There existed no common bond to assure a unity of mind and action. A link in the chain of command was missing; there was nothing to unite command and execution.

When that great German student of the art of war, Moltke, became chief of staff, he at once started to forge the missing link in the chain of command of the Prussian army.

The successes of the Prussian campaign in Austria were soon followed by the victories of the Franco-Prussian War and clearly demonstrated the wisdom of Moltke's policy. The doctrineless armies of France lost the war, but thanks to their many able military students and writers, the lessons learned were clearly set forth and at the present moment the indoctrinated armies of France are holding at bay the indoctrinated German troops.

Flexibility of command spells "initiative." Initiative may be either reliable or unreliable. The introduction of doctrine means *reliable initiative*.

Moltke, the great exponent of doctrine, required of detachment commanders "a high degree of technical skill with minds trained to work in unison with that of the higher command, even when separated from Headquarters by a distance which made control impossible."

It was the inculcating of doctrine into the Prussian army which permitted the introduction of the "cult" of the offensive which now permeates the German army.

Even with the modern systems of communication which bind together the various units of an organization, the need is as great, if not greater, for a unity of thought and action permitting of a reliable initiative.

The usual illustration for the necessity of a doctrine is that of a number of separate columns advancing on a broad front. Each column commander knows that on making contact with the enemy he can boldly take the offensive with the full assurance of the absolute support of the columns to his right and left, and with the knowledge that their interpretation of the various situations that may arise will be the same as his own.

Consider the well worn simile of the football team. Let us take two teams, "A" and "B." The first has been indoctrinated, the second has not. When a certain signal is given by the captain of "A" team, all the members of that team know that the ball is to be kicked; they know that the fullback will fall back; each member of the team on the line knows that he must hold his man at all cost (the strong defensive); the ends know that they must take a strong offensive, break through the opposing line, and get down the field as the ball is snapped back.

On the other hand, "B" team has no doctrine. There exists no mutual understanding as to what is expected of each and every member of the team. The end knows that he should get down the field, but the man next to him does not know it and permits an opponent to block him. The line does not realize the necessity for putting up a strong defensive, and consequently "A" team succeeds in breaking through and blocking the kick. On which team would you bet to win?

In this case the units are in touch with each other. How much more difficult is the situation in the case of a military organization where the units, or some of them, are separated.

Let us examine, for a moment, our Field Service Regulations (1914), the sacred book of every officer.

Under Articles I, II, III, IV, V, and VI we find at the beginning of each article certain "general principles" to which, in most cases, many pages are devoted. As a matter of fact, a casual reading of these pages will show that principles, doctrine, instructions, regulations and customs are all jumbled together in one almost intangible mass, which many officers no doubt take at their heading value—general principles.

Military principles and doctrine should form a Creed for every officer, but when we obscure them by mixing them in with numerous regulations, instructions, customs of the service and other data, they at once lose all force, if they do not become unrecognizable.

Why not cull out the principles and doctrine? Add to them what is deemed necessary, place all in clear and concise language, and make it form the military creed of our officers.

For example, in Article IV, under the heading general principles, we find the following: "The march is habitually at route order." This is certainly not a military principle, it is essentially a doctrine. There is a military principle of the conservation of energy. From this principle flows the doctrine: In campaigns the march is habitually at route order.

Other sentences in the above-mentioned article and under the same heading are: "When possible, ample notice is given so that preparations can be made without haste. Troops are informed of the length of halts so that they can take full advantage of the same. The men are kept under arms no longer than necessary, nor required to carry burdens when transportation is available. As a rule troops on the march pay no compliments; individual salutes, etc." All of this and much more in this paragraph consists of neither principles nor doctrine. It is purely administrative.

Again, the first sentence of Article IV reads: "A successful march, whether in peace or war, is one that places the troops at their destination at the proper moment and in the best possible condition." The first part of this doctrine, for doctrine it is, flows from the principle of the economy of forces and the second part from the principle of the conservation of energy.

Under Article VI, F. S. R., we find under the heading general principles no principles but definitions, administration, instructions, etc. The military principle covering all of these, but which is not stated in the text, is the principle of the conservation of energy. Turning to Article I we likewise find no principles.

The second paragraph of Article V under combat, placed in the text in the nature of a comment, reads as follows: "Decisive results are obtained only by the offensive. Aggressiveness wins battles. The purely passive defense is adopted only when the mission can be fully accomplished by this method of warfare. In all other cases, if a force be obliged by uncontrollable circumstances to adopt the defensive, it must be considered as a temporary expedient and a change to the offensive with all or part of the forces will be made as soon as conditions warrant such change." The underscoring is not in the text.

If we cut out of this paragraph all except the underscored words we have a military principle, not stated as such in the text, from which naturally would flow the doctrine of the offensive, except when the defensive is adopted as a temporary expedient. As a corollary we would have, the defensive is a method of creating opportunity for offensive action. In the same article under the heading combat principles we find few if any military principles, much doctrine, and instructions. For example, "Avoid putting troops into action in driblets" is not a principle, it is pure doctrine. Again, "Flank protection is the duty of the commanders of all flank units down to the lowest, whether specifically enjoined in orders or not." This is pure doctrine and cannot in any way be construed as a military principle.

In Article II the service of security is covered by the military principle that a command protects itself from observation, annoyance, or surprise by an enemy. From this principle springs the doctrine that the "primary duty of an Advance Guard is to insure the safe and uninterrupted advance of the main body." The greater part of the information contained in the paragraphs in this article under the heading general principles are definitions or instructions.

Turning now to Article III. This article deals with the subject of orders and contained in the paragraphs under the heading general principles we find definitions, information, instructions, but little doctrine and few military principles.

An examination of our Drill Regulations (1915) shows a similar condition to prevail. We find, for example, "combat principle" for the battalion, regiment, and brigade (pages 209–218). A careful reading fails to disclose a single principle under these headings.

A military organization, to be efficient and powerful, must be so indoctrinated as to acquire a uniformity of mind and action on fundamental military truths. Would not a commander in the field be reassured if he knew that an unsuccessful attack by the enemy would be a signal for a strong counterattack by all parts of the line attacked, or that the offensive, once begun, would be carried on by all parts of the line with great vigor until order to cease? All the German military teaching is based on the "cult" of the offensive. Their teachings say, "It is not even necessary to delay looking for too many advices about the enemy; the time for research is being wasted from the operations; it allows the adversary to do as he pleases and to impose his plan on us when we should impose our plan on him." This is part of the doctrine with which every German officer is indoctrinated. The offensive, in spite of everything, has permeated their very blood and marrow. But to permit of the placing in the hands of subordinates so powerful a weapon as "initiative" the subordinates must one and all be carefully trained to a uniformity of thought and action. It has been well said: "Initiative is a double edged weapon, dangerous to trust in the hands of subordinates who are liable to misconceive the mind of the Chief and are unable to read a situation as he would read it."

We demand "initiative" of subordinates and yet fail to train them for an intelligent initiative. What then can we expect?

In our Field Orders the first paragraph is the information paragraph. The second contains the general plan, and the third, the details of the plan, etc. A subordinate officer of an indoctrinated force serving with a detached command receiving the order reads the information paragraph and "understands the train of thought to which the information paragraph has given rise. The information being so and so, naturally, the Commander wishes to do this, therefore, I must do that. Obedience at once becomes intelligent because the purpose of the superior is understood and unconsciously approved."

Colonel (now General) Foch in his conference lectures, at L'Ecole Superieure de Guerre, puts it as follows: "An activity of the mind to comprehend the views of the Superior Commander and to enter into his views. An activity of the mind to find the material means of realizing them. An activity of the mind for realizing, in spite of the methods of the adversary, the conserving of freedom of action."

If an organization is doctrineless, a subordinate cannot arrive at an intelligent understanding of orders as now written, in the Moltke style. For a doctrineless force detailed orders are necessary with a consequent absence of initiative and poor results. Since we have gone halfway and adopted the modern system of writing orders, why should we not adopt the modern method of inculcating a doctrine? The one is dependent on the other.

Our Drill Regulations tell us that "In extended order the Coonpatty is the largest unit to execute movements by prescribed commands or means," and further, "In every disposition of the battalion for combat the orders of the bt. c. should give subordinates sufficient information of the enemy, of the position of supporting and neighboring troops, and of the object sought to enable them to conform intelligently to the General Plan."

How can they conform intelligently if they have no military doctrine, no interpretation of the military principles to act as a guide for them? It is as impossible as the command of the famous king that all clocks and watches in his kingdom should keep the same time. He established no method of regulating them and yet he ordered that they must all synchronize.

The mind of the subordinate must be "tuned" by the introduction of doctrine to work in harmony with the mind of the commander. The Marine Corps has no doctrine and the lack of this important factor must necessarily greatly reduce the "efficiency" of the Corps.

It is possible, some say probable, that the Marine Corps may be called on in the near future to face trained, seasoned, highly disciplined, and indoctrinated troops. Lacking a doctrine, no matter how good our organization, equipment, personnel, discipline, and morale, we would unquestionably be badly handicapped, perhaps fatally. We have no creed to bind us together, to help us to understand one another, to guide us to assist one another, to concentrate all our effort; we are as helpless as a ship without a rudder.

The formulation of a doctrine rests with the Marine Corps. It does not require congressional action or outside advice. It would require but slight expense and little effort.

For the purpose of formulating a doctrine it is suggested that a similar course be employed as to that suggested for determining on the general mission. Field officers of the Marine Corps, or as many as are available, should be assembled, under the direction of the major general commandant of the Corps, for a conference. The result of the work of such an experienced reflective body would be a *tentative doctrine* or *creed* for the Marine Corps, to be preached by every commanding officer and taught to young officers on entry. It would thus soon permeate the very blood and marrow of the commissioned personnel.

Such a doctrine, or at least the results of the first conference, would only be tentative and might require changes in it as we became more experienced, but it would certainly be a start in the right direction and establish a bond of sympathy among the officers of the Corps.

Why should we not, in terse language, lay down certain military principles that we believe are applicable to the Marine Corps? Why should we not formulate a concise and clear doctrine to bind us together? Why should we not formulate our traditions and incorporate them in our doctrine? Why should we not have a "cult" of the offensive?

Such action would greatly increase the usefulness, efficiency, and prestige of the Marine Corps and tend to unite this organization into one organic whole.

Let us remember the words of General Langlois: "Without doctrine, text books amount to nothing; a doctrine without text books would be much better than text books without doctrine, as was the case in the Napoleonic age."

A Naval Expedition Involving the Landing of a Marine Expeditionary Force

Col. E. B. Miller, USMC

Marine Corps Gazette
February 1933

In a paper published in the *Marine Corps Gazette* for November, 1932, it was pointed out that the Marine Corps has two missions involving the operations of an expeditionary force.

a. To assist the fleet in establishing and maintaining American sea-power in the theatre of war by land operations in the seizure, defense, and holding of temporary advanced bases until relieved by the Army, and by such other land operations as are essential to the prosecution of the naval campaign.

b. To support the Navy by the prompt mobilization and dispatch to designated areas of such expeditionary forces as may be required by the Navy in protecting the interests of the United States in foreign countries, and in carrying out government policies in emergencies not involving war.

Emphasis was laid on the facts that the Marine Corps has a mission vital to the successful operation of the fleet in war; that the naval officer should understand the powers and limitations of the Marine Corps; that the power of the Marine Corps to accomplish its mission depends greatly upon the possession of adequate material and equipment; that the Marine Corps organization is very flexible and easily adapted to meet sudden and unusual emergencies; and that the Marine Corps is ready and prepared to operate under either of these missions up to the limit of its powers.

It is my purpose to present in this paper some of the problems involved in the preparation, planning, and execution of the expedition involving the landing of Marines under the two missions referred to.

In considering these two missions, we must remember that in seizing an advanced fleet base, the primary consideration is a naval one. If it is an excellent harbor and meets the requirements of the fleet, then the considerations affecting landing operations, even though unfavorable to land operations, must be relegated to the background and our task must be accomplished irrespective of those unfavorable conditions. Here is an operation, which must succeed or fail. There is no half-way measure—no stalemate. We must accomplish our mission or withdraw. No base, half secured, can be made a refuge for a fleet. A beach-head with insufficient depth, is no beach-head—we merely have our feet on land but no place to put our head.

On the other hand, in emergencies not involving war, the primary consideration may not be naval, thereby permitting more latitude in the selection of landing places and the operating area for land operations.

In case war with a major power is imminent, we may assume that by executive order, the Marine Corps has been recruited up to its authorized strength of 27,400; that the Marine Corps Reserve with its 10,000 officers and men, although not yet inducted, are prepared and ready for immediate mobilization; that at Quantico, a base defense force, a reinforced infantry brigade, and certain special troops are already organized; and that the nucleus of a Marine Infantry Division is being assembled and ready to mobilize the division at Quantico or San Diego, depending upon the theatre of operations, as soon as mobilization is ordered.

War plans are prepared with meticulous care and cover a vast amount of detail, but these plans, locked up in the archives of the Department or high command, though they may be safe and secret, do little to make the solvers more familiar with their problems.

General Hamilton, when referring to the lack of plans regarding Gallipoli, says he never heard of the existence of the General Staff study of the Dardanelles made in 1906, "until I had been back some months, when the whole of our troops had been evacuated."

If we know our objective, have accurate and detailed charts and topographical maps of the area, have reliable information of the strength and location of the naval and military forces that might oppose us, we can prepare our plans and have a reasonable expectation that we can execute them as planned. But unfortunately, many factors intervene between departure and actual landing which make such a plan unlikely in a war against a first-class power, though quite possible against a non-maritime and poorly organized military country. Therefore, we must have not one but several plans.

Doctrine covers a large part of the preparation of naval plans. The *what* and *where* to do is told and the *how* is frequently covered by doctrine. But doctrine does not provide for the coordination of effort so essential in operations of this nature.

This is strictly a naval operation until the troops have been actually landed on the beach and the responsibility up to that point rests with the Navy. Therefore, the composition and organization of the force as a whole should be determined as early as practicable after the decision is made to embark on the expedition, in order that the tactical plan of the land forces may be prepared with full knowledge of the nature and amount of naval support.

Let me mention some of the plans that must be prepared by the naval force prior to the landing:

1. Composition and organization of forces.
2. Preparation, collection, and distribution of special equipment and material.
3. Allocation of transports and cargo ships to loading ports.
4. Loading plan.
5. Embarkation plan.
6. Liaison between Naval and Marine Corps staffs.
7. Selection of operating area.
8. Route embarkation points to debarkation points, with rendezvous of transports, if any.
9. Intelligence plan. Naval and Marine intelligence section must cooperate in the preparation of their respective reports before they are promulgated, as much information usually contained only in military intelligence reports will be of great importance to the naval commanders. Preparation of maps and charts.
10. Use of secondary base, if available, and necessary.
11. Rendezvous off landing place.
12. Selection of debarkation area with a subdivision of this area into transport, train, and support areas to support the tactical plan of the landing force and the methods and formation of approach thereto.
13. Attack and defense against enemy surface vessels, submarines, and air.
14. Execution of tile landing—including means of landing; boat plan; officer in charge of the landing; order of landing; formation and advance to the beach; boat traffic between ships and ship to shore and return; disposition of transports and train vessels after troops and material have been disembarked.
15. Naval support to the landing—including preliminary reconnaissance: mine sweeping; mine laying; air plan in reconnaissance, attack and defense; SS plan in reconnaissance and attack; gun fire-preliminary and supporting, close in, distant, and flank; smoke; communication plan: organization of the beach and lauding place by beachmaster.
16. Supply plan—for immediate use—water, ammunition, and food: for use as soon as practicable—heavy equipment, material, and supplies to sustain the contemplated operations.
17. Evacuation and hospitalization of sick and wounded.

The Landing Place

A leading force at sea is on its *line of maneuver* and as it maneuvers, fights, feints, demonstrates, and mystifies the enemy while on that line of maneuver, so will it effect the final line of operations at the decisive landing.

Initially, that is, prior to landing, the attacker has the advantage of mobility and selection of point of attack, but this advantage is surrendered as soon as he has landed.

The basic idea of the defense is to deny access where the enemy can land and quickly establish himself, and to observe those difficult places where he might land but may be thrown out by counter-attack before he can establish himself. The enemy was in the dark as to where the blow would fall, but once he knows, his plans work according to plan, while the attacker flounders forward into an unknown area, over unknown terrain, opposed by groups of unknown strength, and with his own units mixed and scattered into small groups seeking such cover as the terrain affords.

Some of the obstacles which must be overcome or eliminated before a landing may be made against organized resistance are:

1. Heavy artillery fire, HE and shrapnel, a long distance from the beach.
2. Bombing and machine gun fire from planes, a long distance from the beach.
3. Light artillery fire, 6,000 or 7,000 yards from beach.
4. 37mm and machine gun fire a mile or so from beach.
5. Murderous fire from machine guns, automatic rifles, and rifles, when stopped by wire just off the beach.
6. Controlled and contact mines, off and close in to beach.
7. Rough sea—making landing difficult and hazardous.
8. Sudden squalls or very rough sea preventing supporting troops from landing and making it impossible for initial waves to maintain themselves on the beach.
9. Difficulty in consolidating your initial hold just in from the beach.
10. Serious losses enroute to the beach and a break up in tactical units forcing you to establish your landing with greatly weakened forces.
11. Encumbrance of wounded in boats.
12. First wave boats get lost and land at wrong beaches making congestion at some beaches and no troops at others.
13. Mixing of tactical units on the beach. This is most difficult to avoid and affects command and advance.
14. No opposition at some beaches. Calls for initiative and hold and prompt action.
15. Landing boats may ground well off the beach with water too deep to wade ashore.

16. Enemy submarine activity may force movement of transports and supporting ships and thereby materially affect the arrival of supports and reserves and naval gun fire support.

General Hamilton, in speaking of the Gallipoli landing, says:

The problem as it presented itself to us was how to get ashore. The dangers and difficulties alive before our eyes were: (1) how to avoid being slaughtered in our boats and on the beaches; (2) how to get food, drink and ammunition as we went on.

Again, he says:

Staff officers who have had only to do with land operations would be surprised, I am sure, at the amount of organized thinking and improvisation demanded by landing operations. . . . The diagrams of ships and transports; the list of tows; the action of destroyers; tugs, lighters, signal arrangements for combined operations; these are unfamiliar subjects and need very careful fitting in.

In selecting a landing place we must consider our objective, the enemy, the terrain and the sea area.

Our objective. What is it? A harbor; a bridgehead; invasion and occupation of territory; a feint; a demonstration; a denial of territory to the enemy; a specific area that may be seized only by landing near the objective, or may a landing at any point in the area suffice?

An area especially desirable for land operations may be entirely impracticable from the naval viewpoint. Here we see our basic considerations affecting the selection of a landing place are very different from a joint Army and Navy landing, where the Army objective may require an area permitting operations a long distance inland from the beach.

Naval forces do not operate inland—that is the Army theatre. But naval forces do require a water area, almost surrounded by land, from which they may operate their forces, and a land area on which they may maintain the installations essential to the operating fleet.

So our objective is generally a limited one and the amount of territory to be controlled by our land forces is, as a rule, only that necessary to seize, defend, and hold the base area securely, and our decision involves not only the ability to land at one or more points but landing at such points as will give the troops the best chance of accomplishing their task.

Our enemy. A thorough consideration of his organization, equipment, material, armament, strength, morale, training, support available, disposition of forces, supply, the commander, and his mission must be made however inaccurate our information may be.

We do not generally know the strength and disposition of the enemy and one of our greatest problems is to avoid overestimating and underestimating his offensive and defensive power. He is probably as afraid of and worried about it as we are of him. He knows his weak points and that we are looking for them. If we assume that he is thoroughly organized, prepared, and ready at all points to receive and deny our advance, then we better go home or assemble a superiority that will succeed regardless of the number of casualties.

General Hamilton committed both of these errors. He overestimated when he waited for his 29th Division (orders from Kitchener) and sent his transports, already off Gallipoli, to Alexandria to be reloaded. These transports carried 34,000 men and 40 guns and, had he landed them in spite of the poorly loaded ships, he might, with the support of naval forces then available, have overrun the Turkish opposition. He underestimated when he misguessed the defensive fighting power of the Turk.

The terrain. I will merely mention a few terrain factors which are of great importance to our landing:

1. The configuration of the beach—is it an open roadstead, concave, or convex, as the point of a peninsula. Does it permit flanking fire from supporting ships and a landing on a broad front?
2. The nature of the beach—is it free from rocks, mud fiats, deep sand; is it firm to permit landing and movement of heavy equipment; steep enough to permit beaching of boats; sheltered to afford protection from surf; and how many beaches are available?
3. What will be the probable effect and damage inflicted by our naval gun fire on the defender's beach and rear area defense?
4. Does it permit a rapid deployment and advance toward our objective?
5. How many routes of advance? If limited to one—may that be successfully defended by a small force?
6. Does it permit the establishment of landing fields for our planes?
7. Must we transport all of our water supply from ship to shore or is there an available supply in the area?

The sea area. Certain conditions are as effective today, in their influence on landings, as they were a hundred or a thousand years ago. Dangers on an exposed coast; wind and weather; surf, still a great protector to the defender and a disadvantage to the attacker;

continuous or even initial landing cannot be guaranteed from hour to hour; gales a long distance off; squalls; strong currents; changes in tide; all affect, interrupt, disorganize, and may stop a landing force in its advance to the beach. And yet all exposed beaches are considered potential landing places.

What we would like to have would be a good anchorage in smooth water; of sufficient area to permit maneuver of AP's and supporting ships; comparatively shallow to reduce submarine menace yet with sufficient depth close in to allow transports to get as close to the beach as enemy fire will permit and at the same time allow supporting ships to approach within gun range of their land targets; a nearby island for use as a temporary base, especially for landing field; and a location with respect to the objective that it may permit of a feint, demonstration or secondary landing at points other than the decisive landing.

And here let me point out that this secondary landing or demonstration should not be a blow in the air with only a possible advantage. It should be tied in to the general plan. It is easy to make too wide a dispersion of forces and leave insufficient strength to take advantage of success gained by the general plan. We must have a strong reserve, and Gallipoli furnished an excellent example of dispersion of forces and lack of reserves.

How are we going to get this information about our objective, enemy, terrain, and sea area? Excellent maps, excellent information, and an excellent plan may permit a surprise landing without reconnaissance. Poor maps, little or no peacetime information, little knowledge of enemy dispositions, no accurate knowledge of enemy terrain, will demand a preliminary reconnaissance, the extent and nature of which will be in inverse ratio to the amount of knowledge on hand.

Information regarding areas of possible naval use as bases cannot be too detailed, too exact, or too up-to-date. Tactical plans may succeed or fail due to the possession or lack of correct and adequate information. It might seem of no importance to an officer visiting a foreign port, bay, or harbor to report that the beach was of soft sand or muddy, but such information might be of great importance to the commander who contemplated a landing in that area.

The harbor, our objective, may be strongly defended but unless the area is a small island, the enemy will not be able to strongly defend all landing places. It is one or more of these undefended places that we must locate, effect a landing, and advance on to our objective.

We must by every possible means be sure to land the troops at the place and beach designated. One beach may appear to be as good as another but the troop commander's tactical plan is based on operating certain troops from certain beaches, and a monkey-wrench is thrown into the plan if troops are landed elsewhere. Witness the landings at Gaba Tepe and Suvla Bay.

I have briefly presented the selection of a landing place, the defense, which may be prepared, and the reception committee that we may expect to meet on our trip to and our arrival at the beach. It looks somewhat hopeless and I think you will agree that to make a successful landing we must:

1. Land where there is no resistance; or
2. Land where resistance is unorganized and hastily assembled; or
3. Land where defense is in observation only and not in strength; or
4. So improve our naval gun-fire support that it may, by preliminary bombard-ment and supporting concentrations, demoralize and weaken the defender to such an extent that a landing may be made against a defended area without such great losses as will prevent our gaining and extending a beach-head prior to the concentration of superior forces against us.

The attackers supporting group with its gun-fire and combat and bombing aviation must break up the enemy concentration, must silence that enemy fire, or they will find themselves defeated before they really get started.

Boiled down still further, we may contend that there are only two ways, under our present system, of making this successful landing:

1. Land where there is no enemy.
2. Have a sufficient superiority in troops and material that you can force your way in regardless of losses and still be superior in personnel and material.

The Execution of the Landing

The marine commander prepares a tactical plan and executes his part of it. The naval commander prepares a supporting plan, which involves the initial execution of the tactical plan and the support of the landing forces to the end of the action.

Corbett refers to landing operations as "the most difficult and the least appreci-ated form of operation." Why is it the least understood? It is because we devote our attention to other phases of training that we consider of more importance, and yet, our geographical situation demands that should we ever make war or have war forced upon us, we must understand this form of operation, first, that we may take the war to our enemy, and second, that familiarity with the methods used in the attack will permit us to successfully defend our own shores.

And who should be better prepared or more familiar with this form of operation than that composite force represented in the Navy and its Marine Corps? The drill ground is ready. The forces are available. Does it ever occur to you that some day we may have to seize a defended base; that some day we may have to take an army of hundreds of thousands of men overseas; and that the Navy will have to do it? Then let us visit this laboratory, this drill ground, more frequently than the missionary takes his sabbatical leave.

Chance—luck—have played important parts in many campaigns, in many battles. Nelson, in his famous Trafalgar memorandum, noted that "something must be left to chance," but Napoleon added, "he who studies the causes of their success is astonished to find that they took every possible step to win it."

In the execution of a landing, we who have given it little thought will be astonished at the number of steps that must be taken to win it. From the conception of the idea to the delivery of the landing force on the beach, it will require the best talent of command and staff that a military and naval organization can produce. Everything must be planned. Every plan must have a schedule. Every schedule must be fitted in to one or more other schedules. Everything must click perfectly.

It is a relay race with the C-in-C on his flagship and the commander of the enemy shore forces each holding the watch while their forces race toward a lonely stretch of beach. The one who "gets there fastest with the mostest men" will be the winner at that goal—but there is another goal, the beach-head, the possession of which is essential before the dash can be made to the final goal. Each side is pouring in men and ammunition toward this decisive area. The landing forces supports and reserves come from the ships, land, and pass on through to extend their gains. The shore forces gravitate from all directions as if drawn by a magnet, hoping to arrive in time to exert their strength in counter-attacks, which will decide them the winner.

How do we get our forces ashore?

Transports arrive at the debarkation point. We have the task of putting these troops ashore in accordance with a preconceived tactical plan which provides that when the troops are on the beach their movements shall be confined to certain zones of advance leading to or converging on a common objective, or diverging toward special objectives.

Let us imagine a group of combatant ships and transports all anchored under cover of darkness in a common group, all disembarking their troops and attempting to dispatch and transport these troops to various and separate landing beaches. We would have a mess that the most expert of experts would be unable to disentangle. Everyone would be wondering—where do we go from here.

To avoid this congestion and hopeless situation; to assure a singleness of purpose; to control the advance of the troops and the support to be rendered during and after their advance; we must extend the lines, designating and limiting the zones of troops' advance, to the rear and thereby divide our sea area into zones that will indicate the area to be occupied by certain transports carrying troops designated for that particular zone of advance in the tactical plan, and the combatant vessels that are specifically designated to support their landing.

Once ashore, the support given to or received by adjacent zones is clearly defined. Cooperation between zones is dictated in orders from higher command; is arranged by conference between unit commanders involved; or by both methods. We see here a clean, clear-cut allocation of units to accomplish certain tasks; these tasks clearly defined; and a higher control of supports and reserves (and by that I mean fire-power as well as man-power) to reinforce and support when and where support is needed.

This same clear-cut allocation of tasks and mutual supporting arrangement must be extended clear back to the last ship involved in the execution and support of the landing.

We know the tactical plan, the main point of attack, the number and type of supporting ships, and the enemy surface ships in the area.

We have estimated the enemy strength at the point of landing, his artillery, air, mining operations, and submarines.

We select a debarkation point as close to the beach as possible but enemy artillery may force us to keep out as far as 20,000 yards, and that is a long haul to arrive at the beach just before daylight. Night visibility for land artillery is limited to 20,000 yards and then only when target is illuminated by star shell or flare. NWC Rules state that beyond 15,000 yards the target is not visible.

We now have the problems of:

1. Sweeping the area to be occupied by our transports, train and supporting vessels, and channels for the advance toward the landing beaches.
2. Getting the supporting ships into position.
3. Getting the transports and train vessels into position.
4. Getting the troops into the landing boats.
5. Getting off the preliminary bombardment.
6. Getting the troops to the beaches.
7. Furnishing supporting fire.

Sweeping. We must sweep under cover of darkness in order to prevent defense artillery from easily picking off our sweepers and we must clear an area in each suppost sector sufficiently large to permit the safe arrival and maneuver in and out for our transports and supporting ships. Land searchlights cannot pick up a target beyond 8,000 yards. Should it be intended to actually beach designated transports and land troops direct from such transports, then sweeping operations would have to go forward to that particular beach.

Secrecy and surprise are excellent weapons in the hands of the attacker, but in operations of this nature, we play these factors to the utmost of their effectiveness up to the moment our mine sweepers initiate their sweep or until we commence our air reconnaissance, and from then on, we must rely on speed and accuracy in the execution of our landing and tactical plan to take advantage of any surprise we may have put over on the defender.

When the mine sweepers have completed their sweeping and dumped their accumulated mines, they should go alongside transports and assist in the debarkation of troops, towing of boats and barges, and transporting troops and material to the beach.

A situation might exist where destroyers, ocean tugs, and mine sweepers could, under cover of darkness, take the initial troops right to the beach. Secrecy and surprise, together with accurate and reliable information of enemy strength and disposition, might make such a movement possible.

Sweeping may have to be done on the night previous to our landing, as the size of the area to be swept and the distance from the disembarkation point to the beach may be so great as to preclude an attempt to land under one period of darkness. Such action would be giving a twenty-four-hour notice to the enemy. However, if we had sufficient sweepers to initiate sweeping in several areas, it might confuse the enemy and react in our favor.

Preparation of the Actual Landing

Battleships, aircraft carriers, heavy cruisers, light cruisers, destroyers, submarines, transports, cargo ships, tankers, hospital ships, mine sweepers, tugs, beetle boats, motor sailers, speed boats, all have to be put in their assigned position at the proper time, on a schedule that is working against time, for the zero hour, when the troops strike their respective beaches, must be *not later* than the first peep of dawn. And this must be done in the dark, noiselessly, and without confusion.

The anchorage plan provides for a certain combatant ship to be in a specified area, in order to utilize its gun fire on targets and at ranges previously determined. This position must also bear an accurate relation to other ships to prevent interference with that gun fire.

Every ship must know the location of every other ship. Destroyers, tugs, motor sailers, and landing boats are directed to go to certain transports for certain troops and equipment and then form in line or column so many yards inshore of certain other ships.

Mine sweepers must lay lighted buoys or gas buoys to indicate the swept channel, to enable ships to pick up their berths, and to enable firing ships to find their firing positions. Submarines may be able to locate their own position accurately just before dark and plant buoys to be used as range marks and aiming points. In any case, some method must provide for accurate navigational aids.

Firing ships. These ships advance into a swept area sufficient in breadth and depth to permit free maneuver and just beyond the arc of enemy-known gun range. They precede the transports in order to afford them protection, and to act as "guide posts" for the transports' anchorage and for tile line of "Tows" to be formed later. We may assume, with the present 155mm gun range, that this line of firing ships would be about 18,000 yards from the landing beaches with each ship in its own particular support sector.

Transports. Transports follow, proceed to their designated berths, and anchor in line 500 yards in rear of the firing ships.

Troops are distributed on transports by tactical units and, if possible, in accordance with a tactical plan. Any redistribution of troops, and there are many reasons why a redistribution might be necessary, must be made prior to arrival at the debarkation point. A redistribution will call for a change in plans and *all concerned* must have accurate information of the changes made and time to inform their subordinates and make and promulgate their own changes, if any.

Destroyers and tugs assigned to transport or tow troops to landing beaches will proceed to their designated transports and go alongside as soon as the transport anchors. Troops for any single wave must be on the same transport. If any one destroyer or tug handles two waves, both waves must come from the same transport. No destroyer or tug must be required to go from one transport to another to procure its load or tow.

Train vessels. These ships have equipment and supplies that will be needed later but we are primarily concerned with getting the additional landing boats carried by them into the water and enroute to their designated transports. These ships anchor in line about 500 or 1,000 yards outboard of the transports and deliver their boats as soon as they anchor.

Plane Carriers. Carriers should be placed where they may be easily located and so they may be approached from the leeward by planes flying low. The leeward flank of the formation, or in rear, best meets this requirement.

Submarines. Should make a close reconnaissance of the beaches, if practicable. This might be done several days before D-Day and men actually landed to make a personal reconnaissance. During the advance to the beach, submarines should lie stationed on the flanks as guide posts and to assist by gun fire.

Disembarking Troops into Landing Boars and the Advance to the Beach

We now have our force headed for the disembarkation point. Mine sweepers sweeping; destroyers and submarines scouting, observing, guarding; light supporting ships; heavy supporting ships; transports; and cargo vessels; each with its own special task to be performed according to plan in order to get the troops from the ships to the landing beaches. It is pitch dark. No lights. Platoon commanders have assembled their troops ready to embark by gangways, over the side, through cargo ports, by any method that is rapid, safe, and quiet. Landing boats have been lowered from cargo ships 1, 2, 3, etc., and directed to report to transports 1, 2, 3, etc., at a specified time. Landing boats from transports have been lowered and are lying off waiting to come alongside. Boat schedule must consider that certain type boats are not suited to carry certain units and equipment and that certain equipment can be transported only in certain type boats. Landing boats come alongside and troops embark. Boats shove off and join a group of similar boats at a designated rendezvous.

Means of Landing

At this point permit me to say a few words about the means of landing.

The requirement is to land the most or required number of men; in the minimum time; and to establish as extensive a bridge head as possible or necessary, in order to protect the landing of other troops and to defend against counter-attacks.

This demands boats and many of them.

The British, at their Gaba Tepe landing, put three brigades, 12,000 men, ashore from 4:00 AM to noon, eight hours. The Turks, after 8:00 AM, always had superiority of forces against them. Had the British doubled their number of boats they would have had 12,000 men ashore by 9:00 AM; all five brigades, 16,000 men, would have been ashore by noon; and the story might have been different. The total number of boats available landed 1,500 men per trip. At Helles, they landed 5,500 men per trip plus the 2,000 on the River Clyde. At Kum Kale, they landed 3,000 men in six hours.

I would like to impress upon you the fact that naval landings are emergencies requiring prompt action in the initial phases of a war. You cannot improvise boats at the last moment. They must be ready to go with the expedition. The fleet cannot withhold its action until proper boats are constructed and allocated to the forces. We must have them ready or utilize the entirely unsuited means now available.

This is a Navy problem.

Others may suggest and recommend, but cannot dictate the type of boats you will use on your combatant and auxiliary vessels. The Marines make a plan and ask you to put them ashore in accordance with that plan—the means is up to you. We only ask that you consider the means available, and, if you agree that it is not suitable, then assist us in the development and procurement of a suitable type.

A boat meeting the requirements of a landing force would, in all probabilities, meet the routine requirements of the fleet.

If we have enough motor sailers and landing boats to land all troops in the initial landing, good, but more than likely we will be fortunate to have enough to land the first two waves. This means that the third and fourth waves must embark on destroyers and tugs—at least to the number that cannot be accommodated in the landing boats.

Here we must consider the priority in disembarking. Shall we load the destroyers and tugs first and have them lie off and wait for the landing boats to be loaded and join them as "tows," or the reverse? This decision materially affects the arrangements on board the transport. The immediate rendezvous of that destroyer or tug must be known, as troops from more than one transport will join the same tow group. Furthermore, boats must be arranged in formation by tactical units so they may land in accordance with the tactical plan.

The initial landing force is now all on board the destroyers, tugs, motor sailers, and landing boats, tows have been formed, and they have taken position 1,000 yards inshore of the firing ships.

At scheduled time, the tows and firing ships advance. Somewhere off there in the dark is a stretch of beach especially designated as a landing place for each group of boats. Each has its own zone of advance outside of which it should not go. If it gets too far to the right it will mix up with boats in the flotilla on its right—if too far to the left, it may miss its beach, land on an impossible stretch of beach, or get lost—in any case, put the tactical plan in jeopardy.

The firing ships and tows continue their advance, the former stopping when at their minimum most effective range and open fire. If this preliminary bombardment is to cover more time than the landing boats required to reach the beach, then the tows remain about 2,000 yards inshore of the firing ships, and, on schedule, cast off and make for their beaches at best speed.

The motor sailers and landing boats of the first and second waves, having landed their troops, return to their destroyers and tugs, which have continued slowly to advance, and embark the third and fourth waves and proceed to the beaches.

Destroyers then withdraw to assist in fire support; tugs return to transports to assist in debarkation; and the motor sailers and landing boats function in accordance with the boat plan.

Now we can figure out our time schedule by working backward from the beach.

Let the beach be represented by zero.

Tows cast off at—4,000 yards and proceed at 5 K—takes 30 minutes.

Tows formed at—16,000 yards, proceed to—4,000 yards at 6 K—takes 60 minutes.

Landing boats shoved off from transports at—18,500 yards and formed tows at—16,000 yards—takes 30 minutes.

We then find it takes 2 hours to get from the transport to the beach.

Therefore, troops must be embarked in landing boats not later than H-2 hours.

Time allowed to load landing boats depends upon many factors especially previous training and weather conditions. Experienced troops and much previous rehearsing will greatly reduce the time. Suppose we allow 2 hours.

Therefore, transports must be ready to receive the landing boats not later than H-4 hours.

Therefore, transports and train vessels carrying landing boats must be at anchor and these boats overboard in time to arrive at their assigned transports by H-4 hours. If we allow 30 minutes to put overboard plus running time to transport.

Therefore, train vessels carrying landing boats must be anchored or in position not later than H-4 hours, 30 minutes.

Therefore, we need 4 hours, 30 minutes to accomplish the above *provided everything clicks perfectly.*

If we make H hour at 0400, our transports and certain train vessels must be in position by 2330.

Assuming darkness at 2000, that leaves 6 hours, 30 minutes for mine sweepers to sweep and get to the flank out of gun fire—2000 to 0230—ships open fire at 0300 or 0330.

If we want to effect surprise, our mine sweepers should not approach the disembarkation point until after dark. We thereby reduce our sweeping time.

Let us throw a few monkey wrenches into the machine and see what conditions may well have to be overcome.

Some of the landing boats fail to report.

Empty gangway—no boat available.

Special boat for particular unit is late, lost, or does not report. Unit must be landed. Takes two boats of another type and a redistribution of this unit's troops in the two boats.

Congestion at gangways getting right troops in right boats.

Weather and sea conditions limit debarkation to the leeside.

Boats straggle in joining their group and getting into formation due to engine trouble, boat officers' unfamiliarity with the plan, or re-allocation of boats, etc.

Wind of force four springs tip and reduces the speed of the boats. Plan was based on boats of a certain speed making a safety-factor speed. Wind and sea reduces the speed below that factor and troops will not be landed in accordance with the time schedule.

Due to reduced speed, the tide turns before we reach the beach and bucking both wind and tide slows its down still more—some boats might be lucky to make headway.

A rain squall suddenly drops its mantle over the entire flotilla of landing boats and makes it impossible to see the blue stern light of the leading boats or to recognize the flash light signals from the boats ahead.

A submarine, which had been sent in close to the beach to act as a guide post for the flank detachment, cannot be located. The officer in charge of this group had depended upon this submarine to check up on his location.

You hear an airplane. A flare is dropped or a searchlight plays and shortly you are bombed and traffed by machine guns from the planes.

Does the job of the officer in charge of landing appear to be an easy one?

One naval officer has said:

"Too much stress cannot be placed on the importance of the work of this officer. He cannot be casually chosen from a vessel of the fleet just prior to landing. He should be an officer of rank, experience and proven ability, detailed to the duty as soon as the expedition is decided upon. He should have ample assistants, be in close touch with the CGEF and have full knowledge as to the forces and material; their proposed use and disposition. He should be embarked on the same ship as the CGEF or with that part of his staff who deal with the order of landing. On him largely depends the success of the expedition once it has reached the anchorage off the chosen landing."

The officer in charge of landing should:

1. Have charts, maps, field orders, administrative orders, tables of embarkation and disembarkation, and the orders involving the movements, disposition, and actions of all supporting vessels.

2. Should go on air reconnaissance of beaches prior to landing, if an air reconnaissance is made.

3. Have best information available regarding tides, winds, currents, reefs, shoals, nature of the beach, and distance debarkation point to the beach.

4. Have a list of boats and their assignment showing size, type, capacity, speed, and boat number.

5. A debarkation table showing:
    a. Wave number.
    b. Hour for landing each wave on the beach.
    c. Beach at which each organization is to land.
    d. Type and capacity of boats.
    e. Number of troops and of what organization assigned to each boat.

     f. Transport or ship from which troops come.

     g. Gangway to be used by each organization.

     h. Time each unit is ready to embark.

     i. Weight of equipment.

     j. Space in cubic feet of equipment.

6. An assistant detailed to act as his representative with each group of boats designated to land at a particular beach or a particular section of the beach. This assistant should be on the transport with the troop commander who will command this tactical group on shore.

7. Have a speed boat for himself and one for each of his assistants.

8. Be able to communicate with the troop officer commanding each wave.

9. Be on the same ship with the CGEF, and join him at the earliest possible time.

10. Prepare boat plan and issue detailed instructions regarding:

     a. Equipment and numbering of boats.

     b. Movement of landing boats:

          i.   To assigned AP's or other troop ships.

          ii. Disposition of boats already loaded and waiting for others to be loaded.

          iii. Disposition of extra boats, if any.

          iv. Assembly of loaded boats.

          v. Formation and organization into waves.

          vi. Formation in breadth and depth for the advance.

          vii. Direction of the advance.

          viii. Navigational aids prepared.

          ix. Intercommunication between groups.

          x. Formation and rendezvous of tows.

          xi. Scheme for transfer of troops from transport to destroyer or tug and then to landing boats.

     c. Duties of boat officers:

          i.   One officer to each landing boat.

          ii. Familiar with approaches, land marks, navigational aids, and compass course to beach.

          iii. See that boat is properly equipped before it leaves its own ship.

          iv. Do not permit boat to be overloaded and maintain the load below capacity load.

          v. A thorough understanding of his orders regarding place of reporting, loading, assembly, place in formation, destination, method of communication, and disposition after troops have debarked on the beach.

We may now see why the debarkation table contains so much detailed information. The troops and equipment to be landed must be coordinated and made to fit the means of landing. The troop commander presents a plan of when, where, and how he would land his troops. The officer in charge of landing must adjust his means of landing to meet this plan or the plan must be modified to meet the means. Weight, size, number, priority, capacity, speed, sea-worthiness, time, are some of the factors affecting men, material, and equipment which must be dovetailed smoothly in the plan by the officer in charge of landing.

No C-in-C can place a greater responsibility upon the shoulders of a subordinate than that demanded of the officer charged with the landing of troops against an organized defense.

Beachmaster. All that has been said of the officer in charge of landing regarding knowledge of plans, orders, instructions, conference with CGEF and staff, information of weather, sea and beach conditions, apply with equal force to the chief beachmaster, who is a naval officer and lands with the first wave.

He controls the beach from high-water mark seaward and has charge of all naval operations on the beach, landing facilities, beach recognition marks, organizes and controls naval beach communications, evacuates sick and wounded, cooperates with the commander of the shore party, and has an assistant beachmaster for each landing beach. A beach party of the necessary personnel accompanies each beachmaster.

Communication between ship and beach must be established at the earliest moment possible and signal parties equipped with radio, blinker, flag, etc., must be in the first landing group and sufficient stations established to give quick communication to flagship, covering fire groups and transport groups.

Wave lengths must be assigned, special pyrotechnic signals agreed upon and auxiliary signal methods provided. When possible, supplement communication by messages via boats bound for the desired ships. Code work should be reduced to a minimum as time lost in coding and decoding may be vital.

The beachmaster should also make an air reconnaissance of the beaches, if air reconnaissance is made.

The beachmaster is the sole connecting link between the troops on shore and the C-in-C, CG, and supporting ships. If his communication system is OK and the information is delivered to him, the supporting ships will know how to support. If this system fails, so may the attack, due to unavoidable ignorance on the part of those still at sea. I will have more to say about communication later.

Share Party Commander. A Marine officer, one for each landing beach, with ample assistance to take charge of all labor, troops, equipment, and supplies as soon as landed by the beachmaster.

He organizes beach facilities such as dumps, collecting stations, prisoners' cage, etc. He establishes information and communication centers, facilitates the movement of troops inland, and cooperates with the beachmaster. He usually has an engineer party that in addition to performing shore party work, assists the beachmaster in establishing and improving landing places for boats, removing obstacles and obstructions, and the erection of temporary wharves.

His communication system *must* function and move forward with the troops as they advance in order that vital information may be promptly relayed back to the ships.

Night or day landing? It seems pertinent here to note the difficulties involved in a night or day landing. We hear many arguments pro and con regarding the approach under cover of darkness and landing just before dawn.

If we consider the difficulties, from the naval viewpoint, of a night move to the debarkation point, we find the factors:

1. Darkness.
2. Navigation aids—removed or altered.
3. Mine fields—more difficult to locate.
4. Sweeping passage through mine fields—more difficult and hazardous.
5. Passage of ships through swept areas—more difficult and hazardous.
6. Defense against submarines—less efficient.
7. More difficult to locate assigned areas for ships.
8. Greater possibility of collision.
9. Greater difficulty of rescuing troops from damaged AP.
10. Greater difficulty of lowering boats without lights.
11. Greater difficulty in debarking troops.
12. Increased difficulty of ranging and spotting supporting gun fire.
13. Difficulty of scouting, observing, and spotting by air.
14. Increased difficulty of opposing an air attack.
15. Difficulty of warding off a DD attack.
16. Difficulty of night counter-battery work.
17. Difficulty of landing at designated beaches.
18. Confusion in landing boat formation.
19. Confusion and congestion at the beach.
20. Difficulty of the C-in-C maintaining a proper conception of the progress of the operations.

Hence, the enemy naval tactical strength influences the C-in-C's decision as to the hour of landing.

Against this we must consider that in a daylight advance:

1. Secrecy and surprise is almost negligible.
2. Enemy naval forces, air, and land batteries may force the embarkation of troops into the landing boats a great distance from the beach. This factor alone will bring on many difficulties.
3. Defender knows, by its excellent observation, the strength and direction of the attacker's approach.
4. The defender's reception committee, referred to before as the things we might encounter during our approach to and on hitting the beach, due to increased efficiency in their observation, fire, communications, and ability to maneuver and deploy for action, may, and if the attack is against an organized defense, cause such serious losses as to make success merely a forlorn hope.

At Gallipoli, the Navy demanded a daylight landing at Helles; concurred in a night landing at Gaba Tepe; and after protest, agreed to a night landing at Sulva Bay.

This decision as to the hour of landing is made by the C-in-C. The CGEG, if not of the same opinion, must present his views to the C-in-C, but there is no question of paramount interest, divided or joint responsibility, as in a joint Army and Navy landing. The decision rests with the senior naval commander and his decision is final.

If there was no other reason involved, this fact alone should cause the naval officer to give serious thought, study, and consideration to expeditions of this nature.

Value of Aviation to the Marine Corps

Maj. Alfred A. Cunningham, USMC

Marine Corps Gazette
September 1920

In common with every new weapon introduced to the military service, Marine Corps aviation has traveled a rocky and uphill road. Its small size has tended to make the jolts more frequent and severe. Nothing short of the firm conviction that it would ultimately become of great service to the Corps sustained the enthusiasm of the small number of officers who have worked to make it a success. The past year has seen the completion of the first of the stages through which our aviation must pass. Prior to this we had practically no official status or recognition. While we sent 182 officers and 1,030 men to the front in France, and they made a splendid record under severe conditions, we had no aerodromes at home, no shops, or other facilities; in fact, nothing permanent, and could very readily have been disbanded entirely. When it was realized that the Marine Corps' permanent strength of 17,000 was entirely inadequate and that a larger permanent strength must be requested, the figure decided upon was approximately one-fifth the authorized strength of the Navy, or about 26,380. It was desired to utilize this number for ground duties; therefore, Congress was asked to authorize an additional 1,020 men for aviation duty, making the total 27,400. This gave us permanently our aviation personnel. The next task was to secure well-equipped home stations for our personnel, and it required the surmounting of many discouraging obstacles before the Navy Department, which handles the expenditure of all aviation funds, approved the construction of flying fields at Quantico, Parris Island, and San Diego. With this much accomplished and our men and pilots well trained, we feel that the time has about arrived when we can demonstrate our usefulness to the Corps, which I am confident will be great.

One of the greatest handicaps, which Marine Corps aviation must now overcome, is a combination of doubt as to usefulness, lack of sympathy, and a feeling on the part of some line officers that aviators and aviation-enlisted men are not real Marines. We look upon the first two criticisms complacently, knowing that we can abundantly prove our usefulness even to the most skeptical, and that when we have done so, we will receive the sympathy and hearty support of all Marine officers. The last criticism we resent vehemently as an injustice, so far as it applies to loyalty, supreme pride in the Corps, and a desire to do what is assigned to us as quickly and as well as it can be done. Conditions arising from the necessity of organizing and training in a short time an aviation section, with practically nothing to start with and the nature of the duty, which does not allow the older officers to keep their juniors continually under their observation and guidance as is allowed in ground work, may have prevented the instillation in the younger pilots of all the qualities necessary in a Marine officer to the same degree as is done in infantry work. We have realized this difficulty and have made an earnest effort to overcome it and believe, with some few exceptions, that we have been successful. Now since the rush of organizing for war service is over, this difficulty will be easily and simply overcome and the task of aviation officers made much more simple by taking into aviation only those young officers who have had enough service with infantry troops to be thoroughly indoctrinated with Marine Corps discipline and spirit.

It is fully realized that the only excuse for aviation in any service is its usefulness in assisting the troops on the ground to successfully carry out their operations. Having in mind their experience with aviation activities in France, a great many Marine officers have expressed themselves as being unfriendly to aviation and as doubting its full value. I am confident that this must have been caused by some local condition, as the French, British, and Belgian troops in the sector over which the First Marine Aviation Force and the British squadrons operated were enthusiastically "full out" for aviation. In our own aviation section we intend, before asking a vote of confidence from the remainder of the Corps, to demonstrate to their complete satisfaction that we can contribute in a surprising degree to the success of all their operations, save many hours of weary, fruitless "hiking," and materially shorten each campaign. Previous to now we have had no opportunity to do this. During the war we were unfortunately not allowed to serve with the Fourth Brigade, but were placed in a sector containing only British, French, and Belgian troops. Since the war all our effort has been required to secure flying fields and the construction of buildings and hangars on them. We would have been hope-lessly handicapped without these facilities. Now since they are nearing completion we are looking forward with enthusiasm to our real work of cooperating helpfully with the remainder of the Corps. All we ask is a spirit of cooperation and encouragement, and that judgment be reserved until the proper time.

Judging from the unfamiliarity of the average Marine officer with what has been accomplished by Marine aviation, we have failed woefully to advertise. A short resume of what has been accomplished will perhaps be of interest.

In May, 1912, when the writer was detailed for aviation, the Marine Corps took very little interest in the subject. In those days it was looked upon more as a crazy sport than as anything useful, and when I look back on the old original Wright 35-horsepower planes I flew, where one sat on a board projecting out into atmosphere, I am inclined to agree with that view. About eight months later another Marine officer was assigned to aviation, and during the next year we accumulated six Marine-enlisted men. There was very little increase in personnel until the World War began. On April 6, 1917, Marine aviation amounted to four officers and thirty men, all part of the complement of the Naval Air Station, Pensacola, Florida. From this time we began to work energetically for expansion. Our ambition was to organize a first-class aviation force to operate with the Marine forces we hoped would be sent to the front. During the next few months we secured a flying field at Philadelphia, organized a full squadron of land planes, and began intensive training, so that we would be ready to go to France with the other Marine Corps forces. In order to have the latest aviation information the commanding officer of this squadron was sent to France to serve with the French aviation forces for three months. This officer made every possible effort, both with the War Department in Washington and the American Expeditionary Force authorities in France, to secure authority for our Marine aviation squadron to serve with the Marine brigade in France. No success whatever attended these efforts. Army aviation authorities stated candidly that if the squadron ever got to France it would be used to furnish personnel to run one of their training fields, but that this was as near the front as it would ever get. Confronted with this discouraging outlook the squadron commander set about to find some other way of getting his squadron into the fight. The only aviation operations abroad planned by the Navy at that time were antisubmarine patrols in flying boats. After visiting the Navy flying station at Dunkirk, France, and talking with officers of the British destroyer patrol, it was realized that Marine aviation's opportunity to get into the fight lay right here. The situation was as follows: Submarines were causing enormous losses to shipping; their main operating bases and repair shops were at Ostend, Zeebrugge, and Bruges, all within easy reach by plane from Dunkirk; the water for ten to fifteen miles off these bases is so shallow that a submarine can not safely negotiate it submerged. If these waters could be patrolled continuously during daylight with planes carrying heavy bombs, submarines attempting to enter these bases could be destroyed. Destroyers were prevented from patrolling these shallows efficiently in daylight by the heavy shore batteries, but could under the cover of darkness and with mines close the channels at night. This was evidently such an effective plan that inquiries were made as to why it was not put into effect. These inquiries developed that the Germans realized the danger of such a plan and energetically suppressed any attempts of the British Navy to patrol these waters with seaplanes, sending out their best land pursuit planes to shoot them down. An inquiry as to why the British did not patrol this area with bombing planes protected by fighting land planes developed the fact that they were so hard pressed on the front in Flanders and northern France that they could not spare the planes for this work.

Why could not the Marine Corps man the necessary number of planes to allow this operation to be carried out? Jubilant at having discovered a prospective field of useful-ness for Marine Corps aviation our squadron commander hurried home and placed the whole scheme before the major general commandant, had a hearing before the general board and the secretary, and as a result orders were issued soon afterwards to organize four Marine land squadrons as quickly as possible and secure from the Army the neces-sary planes to carry out the operation. It may well be imagined that with the prospect of getting into some real thick fighting all hands turned to with a rush, and by May, 1918, we had our planes and four of the best-trained fighting squadrons that ever went to war. A short time before going overseas a British ace and all-round aviation expert was ordered to spend a week with these squadrons to give them their finishing touches. After three days he stated that they were the most thoroughly trained squadrons he had seen away from the front, and that he could offer no suggestions for improvement—that they were then ready to go over the front lines.

Before the Marine squadron arrived in France the Navy decided to make the main objective the destruction of the bases at Ostend, Zeebrugge, and Bruges, and to increase the number of land squadrons, manning the additional squadrons with Navy personnel and assigning a naval officer to command the whole operation. It was somewhat of a disappointment that the status of this operation, which was originated and organized by the Marine Corps as a Marine operation, should have been changed. But with the prospect of getting into the fight, nothing could discourage the squadrons.

The Northern Bombing Group, which was the title given the combined Navy and Marine Corps land plane bombing operation in Belgium and northern France, although supposedly operating under the British, was in reality almost an independent body. It was composed of four Marine squadrons of eighteen DH4 planes each, known as the Day Wing, and was to have had four Navy squadrons of six Caproni night bombing planes each, known as the Night Wing. Only one Navy squadron was organized and it got into difficulties and sent, prior to the Armistice, only one plane over the front on one raid. Although handicapped on account of the inability of the Naval Bases at Pauillac, France, and Eastleigh, England, to furnish us our planes, spare parts, and tools, the four Marine squadrons accomplished a great deal. The results of one of our raids, verified after the enemy had evacuated Belgium, showed that we totally destroyed a troop train, killing about sixty officers and three hundred men. The Marine aviators also introduced an innovation at the front. A French regiment was isolated during an offensive near Stadenburg, and it was decided to feed them by plane. Sacks of food were bundled into planes and they flew low over the isolated regiment and made good deliveries of much-needed subsistence. This necessarily had to be done at a low altitude and under a heavy fire from every weapon the enemy could bring to bear. It is believed to have been the first instance of its kind. This organization participated in the YpresLys offensive and the first and second Belgian offensives.

In the meantime other activities were being worked out by Marine aviation. An organization of twelve officers and one hundred and thirty-three men was organized and sent to the Naval Base at Punta Delgada, Azores, where they carried on an anti-submarine patrol with seaplanes and flying boats until the Armistice. A temporary flying field was secured at Miami, Florida, where approximately 282 pilots and 2,180 aviation mechanics were completely trained, including advanced and acrobatic flying, gunnery, bombing, photography, and radio. A Marine aviation unit of six officers and forty-six men was organized and attached to the Naval Air Station, Miami, Florida, and performed practically all the long overseas patrols for that station.

In March 1919, a squadron of six land planes and six flying boats was organized and attached for duty to the First Brigade in Haiti and in February 1919, a flight of six land planes was organized and attached to the Second Brigade in Santo Domingo, Dominican Republic. These organizations have been seriously but unavoidably handicapped by a lack of suitable planes and not enough personnel to properly carry on the work. These handicaps will be removed in the near future. However, both brigade commanders have requested that the number of planes be increased, and very complimentary reports as to the value of the aviators' work have been received. They patrol regularly the whole island and have saved many long, hot, and fruitless "hikes." They have located bands of "cacos," dispersed them with machine gun fire, and performed many useful services that will be explained later.

Naturally our first and most important peacetime duty was to secure permanent well-equipped flying fields as close as possible to large Marine Corps posts, so that we could by actual demonstration prove our usefulness. The difficulty of accomplishing this was greater than all our previous endeavors. We received abundant proof that, whether the government wastes money or not—as is claimed by the public—it certainly does not waste it on the Marine Corps. It was finally accomplished, however, and we now have nearing completion well-equipped stations at Quantico and Parris Island, and the establishment of a similar station at San Diego is approved and work on it will begin when the ground at the Marine base is in condition.

The question regarding aviation, that is of most interest to the Marine Corps is: Of what practical use is it to us? We see the planes flying around and they seem to be enjoying themselves, but how will they help us perform our mission? It is confidently believed that this question can be answered to your satisfaction. This article will mention some of the ways aviation will be helpful to the Marine Corps. These suggestions will not attempt to cover every use aviation can be put to or to mention anything that is not practical with the present development of planes and the art of flying them. No one can more than prophesy what the future development of aviation will allow it to do.

It is my opinion that a great part of the evident lack of belief in aviation shown by officers serving with ground troops is caused by the entirely unnecessary amount of flying that is done with no specific object in view, except the practice the pilot gets in handling his plane. This naturally creates an impression that the only use the planes have is to give their pilots practice in handling them. This impression should and will be removed. There are many important military problems that must be worked out by aviation and so many interesting opportunities to work in cooperation with troops on the ground that flights should rarely be made in future except with some useful military purpose in view.

The following paragraphs give some of the duties we believe we can perform satis-factorily, provided always that suitable equipment is furnished. They require no equip-ment impossible to secure with the present state of development.

Every officer who served at the front in the World War was given a rather impressive demonstration of the damage and demoralizing effect of bombs dropped from the air, and was perhaps "extremely annoyed by being shot up by a machine gun in an airplane which it seemed impossible to hit from the ground". It will be remembered that troops in this war were, for the most part, well protected in trenches and dugouts from aerial attack as well as from attacks on the ground, and that both bombing and gunnery from airplanes will be much more effective against guerrillas and troops with less perma-nent protection. During the late war proper advantage was not taken of the possibilities of radio and radio-telephonic communication between planes and between ground troops and planes.

Let us assume that the commanding general of a Marine expeditionary or advanced-base force with his troops on board transports is approaching a port at which he is supposed to land in the face of enemy opposition. Would it be of value to him if one or more of his Marine aviators left his ship a hundred or more miles off shore, flew over the port, photographed the harbor, and returned in time to have the finished photographs in the hands of all subordinate commanders before land was sighted? This would allow the commander to plan his operation, not with inaccurate maps, but with actual photo-graphs showing every detail of any effective plan of resistance. Pilots would hardly be available at an enemy port. The photographs of the harbor in practically all tropical waters show clearly the channels, buoys, reefs, sandbars, and minefields, if any exist, allowing the ship to be navigated into the harbor without a local pilot.

If the commanding general desired to prevent the removal from any locality of enemy stores, railway equipment, and locomotives, would it not be of service to him if the aviator left the ship before the enemy was aware of its presence and destroyed the railway tracks or bridges and made the highways impassable by bombing? During the actual landing the planes could with machine gun fire and small fragmentation bombs so demoralize resistance as to make the task of landing much easier and safer.

After having landed, the following are a few of the ways the planes can be useful to the troops:

They can locate quickly bodies of the enemy and communicate instantly their approximate strength, location, disposition, and actions. The enemy can be watched and any movement instantly reported. In this connection there has been developed a portable radio and radio-telephony ground set that is so small and easily set up that one can be carried by two or three men or on the back of a mule, horse, or donkey. In future operations, every unit which, has one of these—and every unit should have one—will be in instant communication with the planes and through them with any other station.

Photographs of enemy defenses, proposed battle terrain, or any other object or area of reasonable size within a radius of fifty miles can be taken, developed, and the desired number of prints delivered to the troops in time to use them in the plan of attack or defense. I have personally seen photographs distributed to the various organizations forty-five minutes after the plane, which took them, had landed.

Planes continuously in communication with headquarters can patrol wide areas daily or hourly, which duty would require large bodies of troops and much fatigue to accomplish otherwise.

By bombing and machine gunnery the enemy can be harassed and prevented from making orderly dispositions.

Enemy troops and population well in rear of the line of resistance can be kept in a demoralized condition, and enemy ammunition and supply depots and other military objects destroyed.

Any railways, bridges, and roads within a radius of one hundred miles can be quickly made impassable.

Rapid communication can be furnished between detached bodies of our troops in difficult country, and officers can be quickly transported anywhere on urgent missions.

In thick and rough country the planes can keep headquarters informed at all times of the disposition, progress, and needs of our troops.

In the event the enemy has planes, we can protect our troops from observation and annoyance and prevent the enemy from securing benefit from his planes.

For the field artillery the following are some of the ways in which we can be helpful:

Difficult and temporary targets can be located quickly, accurately described, and changes in targets promptly reported.

The bursts of our shell can be accurately spotted and corrections for the next shot instantly reported.

Targets invisible from the ground can be kept under accurate fire by corrections given by the planes.

Photographs of targets can be furnished showing progressively the results of artillery fire.

The location of hidden artillery batteries causing damage can be discovered and reported.

At night designated areas can be kept lighted by parachute flares, etc.

Through its speed and remarkable visibility, and by the use of its radio and radio-telephone, together with visual signals that must be developed, the airplane will cooperate with the signal and communication troops so as to greatly increase their effectiveness.

For advanced base work:

In addition to the duties mentioned above which aviation will perform—and nearly all these will enter into advanced base work as well—the planes will cooperate in the following ways:

- Offshore patrols to prevent surprise raids by enemy light forces.
- Antisubmarine patrols.
- Spotting for shore batteries in attacks by enemy ships.
- Communication between the base and our vessels offshore.
- Photographing, bombing, and torpedoing enemy craft and bases within reach.

On account of the aviator's ability in most localities to pick up and chart enemy mine fields, airplanes should furnish valuable assistance in countermining and mine sweeping.

A large part of the work performed by the Marine Corps is to combat guerrilla and bandit warfare, usually in tropical countries where roads are few and ground communications almost nil. We must not overlook the valuable assistance aviation can render in this kind of fighting or fail to realize its many helpful possibilities in the occupation of such territories whether fighting is in progress or not. The enemy encountered under these conditions are usually unstable and cannot withstand punishment. They are nearly always superstitious and easily stampeded or cowed by methods of warfare with which they are unfamiliar. They base their hope for success on their ability to make raids and get away before the necessary number of our troops arrive. When an attempt to round them up is made, their knowledge of the country and their ability to travel light and fast allow them to lead our troops an exhausting chase for some time before they are dispersed, if that is accomplished. The work of the Marine Corps aviators in Haiti and Santo Domingo has abundantly shown the possibilities in this class of operations. Difficult country can be patrolled so completely and frequently that it is impossible for bands to form without being discovered. To cover an area as thoroughly and frequently as can be done by airplanes would require a prohibitive number of troops and a weary amount of "hiking." The planes in Haiti have already proved that they can, without assistance from the ground, disperse and almost destroy bands of cacos with gunnery and small bombs. When these *insurrectos* realize that they cannot congregate without being attacked within a very short time thereafter by our planes, their enthusiasm quickly disappears and the unfamiliar form of attack from the air greatly assists in their discouragement. If the planes could perform no other service for our expeditionary troops than to make unnecessary the long marches formerly required in searching for cacos they would be worth their keep, but a little imagination will suggest to any experienced Marine officer numerous duties the planes, on account of their special abilities, can perform for them.

It is believed that enough has been said to show those who are students of Marine Corps operations that an intelligent development of aviation and an encouraging spirit of cooperation between it and our troops can only result in enabling the Corps to perform its function much more quickly and efficiently. Marine officers very properly "like to be shown," and nothing is more desired by Marine Corps aviation than a chance to work out with our troops the problems suggested above, as they feel assured that such an opportunity can result only in mutual respect and confidence.

Before closing this article I would like to mention something, which might interest prospective pilots. Above all, aviation is a young man's game. It requires a young heart, nerves, lungs, eyes, and reflexes. It has been said that after a man reaches a certain age he has too much sense to do what an aviator is required to do. There are exceptions, of course, and older men have been good fliers, but I believe they are exceptions, and my eight years' experience and observation has shown me that, provided they have the necessary amount of judgment, the younger the pilots are the better. I believe it is good policy to set the maximum age for applicants for pilot's duties at around twenty-five years. I am also led to believe that the average term of usefulness for a pilot flying regularly is not over five years. At the end of that time they know the work thoroughly, but those who are still alive have lost the "pep" and enthusiasm, which is essential.

The established policy regarding pilots is that they will not be ordered to aviation duty until they have had enough experience with troops to have become thoroughly qualified Marine officers. The ordinary length of the detail will be five years, after which they will return to duty with troops.

Aviation is probably the most highly technical branch of the military service. It differs from other arms in the unusually fast development of its equipment, planes, motors, etc. The administrative and technical part of it is really a profession which requires long experience and constant study to fit one to properly make decisions, which decisions must necessarily be correct, as the life of the pilot, even in peace times, depends upon their soundness. For self-evident reasons it is necessary for any aviation organization to have enough old experienced aviation officers to run the technical part of it on sound principles proved by experience, and to prevent the enthusiasm and inexperience of younger pilots from causing harm. This necessity for officers of long experience is recognized and unquestioned, and for this reason a very small number of pilots who show special aptitude will be continued in aviation duty indefinitely to furnish the number of expert and experienced officers required.

The men in aviation are enlisted especially for aviation duty, and are sent through the regular recruit course at Parris Island or Mare Island, after which they are given a thorough education in gasoline motors, as shop machinists and in practical and theoretical airplane repair and upkeep. Our main trouble with enlisted men has been that, after giving them an excellent education, they discover that men performing identically the same duties in the Army and Navy draw much more pay than they. As a result they become dissatisfied and do not reenlist. It is hoped and believed that this will be remedied shortly and their pay put on a par with men doing similar work in the Army and Navy.

For fear that by mentioning in this article the skeptical feeling regarding aviation, which is supposed to exist among some officers, I have given an erroneous impression, I would like to state that I believe the number of officers who hold this attitude constitutes a small minority of the officers of the Corps. The subject is only mentioned here because the whole article is an effort to show Marine Corps officers that, with encouragement and cooperation, we can be of real service to them, and to show commanding officers what parts of their problems they can use aviation to perform. Naturally, the ones we wish most to convert are those who at present do not fully believe in us.

FMF Organization and Composition Board Report

The Division

Marine Corps Gazette
April 1957

In order to give Gazette readers a comprehensive account of the new organization and structure of the Fleet Marine Force, this issue initiates a series of articles on this important subject.

The articles were prepared by officers of the "FMF Organization and Composition Board." Headed by Maj. Gen. Robert E. Hogaboom, the Board met at Quantico from June to December 1956.

Insofar as possible, the articles not only describe the new organization, but also narrate some of the background thinking, which led to the final decision.

This first article deals with the new Marine division. Subsequent issues of the Gazette will contain material on FMF aviation, artillery, and logistics.

No football coach would last long in his profession if he did not scout next Saturday's opposing team and organize his offense and defense to win that particular game. Nor would his contract be any safer if he attempted to meet a heavier team excelling in power plays on their own terms rather than relying on speed and deception to come out the victor. Yet in the game of war we too often forget these basic tenets, trust only our past experiences, and end up organized and trained to "play" our opponent according to his rules of the game rather than our own.

The Organization and Composition Board was charged with the mission of determining the optimum Marine division organization and composition.

It was apparent that the optimum division should be one with a clearly defined basic capability. A capability that would be required in any type of mission whether in a conventional or a nuclear war. Recognizing that a force-in-readiness would encounter missions with unusual aspects requiring an extension or addition to the basic capability of the division, the need for a well-balanced Force Troops structure was, of course, mandatory. As a result, every effort was made to keep from creeping into the division the "in case" and "nice to have" type units and equipment that can so easily put unmanageable blubber on the muscles of a hard hitting fighting entity.

Another characteristic required was what might be called a "change potential" in order that new equipment and techniques could be readily adopted in the future without requiring a major reorganization. Consequently, although restricted by hardware presently available, consideration of future weapons and equipment gives the proposed division increased stature.

Thus, the Board established five basic criteria which it believes the division and its subordinate commands must meet in the period beginning FY 58. These criteria are:

1. The Marine division must be organized and equipped to conduct an amphibious assault against the most modern defenses.

2. The division must have the greatest possible capability for executing an amphibious assault in accordance with the Marine Corps' modern concepts for amphibious operations and tactical atomic warfare.

3. Combat elements must shed maintenance and service functions to the greatest possible degree in order to attain mobility, freedom of action, and a homogenous tactical structure.

4. The organization of the division, and its subordinate elements, must facilitate the rapid creation and smooth operation of temporary task groups.

5. The Marine division, to answer the requirements of a force-in-readiness, must be capable of making rapid strategic movements by limited air, sea, or land transportation means.

The proposed division that evolved from these criteria is markedly different in some areas and surprisingly similar in others to the present L Series T/O.

To start at the top and work down, the division headquarters battalion has been designed to provide the facilities for a division CP, an alternate CP, and an administrative CP. All general staff sections are increased slightly to provide the necessary personnel for the alternate CP, and the G2 section includes ten air observers who are organic because of the increased dependence on air observation for enemy information. Special staff sections are reduced to the minimum consistent with effective operations. The present Headquarters Co is reorganized into an H&S Co. The Headquarters Co consists of the Div Headquarters, Bn Headquarters, a CP Security Plt, and the Div Band. The Service Co contains the Reproduction Sec, Photo Sec, Disbursing Sec, MT Plt, and Service Plt. Additional units in the Div Hq Bn are a MP Co with four identical military police platoons, a reorganized Communication Co with reduced wire-laying capabilities, and increased radio relay capabilities, and a Communication Intelligence Co with the same capabilities now possessed by the Force Radio Co.

The deletion of the Recon Co was occasioned by the addition of a Recon Bn to the division organization. This was necessary in order to provide more adequate means for gaining enemy information in extended formations of modern warfare, and to provide better target acquisition in order to exploit more fully our nuclear and conventional fire support means. This battalion consists of an H&S Co and three Recon Cos. Its concept of employment is that it will conduct:

1. Helicopter and ground reconnaissance beyond combat area but short of distant reconnaissance missions.
2. Flank, separation, and rear area reconnaissance.
3. Road reconnaissance.
4. Battlefield surveillance by establishment and displacement of helicopter lifted observation posts.
5. Counter reconnaissance.

Necessarily, in order to accomplish these missions, the entire battalion is capable of being helicopter borne and a helicopter reconnaissance squadron has been structured in the light helicopter group of the marine aircraft wing specifically to support this battalion. This is not to imply, however, that the battalion will not be trained and equipped to conduct ground and amphibious reconnaissance.

A significant and perhaps controversial change in the proposed division is the deletion of the tank battalion. Tanks were removed from the division because of the tactical requirements of nuclear warfare with its emphasis on mobility, night operations, and dispersed operations. In view of the fact that the Communist force as well as many of our allies still rely heavily on armored forces, the opinion of both British and American tank officers as well as the recommendation of the Fleet Marine Force were taken into careful consideration. From this investigation, several agreed upon, if somewhat contradictory, facts emerged. Briefly these were first, that the old concept that only a tank can defeat a tank is no longer valid in view of the effectiveness of the rocket, recoilless rifle, and close support aircraft. Officers with tank experience, both British and American, agreed on this without including consideration of the greatly improved infantry anti-tank weapons now in the test stage that will eventually replace the 3.5-inch rocket and the 106mm recoilless rifle. The same officers were also unanimous in their agreement on the second fact—that the great shock power of the tank in the assault was an essential necessity on the modern battlefield. Further, there appeared to be complete agreement on the third fact which concerned the necessity of utilizing operations executed under conditions of reduced visibility or total darkness, possibly to the exclusion of daylight operations because of the devastating effect of one well-placed nuclear munition. The contradiction between facts two and three lay in the complete agreement that tanks are somewhat less than effective under conditions of reduced visibility or total darkness. Consequently, here was a case in which it appeared desirable to "play" the game according to our own rules and turn the enemy's armor advantages into liabilities rather than accept his concept and attempt to meet him on his own terms.

Although it was considered that tanks were no longer required in the basic division, it is believed that various missions or situations may arise requiring that tank Force Troop units be attached to the division. Once the tactical requirements for tanks had been decided upon, which moved them from division to Force Troops, a chain reaction was set off that eliminated a great amount of heavy maintenance equipment and supplies as well as engineer and bridging formerly carried in the division, either in support of, or organic to, the tank battalion. Therefore, when time, method of transportation, terrain, and the enemy permit, the utilization of tanks, force engineer, and bridging units will also form a part of attachments required by division. The possibility of a completely air transportable division sought for, but not absolutely required by the fifth criteria, appeared at this time.

The direct fire punch of the tank gun in support of the infantry, as well as its anti-tank capability, was replaced to a degree by inclusion of recoilless weapons and a greatly increased number of rocket launchers in the infantry units as will be outlined shortly. However, the need was realized for additional weapons to provide antitank and close support to infantry and reconnaissance units, at the division level. The Ontos consequently was chosen to be the heaviest anti-mechanized weapon organic to the division because of the lethality of its 106mm recoilless rifles, its speed mobility and great cross-country maneuverability, and the fact that the vehicle is air transportable.

The forty-five Ontos vehicles that are included in the ordnance of the division are carried in an Ontos Bn, consisting of an H&S Co, and three Ontos Cos. Each company has three platoons, five vehicles per platoon. The principle mission of the Ontos Bn is the destruction of hostile tanks and other gun or personnel carrying, armored, tracked vehicles. Its secondary mission is to provide direct fire support to infantry and to motorized reconnaissance patrols as a close support weapon rather than as an armored spearhead vehicle. It is considered that the battalion's most probable employment will see the attachment of subordinate elements to infantry units with unattached elements assigned specific tasks under division control.

The artillery regiment provides the division commander with an organic means of close and intermediate non-atomic artillery fire support and is organized to meet the criteria set by the Board for the optimum Marine division.

The regiment consists of a Hq Btry, three Close Support Bns and one Intermediate Support Bn. Each battalion is composed of a headquarters battery and three firing batteries. As differentiated from present organization, however, each firing battery is organized into two 1-gun platoons.

The close support battalions are equipped with the 105mm or 120mm mortar rather than the 105mm howitzer and jeeps have replaced 2½ ton 6x6 trucks as prime movers. The only 2½ ton 6x6 trucks remaining in this battalion are those in the Battery Ammo Sec and bulldozers have been deleted. Consequently, the battalion has the same ground and air mobility as the infantry regiment.

The Intermediate Support Bn is equipped with the 105mm howitzer rather than the 155mm howitzer and 2½ ton 6x6 trucks have replaced the 5-ton 6x6 trucks as prime movers. The added range capability of the battalion over the close support battalions provides a source of fire support to engage targets deeper in enemy territory and to reinforce fires locally available to infantry unit commanders. A detailed study of the new artillery organization will appear in a subsequent issue of the *Gazette*.

As in our present organization, the infantry elements of the division were organized into three regiments of three battalions each. The triangular structure was, retained at the regimental level since, in the dispersed formations that the division may adopt in nuclear warfare, it is considered that the division commander requires an intermediate headquarters to properly direct and control his nine infantry battalions. The increased emphasis on mobility and night operations, required in fast-moving, highly fluid combat situations, highlights this need for well-trained and efficiently directed battalions.

Therefore, the organization and composition of the infantry regiment is designed to accomplish the following:

1. *Provide a tactical headquarters for the command of organic battalions and attached units.* Certain administrative and supply personnel have been removed from regimental headquarters and placed in division headquarters so that the personnel administration and supply chain extends direct from division to infantry battalion. Insofar as the personnel administration is concerned, we have already had considerable experience with this system in that during combat, divisions invariably set up "administrative villages" in the rear to which subordinate units assign certain administrative personnel and records, As was stated earlier, the division headquarters is organized to provide, in addition to the division CP, an alternate CP and an administrative CP. The proposal, therefore, is that the administrative organization and procedures be the same in training as they are in combat. Explanation of how the supply chain will function will be contained in an article on the division logistic system.

2. *Provide for the coordinated training of subordinate elements.* The Board considered that, since the basic prerequisite for success in combat is effective training, the responsibility for training must be firmly, permanently, and clearly

fixed. Although it is conceded that battalions could be grouped under combat command headquarters for tactical operations, it is believed that battalions that have trained together under a regimental commander will operate as a more efficient team on the battlefield. Therefore, the Board rejected the concept of tactical groupment of battalions under command groups, a principle that is utilized in some modern theories of infantry organization.

3. *Facilitate the organization of task groups of infantry battalions and reinforcing units from division or Force Troops.* The Board considered that the organization of the regiment into three infantry battalions facilitates the creation of three major tasks groups by reinforcing each battalion with artillery, antitank, or other supporting units from division or Force Troops.

4. *Provide maximum mobility.* The regimental headquarters has been made smaller and more mobile by the deletion of certain functions and the elimination of such weapons as the 4.2-inch mortars and the tanks from the regiment. The 4.2-inch mortars, it should be noted, were eliminated completely from the division weapons systems since they are so inferior to either the 105mm or 120mm mortars. The type mortar support formerly provided the regiment by the 4.2-inch mortars will now be provided by the close support artillery. The headquarters, as well as the three infantry battalions, are therefore completely helicopter transportable and possess sufficient organic transportation in the form of jeeps and "mechanical mules" to ensure cross-country mobility of heavier weapons and equipment. The cross-country mobility required in this instance is that necessary to move the heavier weapons and equipment at the same rate of march as the troops on foot.

The concept of employment of the infantry regiment is that it will normally have supporting elements such antimechanized, engineer, motor transport, and service, attached to form a regimental landing team for assault operations.

The organization of the infantry battalion is designed to provide maximum mobility, reconnaissance capability and shock power necessary to implement the modern concepts of warfare. The increased mobility has just been mentioned in the description of the regiment. The increased reconnaissance capability and shock power is a combination of several factors, the major one being the organization of the battalion into four rifle companies. The addition of a fourth rifle company will:

1. Meet the increased reconnaissance and security requirements. The Board considers that, rather than one specially organized and equipped reconnaissance unit within the battalion, each of the four companies must be thoroughly trained in this type of mission.

2. Increase the shock power of the battalion by providing more tactical units and weapons. Firepower is increased.

3. Permit the battalion commander to commit sizeable forces to the initial attack, while retaining immediately at hand a powerful reserve with which to influence the action, and at the same time provide strong security to exposed flanks and rear, while attacking. Therefore, when security requirements are present, the old "two up and one back" concept still pertains but when operating as an interior battalion, the formation might well be two up and two back. Under no circumstances should the addition of a fourth company be used as an excuse to simply increase the frontage assigned the battalion.

4. Provide increased staying power in battle by allowing the battalion to continue effective combat for protracted periods, even though sustaining heavy casualties. It will also decrease the infantry fatigue in combat. Frequent passage of lines is visualized as a necessity in order to sustain the momentum of the attack.

5. Allow the battalion commander to helicopter lift two or three tactical elements, and, at the same time, provide him with a sufficient security element for those reinforcing units not helicopter transportable, or those awaiting a subsequent lift.

Additionally, the infantry battalion is organized to allow the rapid creation of temporary subordinate task groups, since it provides in its mortar, antitank and assault organization, squads and sections which facilitate their assignment to rifle units. To meet the requirement for a major task group formed around the battalion, it also has the necessary staff and communications to control and co-ordinate reinforcing units from division or Force Troops.

In spite of the greatly increased capabilities of the proposed infantry battalion, it is only one Marine officer, 58 Marine enlisted, and 11 Navy enlisted larger than the present battalion. In addition to the inclusion of a fourth rifle company, for the reasons stated above, changes include the deletion of the battalion weapons company. Battalion weapons are carried in H&S Co and consist of a platoon of 106mm recoilless rifles, a platoon of 81mm mortars, and a flame thrower section. The heavy machine gun has been eliminated but 11 light machine guns have been added for use H&S Co in emergencies. The number of 3.5-inch rocket launchers in the battalion has been increased from 18 to 32, 8 of which are carried as T/E ordnance items to be manned by H&S Co personnel in an emergency.

The infantry battalion is considered to be the basic tactical unit. It has sufficient fire support and antitank weapons to operate on an extended front and is organized to provide a balanced firepower and maneuver team. It is equipped with special surveillance and reconnaissance equipment and with vehicles, which can be furnished any of its organic rifle companies for reconnaissance missions.

Although the rifle company is smaller than its L Series counterpart, it retains a machine gun platoon and an enlarged 3.5-inch rocket section combined into what is designated the weapons platoon.

This platoon consists of three machine gun sections of two squads each; however, the size of the L Series squads are reduced from eight to five men. The rocket squads are the same as presently provided for in the L Series T/Os; however, an additional squad is added to the rocket section to provide greater flexibility and increased firepower.

The 60mm mortar has been eliminated from the battalion weapons system in view of the antipersonnel lethality of the 106mm HEAP round and as the first step in simplifying the weapons system. The 3 rifle platoons and their squads remain unchanged from the L Series T/O. Therefore, the proposed strength of 6 officers and 197 enlisted Marines, rather than the present strength of 7 officers and 231 enlisted Marines, results from the elimination of the 60mm mortar section, a reduction in the size of the machine gun squad, and a slightly smaller company headquarters.

The problem of organizing the service elements of the division to meet the five basic criteria established by the Board was possibly more difficult than the tactical elements.

In this case it was essential to ensure the staying power of the combat units by providing service and support units that could, in fact rather than in theory, support highly mobile, widely dispersed task groups. Consequently, major organizational changes were made in the engineer, service, and medical units and a sizeable reduction was made in the motor transport capability.

The organizational title of the Eng Bn was changed to Pioneer Bn as being more appropriate to its assigned functions and to establish a ready distinction between this unit and the Force Eng Bn.

The Pioneer Bn is designed to provide both tactical and logistical type support. It is organized into an H&S Co, a Pioneer Support Co, and three Pioneer Cos.

The present division Service Regt has been redesignated a Service Bn and has been reorganized to provide for more flexible employment in support of tactical operations. The present division shore party function is incorporated in the division Service Bn and a considerable saving in personnel and equipment has been effected by this move.

The battalion is organized into an H&S Co, three Light Support Cos, a Medium Support Co, and two Landing Support Cos.

The principal change in the Medical Bn has been the deletion of the two hospital companies that were formerly organic, and the addition of one collecting and clearing company. The battalion therefore is organized into a H&S Co and four Collecting and Clearing Cos.

The Motor Transport Bn is organized essentially the same as the L Series battalion except that one truck company has been removed. The size of the H&S Co has, however, been reduced to reflect the support of one less company. With the increase in helicopter support available to the division, the Board considered that a corresponding reduction in ground transport could be effected at this time.

The Battalion, which now consists of an H&S Co and three Truck Cos, has the capability of lifting the assault elements of two infantry battalions. A detailed study of the reorganized service units will appear in a coming issue of the *Gazette*.

In summary, the major changes from the division of today that are represented in the division of tomorrow, will have the following general effect on the capabilities of the Marine division:

1. The capability for continuity of command and control in case of atomic attack is increased.
2. The division is less dependent on land lines of communication.
3. The overall mobility has been increased without sacrificing essential fire power. The organizational flexibility of the division has been increased in that it has a better capability for rapidly establishing subordinate task groups for accomplishing a specific mission.
4. The infantry strength has been increased and a better balance has been created between fighting elements and headquarters and supporting elements.
5. The antitank capability has been increased although the offensive value of the tank has been lost through the elimination of the division tank battalion.
6. The division has a greater reconnaissance capability.
7. An overall personnel reduction of 10 percent has been made.
8. The heavy equipment has been reduced to the point that the assault elements of the division are helicopter transportable and the entire division is air transportable.

FMF Organization and Composition Board Report

Aviation

Marine Corps Gazette
May 1957

Survey and revision of the structure of Fleet Marine Force aviation requires detailed consideration of a variety of important factors. Of overriding importance is the mission and character of the FMF as a whole, and any organization forming a part of it must be tailored to reflect the changing concepts for discharging that mission.

The concept of helicopter mobility influences all FMF structure. Many of the changes in the division are permitted by reliance on the helicopter as a transportation and reconnaissance means. Other changes are feasible because of the capability of the Marine air-ground team to employ its organic air attack capability in the heavy fire support role. Further, wide frontages and basic combat unit separation owe their ready acceptance, in large measure, to expanded and more efficient employment of aerial reconnaissance. In sum, it is apparent that the concept of vertical assault places greatly increased requirements upon FMF aviation to provide direct tactical support.

Attempts to provide increased tactical air support are at present categorically limited by two external factors—aircraft and personnel ceilings. Aircraft are in a category quite apart from other military equipment. Not only are they expensive and complex, but they have a relatively short useful life, they require extensive lead time in development and production, and they require highly trained personnel for operation and maintenance.

In this era of restricted budgets and rising costs, the Department of Defense places certain limits on naval aviation with regard to total and operating aircraft inventories. The air component of the Marine Corps is in turn affected by these restrictions, and for the foreseeable future, authorized aircraft allowances cannot be increased.

In a similar manner, the more familiar limits on authorized personnel are essentially rigid, nor does it seem reasonable to alter to any appreciable degree the current allocation of Marine Corps personnel between air and ground. Thus, certain inflexible guidelines circumscribe the size of FMF aviation.

FMF aviation cannot be drastically altered in character, for the Marine Corps is responsible for performing certain combat air functions. Inherent within the roles and missions assigned the Marine Corps is that of providing combat forces, both ground and air, to achieve the initial accretion ashore of combat power transferred from the sea. Landing forces with fleet assistance, therefore, must be capable of seizing and defending, against ground and air resistance, the designated objective area ashore. Obviously, this view of the landing force carries with it the requirement for an appreciable capability to repel enemy air attack.

This capability must be truly expeditionary. By so specializing, the Marine Corps fills a distinct slot in the defense structure of the country. Recommended changes in lower echelon units of the Marine Aircraft Wing are pointed toward reduction of weight and cube of squadron equipment with this idea in mind.

The FMF aviation structure discussed below provides a maximum capability to meet the requirements for tactical air support imposed by the vertical assault concept. At the same time it maintains sufficient combat air capability to provide a reasonable landing force contribution to the overall offensive and defensive air effort.

FMF Level

No essential change is made at the AirFMF command level. A headquarters and headquarters squadron for the support of each AirFMF headquarters is provided. The AirFMF commander will command the FMF units assigned, will be responsible for their training and readiness, and will coordinate naval aeronautical logistic and administrative requirements with the respective fleet air commander.

Subordinate to the AirFMF in recent years have been the force aviation headquarters groups and the marine aircraft wings. Designation of certain units as force aviation serves no useful purpose, and the title of force aviation headquarters groups will be changed to Marine training groups with the primary mission of training and refreshing pilots and other personnel in new equipment and techniques.

Two such groups are provided, one for each AirFMF; each to be composed of a headquarters and maintenance squadron, a Marine fighter training squadron, a Marine all-weather fighter training squadron, a Marine attack squadron, and a Marine instrument training squadron.

Wing Organizational Philosophy

The squadron is the basic unit for operation of air craft; it is the basic unit for structuring an air organization. It is a T/O type limit. Each squadron is designed to carry out a specific function, that is, attack, intercept, reconnaissance, transport, control, and service support.

Combining squadrons into groups for specific purposes, and further combining groups into wings is sound organizational practice, either for administrative or operational purposes. Such combinations permit centralized control of training in the functions to be carried out and at the same time provide a flexible framework for transfer of squadrons between groups and groups between wings to permit the air commander to accomplish any particular mission. In this sense, groups and wings closely resemble task organizations designed for a specific purpose.

A wing, composed of either functional or composite groups, is the smallest air unit with the capability of command and control of subordinate elements in the execution of air and direct air support operations.

The Marine Aircraft Wing

Despite the fact that rarely do two Marine aircraft wings resemble each other in detail, a Marine aircraft wing is a distinct entity. As indicated by the organizational chart, the typical wing is composed of functional groups that provide a balanced aviation force capable of executing all essential air support tasks for an air-ground task force of wing-division size.

The Marine Wing Headquarters Group

The wing headquarters group is composed of a headquarters and headquarters squadron, one Marine air support squadron, and three Marine air control squadrons. This group contains all the essential elements of the wing command echelon and the air control system. The Marine composite photographic squadron is no longer included in this group in order that the group need not be established at or near an air base. It can, therefore, land early in an amphibious operation to establish ashore the means to command and control landing force aviation and such other air units as may operate in the area.

The capabilities of the Marine air support squadron of this group are enhanced by an additional air support radar team. Essentially the best current means of providing all-weather air support, three such teams in a Marine aircraft wing add valuable flexibility to its combat employment.

Marine Wing Service Group

An essential element of the wing is the service group that is normally established at a rear base within supporting distance of the objective area. It consists of a headquarters and headquarters squadron, a Marine air base squadron, and a Marine aircraft repair squadron. These subordinate elements of the group provide wing-level service for all squadrons and groups of the wing. Principal among these service responsibilities are centralized control of supply (H&HS), wing-level aircraft maintenance (MARS), and operation of the rear area air base (MABS). Normally the transport group operates out of this base.

Transport Capability

Approximately 30 percent of the assigned aircraft of the wing are in the transport category. Two helicopter groups and one fixed-wing transport group are provided. The light helicopter transport group, in addition to a headquarters and maintenance squadron and an air base squadron, contains a Marine observation squadron (VMO), a Marine helicopter reconnaissance squadron (HMO), and two Marine light helicopter transport squadrons (HMR[L]).

The VMO is a small squadron to operate twelve light fixed-wing observation aircraft of the OE type. It is the only squadron in the group that requires anything at all approximating a prepared runway.

The HMO is a composite squadron of twelve HUS/HRS types and twelve HOKs. This squadron is designed specifically to provide tactical support for the new division reconnaissance battalion in the conduct of reconnaissance operations. In addition, it can provide air evacuation for all division units, and perform such miscellaneous tasks as courier service and wire laying by helicopter.

The two HMR(L) squadrons are composed of twenty-four HUS helicopters each.

The total complement of the light helicopter group is sixty-four HUS type aircraft, twelve HOKs and twelve OEs. Its mission is oriented explicitly to fulfill division requirements.

The medium group contains a headquarters and maintenance squadron, an air base squadron and two HMR(M) squadrons, each of fifteen HR2S aircraft.

The total lift capability of the two groups at one time is on the order of fifteen-hundred personnel, or the approximate equivalent of a battalion landing team.

The longer range transport function is handled by the Marine transport group. It consists of a headquarters and maintenance squadron and two fixed-wing aircraft squadrons of fifteen aircraft each. These squadrons will be capable of providing in-flight refueling interchangeably with cargo and personnel transport when aircraft are available to the Marine Corps with the potential for carrying out that dual role.

Combat Capability

The combat power of the typical wing is contained in three functional groups: one fighter group, one all-weather fighter group, and one attack group. The command, support, and maintenance capability of each group is compartmented into two squadrons: a headquarters and maintenance squadron and a Marine air base squadron. Each Marine aircraft group is designed to command and support two to four tactical squadrons. Under the assumption that short of a general war, not more than two Marine aircraft wings will be simultaneously deployed, the best functional balance of combat aircraft types for the typical wing is set in the ratio of three fighter squadrons, two all-weather fighter squadrons, and four attack squadrons. This balance, adjusted as necessary between the three Marine aircraft wings, provides optimum flexibility in task regroupment for strategic deployment and operational needs.

Reconnaissance

The composite reconnaissance squadron (VMCJ) is a separate squadron with a distinctive functional capability. In actual operations it will be based on an airfield with one of the combat groups and receive its group level logistic support from that group. It is equipped with ten photo reconnaissance aircraft and ten configured for electronic reconnaissance.

This squadron together with the VMO and HMO represent the Marine aircraft wings' contribution to the overall reconnaissance system that has been formed in the division-wing team.

Manning Levels

The typical wing will operate slightly less than four hundred aircraft of all types. Personnel are provided in the proposed T/Os to operate and maintain them at an aircraft utilization factor of approximately sixty-five flight hours per aircraft per month. Because peacetime budgets for operating expenses usually preclude realization of such high utilization factors, it is neither necessary nor desirable to actually man the wings at full strength.

The recommended overall FMF aviation structure, manned at approximately 80 percent for pilots, 65 percent for aviation ground officers, and 90 percent for Marines enlisted, is adequate for employment short of general war. It should be adequate at such manning levels to meet force-in-readiness requirements and limited combat employment.

Summary

The essential differences between this wing and the current L Series T/Os are summarized as follows:

a. *Squadron level.*

1. Reduced maintenance, supply, and supporting personnel in VMF/VMA squadrons, caused partially by the reduction in aircraft from twenty-four to twenty, and partially by movement of some service functions to higher echelons.

2. Reduced number of pilots due to lowering of pilot/seat ratio in combat squadrons and reduction in aircraft from twenty-four to twenty.

3. Consolidation of S1 and Adjutants' sections accomplishing a reduction in administrative personnel.

4. Increase in the VMCJ squadron from eighteen aircraft to twenty.

b. *Group level.*

1. Elimination of all exchange and special services personnel except for a special staff section at wing level; elimination of all barbers, and reduction of security personnel in VF/VA Groups.

2. Addition of communications personnel in helicopter groups to permit those units to operate air control teams in embarkation and landing zones during tactical and logistical air lifts.

c. *Wing level.*

1. Addition of one ASRT to the MASS with no increase in number of personnel.

2. Increase in responsibilities of the Marine wing service group to provide pool-type motor transport resources to operating groups and squadrons.

3. The formation of the helicopter reconnaissance squadron as the air counterpart to the division's reconnaissance battalion.

In summary, the results of this reorganization provide a closer balance between air capabilities for direct tactical support and for air defense operations. They, in addition, accomplish significant personnel savings. Finally, by further centralizing servicing capabilities in the wing service group, squadrons and operating groups have been lightened to promote early establishment ashore of operating units.

FMF Organization and Composition Board Report

Fire Support

Marine Corps Gazette
June 1957

The fire support concept, organization, and weapons of the M Tables represent a significant evolutionary step forward toward the full realization of the Marine Corps' modern amphibious doctrine. With the weapons, communications, and other equipment available today, and within the next few years, the M Tables provide the fire support required by Marine infantry on a modern amphibious battlefield. To meet the foreseen fire support needs of this period, the M Tables have provided a fire support system that emphasizes versatility and speed of response to the infantry's fire support needs.

The greatest changes in organization and tactical employment in the fire support system are found in the artillery. The artillery is now organized to fight as task-organized battery and battalion-sized groupments of varying calibers and types of weapons instead of in rigid T/0-battalion organizations. As a result, the battery, rather than the battalion, has become the basic fire support unit. While the battalion, as a T/0 command organization, has been retained in the artillery regiment, it has been eliminated in Force artillery. The battalion organization was retained in the regiment because of the necessity for intimately relating the artillery organization to that of the infantry it supports.

Every battery in both the regiment and Force artillery is now capable of operating independently of a battalion or group headquarters. It has the means to provide its own observation, communications, prepare its own firing data and provide its own supply, and organizational maintenance. Batteries are further sub-divided into platoons, which can also prepare their own firing data and have varying degrees of self-sufficiency in other areas.

In the artillery regiment the close support battery has eight heavy mortars (105mm or 120mm) divided into two platoons of four mortars each. Each platoon has a platoon fire direction center (FDC). The battery commander and his fire direction officer (FDO) establish the battery FDC at the infantry battalion CP. The four forward observer sections in the battery operate with the battalion's rifle companies. This organization of the close support battery enables it to engage simultaneously two targets in different sectors of the infantry battalion's front. It can also provide continuous fire support to the infantry, even while displacing, through its ability to leap frog its platoons.

Locating the battery CP and FDC at the infantry battalion CP ensures that there is the highest possible degree of integration of infantry and artillery plans, operations, intelligence, and communications. By establishing continuous command liaison between the infantry and artillery, it eliminates the need for an artillery liaison officer and party at the infantry CP. The artillery battery FDC provides the ideal location for the infantry battalion fire support coordination center (FSCC). This will facilitate the collection and exchange of target information and provide a higher and more intimate degree of fire support coordination than ever before.

Task organization of supporting artillery can now start right at the close Ssupport battery level. Newly developed gunnery and fire direction techniques, which have made the new battery organization possible, enable another platoon of any kind or caliber of artillery to be attached to the battery.

The battalion headquarters battery is now tactical (and administrative) only. It no longer provides any maintenance or supply support to the close support batteries. Its FDC is established within the infantry regimental CP to provide the same close and intimate working relationship at the regiment-battalion level that is achieved at the battalion-battery level. The battalion FDC no longer prepares firing data for its batteries as it has done in the past.

Its fire direction responsibilities are now tactical in nature, similar to what we have been accustomed to only at artillery regimental level in the past. The battalion exercises fire direction over its organic and attached batteries through the maneuver and massing of their fires and the assignment of targets. It plans close and general support fires to support the regiment as a whole in accordance with the regimental commander's tactical plan. It is responsible for countermortar intelligence and operations.

The close support battalion CO coordinates and controls the emplacement of all artillery units under his command to ensure that the artillery deployment is always in accordance with the infantry regimental commander's tactical plan.

Now that the battalion FDC is no longer involved in the preparation of firing data, it may easily control the fires of additional reinforcing or attached batteries from regiment or Force artillery. It may exercise fire direction over as many as six batteries of any kind or caliber. This permits us, for the first time, to have truly task-organized artillery fire support at the infantry regimental level.

The fires of attached or reinforcing batteries may be controlled at the battalion level or, when the situation so dictates, platoons or batteries may be attached to close support batteries. The ability to task-organize all kinds and types of artillery at the close support battalion level, in conjunction with the high order of mobility of the artillery, enables the artillery to provide the supported infantry commander whatever type or kind of fire support he needs at any given moment on the battlefield.

Because continuous command liaison is now established between the infantry regiment and its close support battalion, the need for artillery liaison officers and liaison party at the infantry regiment is eliminated. Again, the artillery battalion FDC provides the ideal location for establishing the infantry regimental TSCC.

The intermediate support battalion, with its three 105mm howitzer batteries, is organized similarly to the close support battalion. The battalion may be employed as a unit to provide general support or reinforcing type fires to the division as a whole. When the situation so dictates, platoons or batteries of the battalion may be attached to close support battalions. When not attached, batteries would normally have a mission of reinforcing the fires of one or more close support battalions. Through the decentralization of data preparation from the battalion to the battery level, we are able to attach batteries of Force artillery to the intermediate support battalion to give weight and depth to its fires. The battalion can control the fires of up to six batteries.

The artillery regimental headquarters battery is again tactical only, the same as the new infantry regimental headquarters company. It provides no maintenance or supply support function to its battalions. Its fire direction function remains tactical in nature as in the past. However, because of the newly gained ability to create and dissolve artillery task organizations of both regimental and Force artillery batteries within the regiment, the regimental FDC will now have a much larger concern than in the past with the frequent maneuver and assignment of missions to artillery units in the division area.

On a modern battlefield of rapidly changing situations, regiments must constantly ensure that the deployment of the available artillery meets the fire support needs of each infantry commander and the division as a whole. The counter-battery mission, which was formerly a Force artillery responsibility, will now become a regimental responsibility and be one of the major fire direction and intelligence tasks of the regiment.

The regimental FDC is capable of controlling and maneuvering the fires of attached Force artillery batteries or groups that are not further assigned to its battalions.

The regimental CP provides a suitable location for an alternate division CP. The regimental commander may establish his FDC at either the division CP or his own CP, depending on the wishes of the division commander and the tactical and communications situation at any given time. When the artillery regimental FDC is established at the division CP, the same intimate working relationship between regiment and division is established as we have at the battery-battalion and battalion-regimental level.

In this case, the artillery FDC provides the ideal location for the division FSCC. When this situation prevails, the regimental headquarters battery T/O provides for a small alternate FDC-FSCC section that remains at the artillery CP to work with the assistant division commander and division staff members at the alternate division CP. If the regimental FDC is established at the artillery CP, this alternate FDC-FSCC group will be located at the division CP to provide the nucleus for the division FSCC.

The artillery regiment now has 96 tubes as opposed to 72 tubes in the L Tables, regiment. This, in large part, numerically offsets the loss of 36 4.2-inch mortar tubes from the 8 infantry regiments. The net result should be an increase rather than a decrease in the fire support available to the infantry as a result of the many advantages gained through the new organization, tactics, and techniques of the artillery regiment.

The replacement of the 105mm howitzer with the 105mm mortar or 120mm mortar in the close support battalion, and of the 155mm howitzer with the 105mm howitzer intermediate support battalion, has resulted in a loss of range and destructive capability in the regiment. This sacrifice had to be made if the artillery of the division was to be able to embark, land, and fight with the division's infantry in a modern amphibious assault.

This deficiency can be overcome largely through the new ability to task-organize longer range, heavier caliber Force artillery batteries with the artillery regiment whenever the situation permits. This course of action appears feasible for the years just ahead. The development of a greatly improved close support weapon over the present heavy mortars will also do much to rectify this deficiency. The prospects for the early development of such a weapon appear promising at the present.

Radio and radio-relay have become the primary means of communication within the regiment. The only tactical wire net remaining is that in the close support battery. This net interconnects the forward observers and battery and platoon FDCs. Designated channels on the division to infantry regiment radio-relay circuits are reserved for use between the regiment and the close support battalions. Additional channels on the infantry-regiment-to-infantry-battalion circuits are reserved for use between the close support battalion and its batteries. Separate radio-relay circuits are established between the regiment and the intermediate support battalion and between the regimental CP and the division CP.

Prompt, effective close air support is an indispensable element of our new amphibious doctrine. Accordingly, the M Tables have improved our capability to employ close air support as an element of the division's fire support system. The addition of a second forward air controller (FAC) to each battalion tactical air control party (TACP) has greatly increased our ability to provide close air support to infantry battalions. Proper deployment of these two FACs, in conjunction with the ability to use the battalion air liaison officer as a controller when necessary, will enable the battalion to be able to use close air support more quickly and frequently than in the past.

Our ability to provide all-weather close air support to the division has also been increased by the addition of a third air support radar team (ASRT) to the Marine air support squadron. Operating under the control of the direct air support center (DASC) these teams will ensure that the division, even though fighting on very broad fronts, will have adequate close air support under all conditions of visibility. The addition of this third ASRT is of especial significance in connection with the division's ability to obtain the precise delivery of air delivered atomic munitions at all times.

The use of atomic munitions in the preparation of the objective area, combined with a reduced necessity to assault a fortified beach, will reduce the requirement for gunfire support from World War II standards. Much deeper initial penetrations and deeper beach-heads will limit the ability of naval gunfire to support the assault and seizure of many objectives. The wider dispersal of ships off-shore, as a passive defense measure against atomic attack, also limits the amount of gunfire support available. As a result of these factors, infantry battalions will often be beyond the range of gunfire support, or not always have gunfire support ships available.

Therefore, the infantry battalion no longer has its own organic shore fire control party (SFCP). Each close support battalion now has two SFCPs and a Naval gunfire liaison team in the headquarters battery. Each SFCP has a spotting team and a liaison team. When the infantry regiment the battalion is supporting is able to use naval gunfire, SFCPs are attached to batteries in support of battalions that are able to use naval gunfire.

If an additional team should be needed, it may be obtained from one of the close support battalions not using its parties. When the FSCP are not being used to conduct gunfire they may be used as additional forward observer teams with patrols or outposts or to man artillery OPs.

The naval gunfire liaison team that remains at the artillery battalion FDC to work in the infantry regimental SFCG does not contain a naval gunfire liaison officer, but only the necessary naval gunfire communications personnel. The training and experience of the close support battalion CO and his staff will provide the necessary degree of competence to properly advise the infantry regimental commander on the use of naval gunfire support. The fact that the FSCP is an organic part of the artillery battalion in training and fighting will result in everyone concerned having a much better understanding of the capabilities, limitations, use, and techniques of each of these two fire support arms and result in a more efficient and better coordinated use of them on the battlefield. At division level, a division naval gunfire officer remains a member of the division special staff. Naval gunfire radar beacon teams are still located in the division communication company.

The modern doctrine for amphibious operations and tactical atomic warfare has rendered obsolete much of our past organization and doctrine for the employment of Force (Corps) artillery type units. This has resulted from the wide and deep deployment of both friendly and enemy forces, the new high order of mobility of the Marine division, the rapid tempo and fluidity of combat, the need to operate more intimately with division artillery, and the requirement for readily available atomic fire support. These factors have dictated that Force artillery have a much higher degree of mobility, a greater degree of organizational flexibility, and an inherent ability to work intimately with the various elements of the artillery regiment.

Accordingly, the battalion organization has been dropped from Force artillery. All Force artillery units are now organized as separate, independent batteries of varying calibers and types of weapons. All of these batteries are either self-propelled or helicopter transportable. All batteries are further subdivided into platoons in the same manner as the batteries of the artillery regiment. Batteries or platoons are capable of being attached to and working with the close and intermediate support battalions or batteries of the artillery regiment.

Field artillery group headquarters batteries are included within the Force artillery structure to command and exercise fire direction over two or more Force artillery batteries having a common mission. Such groups may either operate attached to an artillery regiment, or under a landing force artillery headquarters battery.

In an operation involving only one division and a limited amount of Force artillery, a landing force artillery headquarters battery may not be present. The group would then be the highest echelon of Force artillery. In this case, the majority of the Force artillery would probably be attached to the artillery regiment, although some might be retained under the Force commander's control.

The Force artillery batteries are of the following types: self-propelled 155mm gun, self-propelled 8-inch howitzer, towed (helicopter transportable) 105mm howitzer, self-propelled (truck mounted) Honest John rocket, and towed (helicopter transportable) Little John rocket. These various batteries provide the foreseen Force artillery requirements for mobility, range, high explosive neutralization and destruction capability, and atomic delivery capability. Because they no longer meet specific needs for fire support, and only serve to complicate logistic support, the 155mm howitzer and 4.5-inch rocket have been dropped from the Marine Corps artillery organization.

The self-propelled 155mm gun batteries are organized into 8-gun batteries of two 4-gun platoons each. Batteries have the same general organizational structure as the division's batteries. The long range (25,000 yards) of these batteries serves in a considerable measure to alleviate the problems brought about by the loss of range in the artillery regiment's weapons. From carefully selected positions, these batteries are able to reach out and give powerful reinforcing fires to close support batteries and battalions. When moved well forward, their range enables them to reach deep into enemy territory and provide general support fires for infantry regiments or the division.

The 8-inch howitzer batteries are organized into 3 platoons of 2 guns each. Because 8-inch howitzers very seldom fire battery-type missions, the 2-gun platoon is considered adequate for their expected normal employment. Whenever battery fire missions for 8-inch howitzers are foreseen or needed, 2 or more platoons can be brought together. Or their fires may be massed if the platoons are within range of the target. When infantry units must operate against an enemy in prepared positions, the 8-inch howitzers provide the means for powerful, accurate destructive fire to destroy enemy fortifications or field works. Their range (18,000 yards) and tremendous power enable them to give decisive reinforcement to close support battalions or batteries.

The self-propelled full-track mounts of the 155 guns and 8-inch howitzers give them a battlefield mobility far greater than any heavy artillery we have had in the past. They are able to go anywhere a tank can go. Their speed, both on the road and across country, is many times greater than that of the tractor-towed version of these weapons. They can go in and out of position in a matter of minutes, instead of hours as in the case of the towed versions. While they have the same general on-carriage traverse as do the towed weapons, in effect they have a 360-degree field of fire because of their ability to shift guns in position in a matter of minutes instead of hours. They have a further valuable ability to act as a direct fire assault gun in support of infantry operating against fortified positions or in built-up areas. Their vulnerability to counter-battery fire is greatly reduced as compared to the towed weapons.

All of these features add up to make them weapons of the highest order of usefulness on our modern amphibious battlefield. Batteries or platoons of 155mm guns and 8-inch howitzers as appropriate, appear to be suitable normal reinforcement for the fires of close support battalions with assault regiments. Other batteries or platoons of these weapons may be attached to the intermediate support battalion or employed directly under regimental control. In an operation involving two or more divisions, additional 155mm gun and 8inch howitzer batteries would probably be held and employed at force level in task organized artillery groups.

The Honest John and Little John rocket batteries are organized as 4 launcher batteries of 2 platoons of 2 launchers each. The 2-launcher platoon is used for the same reason as in the case of the 8-inch howitzer platoon. Again, both the battery and platoon FDCs are capable of planning for and executing atomic fire missions. The Honest John, being truck mounted, has a high degree of road mobility. The Little John, being helicopter transportable, can go anywhere assault infantry and close support artillery can go. Although these weapons were designed primarily for the delivery of atomic munitions, the development of extremely effective high explosive warheads for them gives them an added utility that will greatly increase their value.

Rocket batteries will probably be controlled at artillery regimental level and employed on division missions, except when platoons are temporarily assigned to a close support battalion for specific missions. In large scale operations, some rocket batteries will be retained at Force level for employment.

A limited number of separate 105mm howitzer batteries are provided in the Force artillery. These batteries are identical in organization to those found in the artillery regiment. Until such time as other Force-level helicopter transportable artillery weapons are developed, these howitzers provide the means to reinforce the division's artillery in a situation requiring helicopter movement. The normal method of employment of these batteries will be by attachment to close support or intermediate support battalions to increase the division's helicopter transportable fire support capability.

The Force artillery organization provides us an extremely powerful and varied source of fire support to meet almost any situation encountered in the amphibious assault. Its organizational structure permits it to be rapidly and readily task organized with regimental artillery units to meet the division's fire support needs. It further permits us, for the first time, to provide appropriate Force artillery units to brigade-size landing forces.

In summary, the M Table organization of regimental and Force artillery units and of the means for the planning, control, and coordination of artillery, naval gunfire, and close air support enhance their ability to support Marine infantry in modern amphibious combat. Infantry commanders at all echelons will benefit by having a greater variety of coordinated fire support instantly available to meet their needs.

Truly a New Corps

Larry James

Leatherneck
April 1975

You know it's a whole new ball game when all Marines no longer receive advanced infantry training before going to their first duty station or being assigned to a school.

Marine Corps training hasn't been revamped. It's become more of a polishing process. Corps old-timers—and today that probably includes Marines who enlisted anytime from '74 on back will find that some dramatic changes are under way. The end result is still the same professional Marine. The means to achieve that goal merely have been altered.

An indication of the shift in training emphasis includes the fact that Marines in the future will not all be required to spend two weeks annually on "range details," with one week devoted to "snappin' in."

In further marksmanship training developments, Marines assigned to aviation units will only need to sight-in from the 500-yard line every three years. Other years, they fire the "B" course from the 200.

And, don't be surprised the next time you spot a woman Marine sporting a qualification badge. Certain women Marines will be required to requalify annually.

Today's truly "New Corps" training also de-emphasizes rigid classroom hours for essential subjects—and less importance will be placed on written tests.

A further revision cuts the number of essential subjects from twelve to ten. At the same time, the mandatory requirement to be retested annually on all subjects is gone. However, performance "tests" will continue in marksmanship and physical fitness.

With all of the cuts and de-emphasizing, the question has to be: Just when are Marines trained? There are two keys to the Marine Corps' updated overall training picture. Considering the needs of the Corps, the individual Marine receives recruit training as either a basic Marine rifleman or basic woman Marine. Following the selection of a military occupational specialty for which the Marine is suited, the next step beyond the recruit depot is skill qualification training. In other words, MOS training.

This may sound similar to the old procedure but the big difference is that, after boot camp, our 1975 Marine goes directly to a formal school or to a unit. The Marine may receive that skill training to be MOS-qualified from either an on-the-job training program or from a unit training setup. This actually pulls the Marine off the "training line" (the length of time spent in Initial or entry-level training) much earlier and makes him available to a unit sooner.

This also saves money by eliminating instructor billets. The in-unit skill training is accomplished by T/O assigned Marines.

The second updated key to training concerns the Marine's instruction after his assignment to a unit. Headquarters Marine Corps has divided this post entry-level training into four main areas: career, mission-oriented, essential subjects testing/ training, and related training.

Under old training schedules, units sometimes found it difficult to accomplish all phases. Now, unit commanders have been given priorities for training. The unit's mission emphasized in the mission-oriented phase has top priority. If other training cannot be reasonably accomplished, it can be delayed until time is available.

Marksmanship, too, has a new look. If a Marine has been a qualified shooter several times, does he really need to spend two full weeks each year in the requalification phase? In fact, is it necessary for an accomplished shooter to fire for five days? Not any more. A shooter who has established a reputation for high scores can arrange ahead of time to fire for record on the second or third day.

Instead of annual essential subjects testing for all ten subjects, time for training and testing is devoted only to those who have problems mastering certain subjects. These individuals will be tested on only the subjects with which they have had difficulty.

While written exams are to be used if the commander feels they're necessary, the real test in all categories is performance.

Marine Corps Order 15110.2H (Individual Training of Enlisted Marines the new ITEM order) stresses: "Performance tests and observation will be the primary means of determining individual proficiency, supplemented when necessary by written or oral tests."

The new training concept is a far cry from the days when Marines crammed for their TT and GMS tests that required passing for promotion. The old technical test (an indication of a Marine's MOS knowledge) and the GMS (the general military subjects test, a forerunner of today's EST) were all geared to reading and comprehending the questions. Now there is peer instruction . . . innovative or imaginative training . . . and job/performance aids. They may be new descriptions, but they're all factors in the improved and updated training.

How do individual Marines "see" the new training trends?

While Brig. Gen. Maurice C. Ashley, Jr., served as director of training and education at Headquarters Marine Corps, he spoke of training as "the father of each generation of Marines."

"The recruits definitely heard about boot camp before arriving," the general said. "The image is there. He knows recruit training is a tough test of the individual. And, understandably. When the young Marine gets to a depot, recruit training lives up to everything he believes about that image. And the training is set up to ensure there is no letdown."

Even during recruit training, there is a new look about measuring a boot's advancement. Recognizing that written tests place huge demands on reading, writing, and interpreting the questions, performance-oriented training (now referred to as "hands-on" training throughout the Marine Corps) and peer instruction are taking over.

Simply, peer instruction employs students to train other students in a controlled environment. Broken into four steps, the student (recruit) observes a skill being performed and then receives instruction in this skill. In the third step, the Marine is required to demonstrate the skill. At this point, another Marine entering the first phase may observe. During the fourth step, our original Marine can instruct, which provides the second step for the follow-on Marine.

General Ashley saw this approach as both interesting and challenging. Additionally, it supports "a hallmark of Marines," he said, "assuming he can do it after instruction." A written test didn't necessarily prove that.

Recently, Staff Sgt. Michael E. Moro, a drill instructor at Parris Island, told *Leatherneck's* Tom Bartlett, "This new program is better than the old package. It teaches a recruit quickly. With the new program, the privates pay closer attention, knowing that they're going to be doing your act next."

However, Staff Sergeant Moro believes that the success of the new instruction can be attributed to the actual handling of the training aids by the recruits. The training session becomes little more than a lecture.

Gunnery Sergeant Joseph Gates, academics chief of the Parris Island Recruit Training Regiment, had been a drill instructor for a year and a half before joining the academics section.

"The new training program really impressed me," he said, running a tanned hand through a graying crew cut. "I'm a grunt, and . . . I learn by doing.

"The new program means fewer written tests. We've only been working with it here for about six months, but we find that it permits us to go into more detail."

Another Parris Island Marine, Gunnery Sgt. Bobby Dixon, NCOIC of the Field Training Unit, which instructs and supervises the training of recruits at Elliot's Beach, has seventeen years in the Marine Corps, and two tours as a drill instructor.

"I've seen many programs tested and tried," he grinned, "but I believe in this one. They come out here, and they either know or they don't know. There's no way they can fake an envelopment or first aid problem.

"As a result of this new application program, the recruits know more about what's going on, and they know how to react."

The training change is probably more noticeable in the period following boot camp. Many Marines wonder whatever happened to ITR. The infantry training requirement for all Marines after boot camp is gone, but for some there is a new training program called field skills training.

On the surface, Marines at Camp Lejeune seem to be getting the same infantry indoctrination as before. They fire crew-served weapons, receive instructions on tactics, and begin to learn the fine points of being a grunt. But a closer check reveals that only four MOSs are involved. There are Marines being trained as 0311 (Riflemen), 0331 (Machine gunners), 0341 (Mortar men) and 0351 (Antitank assaultmen). The field skills training (FST) schedule resembles the ITR package but it applies to only the four MOSs.

And, the Marines already belong to a unit. Using the Second Marine Regiment as an example, the FST instruction unit consists of one officer and twelve enlisted Marines. But, in place of the cadre of special instructors and troop handlers that was necessary for ITR, all of the guidance is provided by these members of the Second Marines.

The regimental commander, Col. John E. Greenwood, believes his '03 Marines are "better trained than when there was ITR." And he thinks the sergeants and staff sergeants involved in the instruction are also benefiting. The enlisted leaders come from his infantry units. After instructing with the FST for a planned twelve to eighteen months, they return to a company. At this point the colonel believes he has a better leader.

The evolution of today's FST in the Second Marines has been polished, and changed slightly, since the last ITR in mid-1972.

Initially, a division-level infantry training program was tried. But, it was decided a stateside regiment was a better answer for training the Corps' grunts. The Second Marines began the field skills training in late 1972. At that time, the young Marines reporting in from boot camp were assigned to a company, went through training in the daytime, and were billeted with the company at night.

Colonel Greenwood said this proved to be a little too much for the young troops to handle. "Things got a little out of limbo for some of the Marines right out of recruit training," he said, "and then listening to those Old salts of six months in the barracks at night didn't help."

"Now that we have gone to centralized billeting for the FST Marines, we believe the problem has been solved," the colonel commented.

Captain John Gaieski, a former company commander in the regiment, is in charge of the Second Marines' FST unit. Of the six weeks—thirty training days—about 70 percent is practical application instruction, he stated. Most classes are geared for twenty-five to forty Marines but entire companies do go through, particularly when a company with a deployment scheduled in the near future is being formed. The equivalent of one battalion a year goes through the Second FST.

The first phase of FST includes five days of assembly, welcoming aboard, unit assignments, personnel processing, equipment issue, and an actual base orientation. The basic Marine infantryman is shown where disbursing, special services, Red Cross, and other important offices are located. It's not the case of a check-in sheet with a list of building numbers.

And, from the beginning, there are troop handlers. These are not T/O assignments like the old ITR. They are squad leaders from units to which the Marines are assigned. This way a corporal from a line company gets six weeks to know his men before they become an intricate part of the company.

"We started with only one troop handler," Captain Gaieski said. "Now we have up to 25, particularly when we have men from the 2nd Recon Battalion going through our FST."

Corporal Walter Haas of I/3/2 is typical of the caliber of Marine assigned as a troop handler by the Second Marines. Last year he was the second rifleman for the third fire team in K/3/2. This unit was selected as tops in the annual Corps-wide squad competition. Haas, who has three years in the Marine Corps, and had gone through ITR about two months before it was phased out, said the FST Marines are really motivated.

"This hands-on training really appeals," he said.

Staff Sergeant Charles Dedmond, an 0311 tactics instructor from C/1/2, believes the FST is "just outstanding."

"Personally, I believe the experience the instructor gets here is valuable when he goes back to the company," Dedmond said.

Staff Sergeant Kenneth Browne, a thirt-eight-year-old mortar instructor with nineteen years in the Corps, definitely has the perspective to discuss FST. Browne has been a member of the FST unit since March 1973. A couple years before that, he spent eighteen months as an instructor at Lejeune's Camp Geiger. Prior to that duty he spent a year as a troop handler. He claims the specialized FST instruction is not as thorough as when he was at ITR.

"But one advantage is that I work with smaller groups than at Geiger," Browne said. "The largest number I have had was 43 Marines versus 150 to 200 in ITR.

"The biggest problem the FST instructor has is to counter the scuttlebutt the young Marines pick up at night in the area. Some of the six-month 'salts' pass out bum dope. At Geiger they were isolated."

Although most of the twelve instructors favored the old ITR since it could accommodate more Marines for the advanced infantry training, much of the original ITR material is now taught during recruit training. FST is not intended to replace ITR. It is strictly meant to qualify Marines in the four infantry MOSs.

The one thing that all of the Second FSTU instructors agree about is the leadership value for the enlisted Marines who will be rotated as instructors or troop handlers.

The Marines have ten days of MOS qualification in the second phase basic skill training. Following this, everything is put together in organizational/mission training. The individual Marines discover how their particular skill blends into the overall infantry picture.

Duty and training with the Second Marines' FSTU is not an eight-to-four proposition.

"All of my instructors pull duty with the night study halls," Captain Gaieski said. And the troop handlers have a lot more to do than merely seeing that their men move from class to class. Corporal Haas said his day starts at 5 AM with the Marines in the barracks. At the end of the training day at 5 PM, the troop handler often spends until 9 or 10 o'clock talking and reviewing with the troops.

This personal interest, along with the centralized billeting, has greatly lessened disciplinary problems for the Second Marines.

This relationship of small unit leaders and the new Marines was one of the points General Ashley stressed from the Headquarters Marine Corps level. It ensures there is no letdown of that Marine image with which the recruit arrived at boot camp.

While still director of training and education, the general cited the Second Marines as "biting the bullet" to accomplish the needed training. At the same time the regiment was able to maintain its combat readiness.

General Ashley also said that he believes the Marine Corps concept in training new Marines will carry its advantages over to career men. Beyond the improved leadership derived by Marine NCOs involved with FST, the possibility of establishing "adventure training" is being considered.

As part of the "no-letdown" idea, a career Marine who is in supply or administration might be able to put in for something like jump training. This would apply to a Marine who desires to continue in his MOS but has always wanted to attend what he envisions more glamorous training. The general felt that if the Corps makes "adventure training" available, the individual will probably have to contribute his share of off-duty time while undergoing the training.

Someday the clerk who always wondered what it would be like to drive an M-60 tank may get the chance.

It is also believed that MOS training for many fields does not have to take a formal school approach. Job/performance aids will allow precise step-by-step directions for Marines to work on equipment or weapons. With very little experience or knowledge of the item, Marines can efficiently perform both simple and complex maintenance and repair activities. Simply, a Marine will be able to accomplish work while actually learning a skill.

Today's Marine training still produces the same professionals who were on Hills 861 and 881 at Khe Sanh eight years ago. But the new look on individual training is now giving the Marine unit's primary mission even greater consideration and significance.

Building Better Infantrymen

Chris Lawson

Leatherneck
March 1998

There's a framed quote by Gen. George S. "Old Blood and Guts" Patton that hangs above Capt. Michael Aubut's desk at the School of Infantry (SOI) at Camp Pendleton, California. Aubut, the infantry training battalion's tactics officer, believes it pretty well sums up his feelings regarding war and a Marine infantryman's role in it.

It reads: "Wars may be fought by weapons, but they are won by men."

Ever mindful of that philosophy, Aubut and other infantry trainers throughout the Corps are hard at work implementing recently approved Headquarters Marine Corps-mandated changes to the way the Corps trains its young gunfighters. The Marines, it seems, are well aware that regardless of all the gee-whiz technology and weaponry entering the fleet these days, infantrymen are still the ones who will ultimately win future battles.

The bottom line to the dramatic changes that took effect last fall on both coasts: shorter training schedules, an emphasis on coaching versus lecturing, higher marks-manship standards, more time spent in the field, and more live-fire opportunities for everyone, regardless of infantry specialty.

"We're looking to the future with a lot of our training," Aubut said. "This is a para-digm shift in our policy."

The new thirty-four-day training package about half as long as the previous fifty-nine-day course, will affect all infantrymen, including riflemen, machine-gunners, mortarmen, assaultmen, and TOW antitank gunners, Aubut said. And while one of the main thrusts of the new program is training many 0311s in other infantry specialties, riflemen will report directly to their infantry battalions once they graduate from SOI while crew-served weapons Marines will get an additional two weeks of intensive, specific weapons training.

The changes to infantry training come hot on the heels of other sweeping changes made throughout the Corps by Marine Corps Commandant Gen. Charles C. Krulak. Last year, for example, recruit training and Marine combat training for non-infantry

Marines were overhauled to embrace the "Transformation" process which begins in entry-level training for both officers and recruits.

General Krulak's Transformation emphasizes realistic, relevant, and demanding training for all Marines, regardless of job specialty. Under new philosophies, the mental demands, such as those experienced in decision-making exercises, are often as tough as the physical.

But in this latest round of changes, there are specific, tangible benefits as well. Aubut said the new package is a more efficient and effective way to conduct training. Adding that the streamlined program will allow Marines to reach the FMF faster than ever before, boost the number of classes being taught in a year from sixteen to twenty-four, and save time and money. In the end, officials are betting they can produce better quality infantrymen in shorter periods of time.

"We've eliminated redundancies, packed training into the weekends and nights, and produced a very demanding program," Aubut said. "If you don't continue to refine and improve yourself, you're losing."

The key objectives in the new training program include:

- Emphasizing urban/night operations
- Training all infantrymen to the 0311 standard
- Realistic/scenario-based training
- Developing a warrior attitude, i.e., the "Hunter/Killer"
- Sustaining the Transformation
- Avoiding ritualistic training

The priorities of training that will receive the most attention, money, and time include:

- Weapons and gunnery
- Combat operations
- Battlefield awareness

Aubut said students and instructors will achieve these goals by incorporating more combat-scenario driven training, the use of force-on-force exercises, training students to expect the unexpected and developing decision-making skills.

Here's how the new program will work. Upon graduating from boot camp, riflemen and other infantrymen with a crew-served MOS will report to SOI immediately following graduation. Within one week, classes will be formed and training begun almost immediately. Instead of having weekends off, as they did under old policies, students will have only two weekends of liberty, in order to pack as much training as possible into the thirty-four training days. In addition, much, if not virtually all, training will be conducted in the field, outside of traditional classrooms.

"We're giving them experience—field experience—not just classroom instruction," Aubut said. "The training will be much more tactical."

Training day one will focus on in-processing students, Aubut said. Training days two to ten will focus on weapons and gunnery proficiency (including the use of night vision equipment). Students will study woodland attack and defend tactics on training days eleven to sixteen and urban attack and defend tactics from training days seventeen to twenty-two. Advanced patrolling will be conducted from training days twenty-three to thirty-one, and out-processing will take place on days thirty-two to thirty-four.

Students will live and learn in the field, Aubut said, remaining as tactical as possible during the entire field evolutions. Weapons, for example, will be carried outboard versus at sling arms, even if a student is just walking to the water bull or portable toilet.

"And we don't just eat chow at a certain time and place," he said. "We eat at tactical opportunities, just like in real operations."

The thirty-four training days will be spent training in the field, and there will be seventeen overnight evolutions. And on those overnights, there will be very few bivouacs, Aubut said. Students will establish "patrol bases" and operate from fighting holes.

Officials will train all the infantrymen to become competent with the M16A2 rifle and grenades, and all students will receive more trigger time with the M203 grenade launcher, M249 squad automatic weapon, AT-4 antitank weapon, the M240G machine gun, the MK-19 grenade machine gun, the M2 .50-caliber machine gun, 60-mm. mortars and mines as well. They'll also learn to call for fire, a skill not normally taught at SOI. Students will also conduct two live-fire day attacks, live-fire night attacks, day and night ambushes, and live-fire room clearing techniques.

The goal: give as much experience and training to as many infantry Marines as possible.

"We're making infantry Marines more interchangeable," Aubut said.

Not only are trainers adding new elements to the course curriculum, such as urban operations, night vision equipment, and weapons cross-training—they're training smarter as well as harder.

For example, under the old program Marines would spend three days in the classroom learning techniques of land navigation. Under the new program, infantrymen will receive a map, protractors, and compass when they report aboard and keep them all during training. It will be a continual learning process.

Instructors will come down off their podiums and teach classes right in the field, where the rubber meets the road, Aubut explained. There's a philosophical change in how the Marines will be taught as well. Instead of simple lectures, involving rote memorization, students and instructors will work together in the field.

"The old 'Techniques of Military Instruction' are a thing of the past. Today, it's more of a mentoring process," Aubut explained. "Today's Marines have to be decision makers. We want to develop independent thinkers. It's a lot like TBS for officers. We realize that the decisions a young pfc might make out there in the Somalias and Haitis of the world could well affect national strategy."

Instructors will have a steeper learning curve as well under the new program. Instructors like Staff Sgt. Leo Varos will now be required to teach a multitude of subjects, instead of specific courses. They will remain with their charges throughout the entire course, adding to unit cohesion, which is so important in the infantry. All instructors will go through a ten-day formal instructor course to prepare them for their new responsibilities.

"I feel like I'm playing a bigger role in developing these young Marines," Varos said. "I've broadened my skills as well. I know more than just how to patrol. I'm not a master of the SMAW [shoulder launched multipurpose assault weapon] or anything, but I can effectively engage targets with it, thanks to this new training."

Since the new training schedule moves at a much quicker pace, both students and instructors will be under intense pressure from day one.

"On the 15th day of training, students will be moving under live fire overhead in the attack," Aubut said. "That's pretty bold. There are Marine infantrymen who have been in the fleet for years who have not even done that sort of thing."

During the course's final exercise, students will do scores of night movements, Aubut said, including one 15-mile hump. They'll also be challenged by lack of sleep and food hardships they can expect if deployed in a real operation. During the FX, they'll get 1½ meals a day and only 5 hours of sleep in a single 24-hour period.

Aubut is excited that the classrooms are virtually abandoned now, except for three times in the training: in-processing, out-processing, and when students are using indoor marksmanship simulators.

"The field is our classroom," Aubut said.

The value of the new training has not been lost on the students. Private Justice Asbury, a student from Squad 6, Weapons Platoon, "Alpha" Company, said he relished the experience.

"It's more fun, I think. More hands on. I really enjoy getting experience on all the different weapons systems," he said during a break from training. "I feel like it has more purpose. It lets us know what to expect when we get to the infantry."

But Pvt. Joseph Thomas, a TOW gunner, probably summed it up best.

"I feel like a total infantryman," he said. "I'm not just a TOW gunner."

Regardless of all the gee-whiz technology and weaponry entering the fleet these days, infantrymen are still the ones who will ultimately win future battles.

Since the new training schedule moves at a much quicker pace, both students and instructors will be under intense pressure from day one.

Your Forever Experience

Robert Church

Leatherneck
November 1975

On this 200th anniversary of our beloved Marine Corps, I would like to write a letter and (if I could) send it back through time to a certain young Marine who marched in the green legions of the Corps more than thirty years ago. Strangely enough, his name happens to be the same as the writer's. . . .

November 10, 1975
Pvt. Robert Church (855313)
Platoon 400, 7th Rec. Trng. Bn.
Marine Corps Recruit Depot
Parris Island, SC

Dear Private Church:

It's May 1943, and you're in boot camp, the threshold to glory! For you (my younger self) and your buddies of Platoon 400, this is where it all starts—your training, your salty pride, your service to Corps and Country, your Marine memories. Here in the sweat and toil of boot camp, you begin the greatest adventure of your life. This is the birthplace of your forever experience.

Your forever experience! You sail away from the monotonous gray of commonplace existence into the exciting blue of life extraordinary! Your odyssey will span all the years, places, men, women, and events of your life in the Marine Corps. You wouldn't trade it for a king's crown, and you'll never forget it. It will be your forever experience, and it started the moment you stepped aboard boot camp.

Of course, right now, in your first few days of training, your experience consists of trying to keep up with everything your drill instructor keeps throwing at you: Push-ups, double-time, drill, and all the other little exertions that leave you with quivering muscles, heaving lungs, and rivers of sweat! There may be times when you wonder if you'll make it—and you want with all your heart to make it! Many Marine boots know that feeling.

Well, don't worry, you'll make it. You'll go all the way to graduation, and you'll come out grinning with the joy and pride of knowing you've earned your place among the elite!

Yes, Private Church, I know just how tough boot camp is. In memory I can still feel the blisters that made you limp in your stiff new field shoes, so many years ago! (You were a mighty hard D.I. back then, Platoon Sergeant Koons . . . and a first-rate Marine!)

It's hard training, indeed, but it's all part of a carefully planned and tested program that's transforming you into a highly efficient fighting machine. No, not a robot. A man. But a very special kind of a man with a toughened body and a trained, alert mind, able to function equally well with others under command, or on your own initiative—like a single bolt of lightning!

At the same time, you're learning the techniques of survival, so you'll have the best chance possible of coming safely through whatever battles may lie ahead. You're learning to hit the deck with enthusiasm. You're learning to "keep that big, bouncing butt down, Church!" You're learning to go over an obstacle faster than a man can aim and fire a rifle at you. You're also learning that often the best defense is a swift, overwhelming offense. And you're learning that, in battle, the Marines take care of their own, by covering fire and other tactics, and by buddy helping buddy.

No, not all Marines survive their battles. Many fall, but not without meaning or purpose, no matter what the armchair critics may say! They fall doing their duty for their country, and with the greatest of honor! And they lie asleep with their fallen buddies until the final reveille calls them forth forever.

Is that such a bad way to go?

Think about it.

Meanwhile, Private Church, you're learning a lot, and you're learning it well. And, as time goes by, you'll also discover that, along with everything else—or perhaps because of everything else—something unique is happening inside you. It began your first day in boot camp, and it will grow as you grow in the Corps. It's the very heartbeat of your forever experience, and you'll have it all the days of your life. They call it esprit de corps.

Esprit de corps. The Marine mystique—the intangible but very real spirit that makes the qualitative difference between a U.S. Marine and any other military man in the world. It's love. It's pride. It's devotion. It's all that and more, too. You can't fully explain it. To understand it you have to experience it yourself. And to do that, you have to be a Marine.

Look at any Marine when he hears a band playing his own Hymn. Look at any Marine when he's saluting his country's flag. Look at his face, and you know he'll go all the way for his country and his Corps. Ah the way to Kingdom Come if he has to!

That's just a hint of what esprit de corps is, Private Church. It's why you'll honor your Corps—second only to the flag you defend.

Which brings us to the moment of truth. The defense of that flag, and the country it represents, has been the primary mission of the Marine Corps for two hundred years of magnificent heroism, and it is still our primary mission!

And what of the flag? What is there about it that makes men willing to lay down their lives to keep it flying? What makes young men actually eager to climb a hell on earth like Mount Suribachi to plant the Stars and Stripes at the summit?

Simply this: that flag, that Old Glory, that beautiful Star-Spangled Banner, symbolizes the very highest principles of human decency ever conceived in the hearts and minds of men!

And your primary mission, Private Church, is to help your Corps defend that flag—with all your might! It's as simple as that. And as worthy!

You see, Uncle Sam and his "few Marines" have come down a long road of years shoulder-to-shoulder. The road began as a narrow, cobblestone street in Philadelphia; it extends down to today; and stretches on into all our tomorrows.

The milestones along this road have the names of places that are shrines to the courage of the Marines who fought there: the Bahamas (where Marines made their first amphibious landing, led by none other than our old friend, Capt. Samuel Nicholas, formerly of Tun's Tavern!); Tripoli (source of the Mameluke sword); Chapultepec (and the Halls of the Montezuma); Guantanamo Bay; Cavite; Samar; Peking and Tientsin (Boxer Rebellion); Belleau Wood; Mont Blanc Ridge; Meuse-Argonne; Guadalcanal; Tarawa; Guam; Iwo Jima; Okinawa; Tokyo; Chosin Reservoir; Con Thien; Chu Lai; Hue—and many, many other milestones, including the decks and rigging of countless ships, in naval engagements starting with the American Revolution and continuing today.

And the two-hundred-year road is paved with the valor of men whose names, coming one after the other, sound like the measured thunder of a mighty bell, tolling liberty through the centuries: Samuel Nicholas, Presley O'Bannon, Archibald Henderson, Archibald Summers, Smedley D. Butler, Dan Daly, John Quick, John A. Lejeune, A. A. Vandegrift, Evans Carlson, "Red Mike" Edson, "Pappy" Boyington, Lou Diamond, and "Chesty" Puller. . . .

And so many others their names would fill an honor roll reaching from here to eternity. And in a very special place on the honor roll would go the legendary Pfc. G.I. Grunt and his buddies, those heroes of heroes, the tired, dirty, sweatin', shootin', unsung sons of the rifle companies!

We salute them, every one!

Marines like these know what every thoughtful American knows, that freedom is not free. The price is high, but we Americans pay it because we happen to think freedom is worth it. And the Marines always pay a lion's share of the bill. Gladly. Proudly. The first Marines thought America had something worth fighting for. Today's Marines still think so.

Nobody likes to fight a war. But until somebody figures out how to establish a permanent peace with freedom for all, somebody has to be able and ready to guard the rights and lives of free people. The Marines have that capability, and use it whenever Uncle Sam calls them into action.

Private Church, the Marines of your generation won your war in the islands of the Pacific, and you won it heroically. But there have been other costly battles between your point in time and the present—Korea, Vietnam—and special missions such as the Cuban missile incident, the Lebanon landing, and the *Mayaguez* rescue.

Now, in the year 1975, two-hundred years since the Marine Corps was established, we live in a world that seems more troubled than ever. There are those who would take away our freedom today, if they could. (But they damned well can't!)

And there are others, sitting on a so-called "neutral" fence, who snipe at us verbally. We Americans are "decadent," they say. "Immoral."

It seems they can see the speck in our eye, without being aware of the plank in their own.

Sure, we have our "lunatic fringe." What country hasn't?

But when there's disaster anywhere in the world, who's the first in with help? Who's the first to land with food, medical supplies, blankets, shelters—plane load after plane load of help—without ever counting the cost? The "decadent" Americans, that's who!

And when innocent people in danger of mass slaughter call out for help—who's the first (and sometimes the only) to go in and guard them, feed them, evacuate them without ever counting the cost? The "immoral" Americans, that's who! With the U.S. Marines leading the way in!

Uncle Sam and his "few Marines" are ready—as they've been for two-hundred years—to go anywhere, anytime, in the cause of justice, honor, and simple human mercy.

These missions have the wholehearted approval and support of the American people. Not the oddballs, of course, who won't support anything, including themselves. Not the cynics who look on from afar with delicately raised eyebrows. No, our strength comes from the vast center of our population, which is as solidly American as it ever was.

We have many millions of decent, patriotic citizens who love our country as much as ever. Gutsy Americans who are not ashamed of a teardrop in the eye when they see

Old Glory still proudly waving. They know what she stands for, and what it has cost to keep her flying.

And we have millions of strong, reverent Americans who are not ashamed to ask God's blessing and guidance for our country, our leaders, our men and women in uniform.

There's a famous painting of Gen. George Washington before a battle, kneeling on one knee in the snow, praying for his men and his country.

That spirit of faith and reverence still prevails in the great heart of America. We're still ". . . one nation under God . . ."

Thank God that we are!

No godless nation or group of nations in the world can prevail against that spirit! And as for the godless cynics in our midst, they can go plumb to hell, which no doubt they will!

Well, Private Church, as you can see, you've got a lot going for you, and a lot to live up to, as you join the elite in the front ranks of our country's defense forces. Your life as a U.S. Marine stretches like a shining road before you, and whether you stay on that road for one tour of duty, or thirty years, you'll find it the highroad of your whole life. You'll never have a greater opportunity to reach so high a level of service and personal fulfillment.

So there's something you should know, something you should be aware of at all times. It is one of the most important things anyone could be aware of—but very few are! It's something I should have been aware of, but wasn't.

This is it: Be aware that you are always building memories! Wherever you may be, whatever you may be doing, you're also building memories.

Now you'll be building memories of men, women, duty stations, voyages, islands, the rattle of gunfire, the coppery taste of fear, the sound of laughter, the many details of life in the Corps.

But most importantly, you'll be building memories of your own performance from moment to moment, and day to day. Some of these will be the big memories that will come winging home to you . . . either like golden eagles, or like vultures. They'll bring you satisfaction, or regret, as long as you live.

Once an action has been completed, once a moment has passed, once today has become yesterday, you can't call it back and change it, or erase a line of it, no matter how much you wish you could! Each moment is a segment of eternity that becomes part of your forever experience.

That is why it is so important—to both you and the Corps—to live the kind of life that produces good memories, ones that will bring joy and pride whenever they come to mind. Private Church, live so the Corps will always say, "We're glad he was one of us." And you'll always say, "Me too!"

There are two simple guidelines that can help you build good memories. One is this: Don't take anything or anyone for granted! Everything, and especially every person, and your personal involvement, is a potential memory, treasured or tragic.

And the second guideline: When you are going to do something, always ask yourself, "Will this deed be worthy of two hundred years of Marine Corps honor? Would a really first-rate Marine do this?"

If the answer is "no"—then by all means don't do it! Because if you do, the memory of it will cast a shadow on your forever experience that will haunt you all the days of your life!

To sum up: The quality of your own service to your Corps and country will determine the quality of your memories, and thereby the quality of your forever experience.

So you see, Private Church, you'll want to be the very best Marine you possibly can so that, thirty-two years from now (way up in 1975), you'll be able to look back at a forever experience that gleams like purest gold in your memories—and in your Marine Corps record!

Well, Private Church, this letter won't reach you in boot camp because you graduated many years ago, and marched away into the mists of time. . . .

. . . and now you're an old-timer who has lived his forever experience. An old-timer full of memories, of both sunlight and shadows. But an old-timer with the fierce love and pride of the Marine Corps still surging through his veins!

I'm wearing civvies now, but just inside lives a young Marine in dress blues . . . forever!

As for this letter, I guess the best thing we can do is make it an open letter to all Marines, everywhere. And we salute you all!

We often think of our own old buddies—the Marines of the World War II generation—and to them we say, "Thank you for the unforgettable camaraderie."

We think of the generations of Marines who served before our time, and we say, "Thanks for what you built, and guarded through two hundred years, and passed on to us."

We think of all the Marines of the future, and we say, "You'll have a lot to live up to. But you'll do it. Marines always have."

We look at the magnificent Marines of today, and we say, "You're doing just fine! You're as good as we were, and better! We wish you Godspeed, a happy voyage, and a treasured forever experience!"

And you women Marines of yesterday and today—did you think we'd forget you? So trim and chic? The prettiest, proudest sight in all of God's green earth! Forget? Ah, no. Love's the word! And respect! We wish you a golden shower of bright memories always!

And now to our beloved Marine Corps in your 200th year of glory—we're overflowing with pride and devotion as we present to you the smartest, most heartfelt salute a Marine can give!

Finally, to the flag of our country—the basic reason for our existence as Marines—we pledge our allegiance, and our lives, forever!

Semper Fidelis!

The Crucible: Building Warriors for the 21st Century

Gen. Charles C. Krulak, USMC

Marine Corps Gazette
July 1997

In a world of international civil unrest and uncertainty, the Corps continues to prepare its Marines for the eventuality of combat on tomorrow's battlefield.

On the May 26, 1997, I delivered a Memorial Day address at a solemn ceremony on one of the Marine Corps' most sacred battlefields: Belleau Wood. The tenacity, valor, and sacrifice displayed by the 4th Marine Brigade during that epic battle forever cemented the Corps' reputation as the world's fighting elite. Since Belleau Wood, Marines have been looked upon as professionals, honed to the highest standard, sharpened for any challenge, warriors without peer.

After the ceremony, I spent the rest of the day walking through the wheat fields, forests, and villages where the 4th Brigade fought. This is hallowed ground. Even to this day, the battlefield bears the scars of vicious combat-fighting positions, trenches, shell holes, and shards of shrapnel are everywhere. It was a wonder to me that anyone could survive, much less prevail, in the cauldron that was Belleau Wood. Survival required much more than just courage and exceptional training. The individual Marine rifleman had to be innovative, resourceful, and capable of making the right decision in extremis—in many ways, a force of one. More importantly, though, each and every Marine at Belleau Wood had to believe in his heart that, although he might seem alone and on his own in the darkness of the forest, he was actually fighting as part of an insep-arable team—his unit Marines who he could never let down.

While walking in the wheat field through which the Marines attacked on June 6, 1918, it dawned on me that the battle of Belleau Wood was won before it was even joined. On the eve of their trial by fire, the Marines of the 4th Brigade were supremely confident in their personal abilities to carry the day, and more importantly, they felt an incredible allegiance to their unit and to their fellow Marines. It was these attributes that enabled them to prevail in the crucible of Belleau Wood. These same attributes—confidence and allegiance—will be necessary for success in the battles that will confront

Marines in the twenty-first century. The Corps' Crucible of today is designed to help Marines prepare for those future battles through the inculcation of these attributes.

I know that many of you have already heard of the Crucible. Some of you are even beginning to receive Crucible-trained Marines into your units. Let me share with you our rationale for starting the Crucible, identify what this training evolution entails, and then discuss the opportunities and the challenges that it poses to us as leaders.

Why the Crucible?

The Crucible was not implemented because we found our tried and true methods of recruit training to be flawed. Nothing could be further from the truth. We developed the Crucible for two major reasons. The first reason is that we saw a change in the operating environment in which our Marines will be employed. Decentralized operations, high technology, increasing weapons lethality, asymmetric threats, the mixing of combatants and noncombatants, and urban combat will be the order of the day vice the exception in the 21st century. Our Marines must be good decisionmakers. They must be trained to the highest standard. They must be self-confident. They must have absolute faith in the members of their unit. This is why we have instituted the Values Program for all Marines. This is why we have enhanced the way we transform America's sons and daughters into U.S. Marines. This is why we have included the Crucible as part of the Transformation process. We must ensure that our newest Marines fully understand and appreciate what the Marine Corps represents, and that, as members of the world's fighting elite, they must uphold the sacred trust we have with our great nation–and the sacred trust that we have with each other. The Crucible is designed specifically to contribute to the making of this kind of Marine. Preparing our young Marines for battle is the genesis for the Crucible.

The second reason for the Crucible was derived from subtle changes in the societal norms and expectations of America's youth. We have all heard the term "generation X," a term often associated with a negative connotation. Yet, it is from this generation that we recruit the Marines who will be our future. It is, therefore, important for us to understand just how the young people of today view the world, to understand what motivates them. Almost two years ago, we brought in a team of psychologists to tell us about generation X. From them, we learned that young people today are looking for standards, and they want to be held accountable. They, for the most part, don't mind following, but they can lead and want to lead. Most want to be part of something bigger than themselves. They want to be something special. Most believe in God. Many don't fully recognize it as such, but they want to have faith. These traits manifest themselves in a tendency to join—join gangs, join fraternities and clubs, join causes. These are exactly the same attributes and attitudes that offer the Marine Corps a tremendous opportunity. Generation X does not want to be "babied." These young Americans are looking for a real challenge. They desperately want to be part of a winning team; they crave the stature associated with being one of the best. These are the Marines of the future, the warriors of the 21st century. The Crucible is giving them exactly what they want—and exactly what we need.

What Is the Crucible?

Remember that Transformation is a four-step process: recruiting, recruit training, cohesion, and sustainment. The Crucible is the centerpiece of the recruit training phase. It is a three-day training evolution that has been added to the end of basic recruit training, designed specifically to make Marines better warriors. It features little food, little sleep, over forty miles of forced marches, and thirty-two stations that test physical toughness and mental agility. The events are designed to focus primarily on two areas—shared hardship and teamwork. We wanted to create a challenge so difficult and arduous that it would be the closest thing possible to actual combat. We wanted to create for the recruits a Crucible that, once experienced, would be a personal touchstone and would demonstrate for each and every recruit and candidate the limitless nature of what they could achieve individually and, more importantly, what they could accomplish when they worked as a team. To accommodate this culminating event we lengthened recruit training to twelve full weeks. The Crucible has been strategically placed in the eleventh week of training, a week we have designated "Transformation week."

The drill instructor is still the backbone of the recruit training process. The drill instructor's role in the first ten weeks of recruit training remains as it always has been. However, during Transformation week the drill instructor trades his or her traditional campaign cover for a soft cover or a helmet, and transitions to the role of a team leader and mentor for the Crucible process. The drill instructor guides the recruits, seeking to build confidence in their individual abilities and to emphasize the importance of the team. The objective is to build a sense of unit cohesion so that by the end of the Crucible the individual recruits see the value of working together, in a common cause, to overcome the most arduous tasks and conditions.

The drill instructor's job is not over, however, when his or her recruits complete the Crucible. There is a week remaining—Transition week. It is the time when our newest members have the opportunity—and the responsibility—to increase their knowledge and confidence so that they are fully prepared for what lies ahead. It is during this last week that the drill instructors debrief the recruits' Crucible experience, identifying and reinforcing the teamwork and values that allowed them to prevail in times of duress and hardship.

The Opportunity and the Challenge

The results of the first iterations of the Crucible have been impressive, not only in the increased sense of pride and maturity in our new Marines, but in other, more tangible, ways as well. For example, liberty incidents of the Crucible-trained companies going through infantry training battalions at the schools of infantry have decreased dramatically. Both schools report that companies composed of Marines who have completed the Crucible are performing better than Marines who underwent the syllabus prior to implementation of the Crucible. Recruiters report that these new Marines, when assigned to the recruiters assistance program, are more responsible and more confident. These are preliminary results, but clearly we have hit the mark. We have taken a proven process that produces the finest fighting men and women in the world and actually improved it!

Now as these Marines—tempered in the Crucible—enter our ranks, it is up to every leader in the Corps to combine the strengths of our experienced Marines with the intensity of our new Marines. This amalgamation will increase unit warfighting capabilities. As always, Marine leaders must capitalize on the strength that every Marine brings to the team.

You have great Marines now. Your new Marines will be the same in many ways yet will be different for their Crucible experience. Think about how you will capitalize on that difference. Think about how you will meet this challenge. While it is true that leadership fundamentals are timeless, the method of application varies with every scenario and with each individual. I have complete confidence that in this organization of leaders you will find the methods to maximize this opportunity wherever you are—in your fire team or shop, in your battalion or squadron, in your Marine air-ground task force, or on your staff.

The battles ahead will be violent, chaotic, and lethal. It is our responsibility to prepare our Marines for these future trials. They, like their forefathers at Belleau Wood, must have complete confidence in their individual abilities and in those of their unit. The Crucible helps instill that confidence. But, it only helps. It is up to us to do the rest with good, old-fashioned, Marine Corps leadership.

Semper Fidelis.

Preparing the Marine Corps for War

Gen. Charles C. Krulak, USMC

Marine Corps Gazette
September 1997

The 31st Commandant reviews the Corps' progress during the last two years, and points the way ahead.

In 1993 we took a major step forward in ensuring that our Corps would always be "the most ready when the Nation is least ready." In that year we published Marine Corps Order (MCO) P3900.15, which defines the Marine Corps combat development Process (CDP), now called the Marine Corps combat development system (CDS). In that order we codified an integrated process by which we identify, obtain, and support necessary combat capabilities for the Marine Corps. The CDS is not about the procurement of things. It is about the procurement of capabilities. Things don't win battles. Marines win battles . . . Marines who can outthink, outmaneuver, and who have the capabilities to overwhelm their foes.

As part of the CDS, the commandant of the Marine Corps is responsible for publishing a document called the commandant's planning guidance (CPG). The CPG is intended to be the foundation of Marine Corps planning, the cornerstone of our efforts to maintain a combat ready Marine Corps. Two years ago, we published the CPG—a comprehensive document that serves as the schematic for how we make Marines and win battles for the nation. Now, at the halfway mark of this Commandancy, it is time to revisit the CPG and remind ourselves that our priority must always be maintaining our focus on preparing the Marine Corps for war.

Unique Contributions

We have made significant contributions to the nation's defense in several new and very unique ways. Identifying a gap in our nation's ability to rapidly respond to chemical and biological attacks, a chemical and biological incident response force (CBIRF) was created. This unit is ready for use in the fight against those who would attack our nation asymmetrically. It has been deployed to several real-world contingencies, making our population and leadership safer—at the Olympic Games in Atlanta, at the president's inauguration in Washington, and at the economic summit in Denver. It is ready for worldwide deployment and is improving on ways in which it can be used to "train the trainers" in organizations and agencies preparing for similar contingencies.

A standing joint task force headquarters (SJTFHQ) has also been created. Recognizing the ad hoc nature in which joint task force (JTF) headquarters are usually created and the inefficiencies incurred in such activations, the SJTFHQ was developed to address those inefficiencies. Resourced by the Marine Corps, it is ready for use by any theater commander. The SJTFHQ has participated in numerous joint exercises and most recently honed its skills in the European Command's exercise AGILE LION.

The special operations capable Marine expeditionary unit, or MEU(SOC), deployments offer our nation the quintessential crisis response force. Our country's reliance on their capabilities over the last several years has dramatically increased. But, rare are the occasions when any Service or Service Department conducts operations solely with its own resources. Because of this, and because the MEU(SOC)s are often the first on scene, we have increased their command and control capabilities so that they might be better prepared to serve as JTF enablers.

The enhanced MEU(SOC) capability to serve as a JTF enabler, the chemical and biological crisis management capability, and the SJTFHQ all provide unique capabilities to our national defense. By anticipating and filling the nation's warfighting requirements we are preparing the Marine Corps for war.

Traditional Capabilities

While adding and enhancing some capabilities, our stock-in-trade remains being able to field well-trained and capable Marine air-ground task forces (MAGTFs). Whether a small, special purpose MAGTF (SPMAGTF) organized for a contained response, or a Marine expeditionary force (MEF) employed in a major theater war, the Marines we send to battle must be well trained, properly organized, and ably led. Necessary combat power will be provided to the MAGTF, particularly at the MEF level, through global sourcing from the total force: one force consisting of Marines, both Active and Reserve.

The Marine Corps maritime prepositioning force (MPF) remains one of the cornerstones of our ability to quickly insert a sustainable and capable force in time of significant crisis or challenge to our national interests. While offloading operations may take advantage of benign port facilities, it is our ability to offload unassisted by such infrastructure that makes MPF such a versatile means of force introduction. Congress has provided the funding, and we have contracted for an additional ship in each of our three

MPF squadrons. This enhanced MPF capability will mean an added expeditionary airfield, field hospital, and additional sustainment for our committed forces.

But forcible entry from the sea remains the Marines' forte. We continue to work with our Navy shipmates to ensure we reach our resource-constrained, programmatic goal of enough amphibious shipping to lift the equivalent of 2.5 Marine expeditionary brigades. The requirement—the capability that we strive to provide to our nation, brigade equivalents. The goal of the Naval Services is to ensure a credible amphibious capability is ready when the nation says, "land the Marines."

Once landed, our ability to maneuver effectively is directly tied to our tactical mobility. The V-22, the advance assault amphibian vehicle (AAAV), and the procurement of the lightweight 155mm howitzer are all part of an overarching architecture designed to make sure we have the mobility to support our doctrine of maneuver warfare. But, we must explore advanced technologies, not just for ship-to-shore movement or for enhanced air and ground mobility, but also for technologies that support the individual Marine's mobility. Their clothing and equipment have a direct and immediate impact on survivability, lethality, and mission accomplishment.

Marine Corps operational forces will continue to be organized as MAGTFs, with the MEF as the principal warfighting organization. We will maintain the amphibious forcible entry option for the national command authorities. We're enhancing our ability to move significant warfighting capabilities to a point of crisis, and we are aggressively working at increasing our tactical mobility. We are focused on preparing the Marine Corps for war.

Doctrine

We are forging ahead with our doctrine efforts, ensuring that concepts and doctrine are synchronized, covering the gaps, and coordinating materials at every level. New doctrinal publications are coming off the presses. And most importantly, the doctrine is sound.

To ensure that Marine Corps capabilities are understood and properly employed, we are fully participating in the joint doctrine development process. Having our capabilities fully inculcated in the nation's quiver of warfighting techniques is vital to her defense. Ensuring that our Marines and our fellow joint warriors have a fundamental understanding of warfighting principles is of inestimable importance. We are focused on preparing the Marine Corps for war.

Harnessing Our Assets

No organization can be truly efficient until it harnesses all of its resources, especially its people. This is particularly true if your business is warfighting. The Corps recognizes that every Marine has something to contribute. We are a diverse institution comprised of men and women representing the cultural and ethnic diversity of our nation. These Marines are our warfighters and race, creed, and gender make no difference. It is paramount that we, as an institution, foster an environment of dignity and respect for all Marines, an environment where all Marines feel proud to be part of something bigger than themselves. Those who cannot act with dignity and respect toward their fellow Marines in garrison certainly have not properly prepared their character for the stresses of war.

Often large organizations fail to take full advantage of their people because there is no mechanism by which good ideas can be surfaced to the top. Recognizing that good ideas come from individuals of all experience levels and from throughout our rank structure, we created Marine mail. When we started, we asked for answers to three questions: What aren't we doing that we should be doing? What are we doing that we should be doing differently? What are we doing that we shouldn't be doing? Since then we have also come to appreciate just how many good ideas are out there with respect to new concepts, tactics, and equipment that might improve our warfighting capability. The response from Marines across our Corps has been tremendous. We are a stronger warfighting organization for the contributions received through Marine mail.

Just as we have empowered the ranks of our Corps, we must ensure that we are making maximum use of the talents resident in our most seasoned leaders. An executive steering committee has been created to make better use of the knowledge and experience of our senior leadership at the lieutenant general level. This more formalized process of coalescing ideas and tracking progress has been very helpful in the decisionmaking process that guides our Corps. Capitalizing on our diversity, emplacing a mechanism to encourage the free flow of new ideas, and maximizing the talents of our senior leaders are all measures designed to prepare the Marine Corps for war.

Innovation

Innovation is our key to ensuring that we provide the nation with a Marine Corps that is organized and equipped to fill our role as the nation's expeditionary force-in-readiness . . . ready not just for the battles of today but of tomorrow and the day after tomorrow. The quadrennial defense review just finished, and the national defense panel underway, seek to define our place in the national defense. It is up to us to develop the operational concepts through which we will effect that role.

Operational maneuver from the sea (OMITS) is our operational concept. Using the quantum leap in capabilities of the V-22, the air-cushioned landing craft, and the AAAV, we will be able to take maneuver warfare to a new level. We will not be constrained by traditional beach landing sites. We will avoid enemy defenses where he is strong and attack through his weaknesses to destroy his ability and desire to resist. Through an unprecedented ability to generate tempo, we will overwhelm our enemies and protect our force.

We are conducting a series of advanced warfighting experiments to determine, among many things, the best configuration of the force that will execute OMITS. The Marine Corps warfighting laboratory will gather the data from these experiments. Based partly on this data, we will then conduct a comprehensive force structure planning group to evaluate the structure of our Corps. It is through experimentation that we will we find the recipe for success on tomorrow's battlefield.

Just as we have done in other interwar periods, we are using experimentation and innovation to ensure we are ready for war as it will be, not as it was. Innovation is one of the keys to preparing the Marine Corps for war.

Professional Military Education

Professional military education (PME) is crucial to our development as warriors. There are few dilemmas that will face our Marines on the field of battle that have not been faced before. Even as the nature of war evolves, the challenges associated with it contain a number of reoccurring themes. The Marine who has not availed himself or herself of the opportunity to learn from the mistakes and successes of others is ill prepared for war. He or she stands a higher chance of needlessly becoming a casualty, endangering other Marines, and failing to accomplish the mission. But, Marines don't fail in battle. We prepare ourselves for it. We ensure we are technically and tactically proficient. We study our trade.

We have placed great emphasis on PME. We want all Marines to receive top grade education at every level, education that will make them better warfighters. Having said that, we have received considerable input that says some of our correspondence course PME may be too time consuming, that it is detracting from the accomplishment of our day-to-day mission. We are examining that. The goal is a continuous and incremental increase in the ability and education of every Marine as he or she progresses in rank.

Formal, residence courses are valuable experiences for those Marines who get an opportunity to attend them. We have not always done as good a job as we could have in filling school quotas. This is an area that requires constant monitoring. These courses are where we accrue the skills necessary to allow us to conduct decentralized operations to fight and win.

The commandant's reading program is designed to help steer our Marines toward books with good lessons. The MAGTF staff training program provides professional education for our staffs. All of our correspondence and resident PME courses cultivate our Marines as warriors and prepare them for additional responsibilities. PME is an essential ingredient in preparing the Marine Corps for war.

Developing the Warrior

We have already spoken of the preparation of our warriors' minds through education, but there is more to being mentally prepared for combat than being well schooled in the art of war. Our Marines must be mentally tough as well. The Transformation process helps make Marines with the depth of character to do the right thing, in the right way, for the right reasons. Marines full of conviction and with strong minds, Marines who have been made to look within for the answers they seek, will be a powerful force on any battlefield to which the nation sends them. The Marine Corps values program is designed to reinforce and help sustain the hardening—the Transformation.

Of all the things we do as an institution, none is so crucial as preparing our Marines for the rigors of combat. Tough physical training hardens our warriors, makes them equal to the challenges ahead. The physical fitness test has been made tougher. We will continue to emphasis fitness as a way of life for Marines.

But Marines are more than body and mind. To be a United States Marine, one must prepare the body, the mind, and the spirit. The experiences of the Crucible are the gateway for the development of the Marine spirit. The cohesion-building phase of the Transformation process is designed to strengthen the bonds between us as warriors. Being a Marine has always been a mystical association of spirit with one's fellow Marines. Capitalizing on this esprit, we have become the band of warriors we are today, feared by our foes, and respected throughout the world.

We make Marines—body, mind, and spirit. Making Marines is all about preparing the Marine Corps for war.

You the Marine

The last paragraph of the CPG states:

In the final analysis, my guidance simply is to be prepared to fight, on the shortest notice, under any circumstances of weather or resistance, in conflicts large or small. Be prepared to integrate Marine combat power smoothly into the overall matrix of other

U.S. Services or other nations. Be prepared, in conjunction with the U.S. Navy, to project power from the sea for as far and as long as necessary. Be ever mindful of technological opportunities to enhance combat proficiency and to promote logistic economy. Be also mindful of the deep meaning in Title 10 of the U.S. Code of the requirement that Marines shall be prepared to discharge "such" other duties as the President may direct, whatever those duties may be. But, most of all, be prepared to fight and win.

We, as an institution, are preparing the Marine Corps to fight. This preparation is reflected in everything we do. From revamping the fitness report system so that we are sure to promote our most qualified warriors, to our aggressive efforts in seeking funding for the tools we need to enhance our warfighting capabilities, it's all about preparing the Marine Corps for war. But we can't achieve our goals as an institution without participation from all Marines—from you. Look for ways to contribute to the readiness of your Corps. Make training for your Marines tough and demanding. Reaffirm your commitment to principle and make a check of your personal character. Conduct or participate in the daily warfighting discussions mandated in the CPG. Send in a Marine mail, write your ideas in an article for the *Gazette,* or share a lesson learned with a peer. Together, we shoulder the awesome responsibility of preparing the Marine Corps for war.

Abstract (Document Summary)

The USMC Commandant discusses the Marine Corps' current warfighting doctrine. Forcible entry from the sea remains the Corps' forte.

PART III

Leadership and Command

There is probably no better expert or practitioner of leadership than Medal of Honor recipient, Col. Wesley L. Fox. This section begins with what Fox believes are the timeless attributes of what it means to be a leader. He examines leadership styles that worked in the past and offers what he believes the Corps needs to do to properly motivate modern day Marines.

Brigadier General Paul K. Van Riper's article discusses the art of preparing to take command, and a memorandum he prepared when he was getting ready to take command of the 2nd Marine Division contains some very sound advice on leadership.

Next are two excellent companion pieces authored by Marine Commandant Gen. Al Gray and retired Brig. Gen. F. P. Henderson. Both generals had numerous opportunities to command at various levels during their lengthy careers with the Corps and offer excellent information on the art of command.

Marine Commandant General Charles C. Krulak provides an additional point of view on the complex subject of leadership. His article focuses on what he believes to be the one indispensable quality all leaders must possess, and this is something most of us call "character." General Krulak asks all leaders to ask themselves: Who are you really? What do you stand for? What is the essence of your character? And he advises all leaders to understand that the basic tenet of character forms the essential building blocks for everything else that follows about leading Marines.

Coincidentally, the next article is by Gen. Charles Krulak's father, a legend of the Corps himself, Lt. Gen. Victor H. Krulak, whose prize-winning essay gives sage advice for officers on how to be an innovator and leader at the same time. Using a number of historical vignettes to illustrate his point, it is an excellent discussion on how to advance an idea that will likely meet resistance.

The final articles in this section provide different points of view on the difficulties of leadership. Captain John D. Kuntz's article is a very innovative piece on the art of disobedience. What he conveys in his article is that there is sometimes a time and place for disobeying orders that violates appropriate professional judgment. Using historical vignettes, he clearly demonstrates that blindly following orders is sometimes the quickest path to failure.

Colonel Bruce G. Brown, USMC (Ret.), provided an invaluable list of "lessons learned" from his long career on leadership.

The final article is by present day commandant, Gen. James T. Conway. General Conway believes that while generals are important to a winning war effort, he emphasizes that we are living in the era of the strategic corporal and that having excellent small unit leaders has never been more important. He strongly confirms the importance of Marine noncommissioned officers as the critical link in battlefield leadership.

Herringbones, Boondockers, and Leggings

Lt. Col. Wesley L. Fox, USMC

Marine Corps Gazette
July 1984

Old Corps–New Corps, when did the former end and the latter begin? Every Marine has his own ideas about when the Old Corps was—namely, just about the time when he joined, if he has been in longer than a year. The recruit, of course, just has to suffer along with being a New Corps Marine.

We have all heard plenty of stories of leadership within the Old Corps; Dan Daly, Chesty Puller, the Raiders, the Para-Marines, and the walk out of the Chosin Reservoir. Leadership is synonymous with the word Marine. Put two Marines together and what happens? The senior is in charge! Well, how do our leaders today stack up against the Old Corps' leaders? To answer that, we would first have to identify the time span of the Old Corps and that is a story in itself, which is not my purpose.

Since I also believe that I joined the Marines back in the Old Corps (for me that is herringbones, rough side out boondockers, and leggings), I will give a personal view of our Corps' leadership over the past thirty-three plus years. The way I will present that viewpoint is by giving some thoughts on leadership as it applies to today's Marine. My bottom line is that today's leaders tend to micromanage. Admittedly, that deduction is the perception of a Marine who is a lieutenant colonel and feels that he and his peers are too involved with the mechanics of the day-to-day operations of the squad and the platoon and who, as a sergeant in 1934, thought that he ran things because he seldom saw officer rank in his area.

Over the years, leadership has come to mean to me more than *Webster's* definition of "the ability to lead." Leadership in the Corps means to me: promptly accomplishing the mission with the smallest number of people, personnel problems, and materiel. Expressed another way, leadership is making the most of people, time, and materiel. Leadership is also selecting or recognizing the right man for the job and leaving him alone to do it.

Some Observations

One of our most obvious changes in leader positions during my time in the Corps is that of the lieutenant in relation to the private. In 1950 I never saw a lieutenant during my eleven weeks of "fun in the sun" at Parris Island. I didn't want to see one either! With the imagined power of life and death held over me by Corporal Reiser, my senior drill instructor, I didn't want exposure to anyone more senior. I will never forget Platoon 88's final personnel inspection held by the company commander, the only Marine officer that I knew of in boot camp. Standing in ranks, aware of the captain's slow move ever closer to me (the feeling must be similar to that of approaching certain death), I wondered if my numb arm could lift my M-1 rifle, if my thumb would contact the operating rod handle smartly to start the rearward movement, and if I could do it strongly enough to lock the bolt open. Would I know the answer to the question he would ask? With a cotton mouth and a pulse rate of at least two hundred beats per minute, I lived through it. I learned two things in boot camp, discipline and the fact that the noncommissioned officers (NCOs) ran the Corps—at least on the private's level.

Years later, recruit deaths resulting from inept NCOs assigned to drill instructor duty were the reason for the addition of lieutenants as series supervisors. I had one year on the drill field at the time of the "death march" at Parris Island in 1956. My second year was cursed with the intrusion of the recruit training command, providing us with our very own general and series supervisor. I was convinced that the Corps would never be the same; Marines could not be trained properly in such a supervised, structured manner. One long war has since put those fears to rest. Our young Marines today are as good as any in the past.

I wonder if our emphasis is in the right place while training our young Marines. It would be great if we had a way to cull out those very few NCOs who might not be trusted to perform properly as drill instructors. The recruit would then see the trust and confidence the Corps has in its NCOs. The NCO Corps rather than the recruit would be the benefactor, a boost that is needed if the NCO is to remain the backbone of our Corps.

All leaders have their strong as well as their weak points, and these extremes are what we notice more and remember longer about those with whom we have served. If one could collect and copy all of the good traits he had observed over the years and discard his own bad or less desirable traits, he could be one super leader.

The way a Marine sees himself and his place within an organization goes a long way toward providing what the organization gains from him. Do leaders influence that image? Checking into the provost marshal's office (PMO) in Marine aircraft group 11 (MAG-11) at Atsugi, Japan, in 1954, the provost sergeant Master Sgt. "Caribou" Johnson, assigned the PMO's driver and jeep to me for use while "checking in." This was my first unit to check into as a sergeant, and needless to say, I was impressed. As PFC Carr drove me here and there, my three stripes got bigger and bigger. That feeling of importance lasted for the entire tour of duty; the sergeants ran the MAG-11 guard, and that was an E-4 sergeant's stripes.

Sometime much later as a technical sergeant, I worked for a captain in a training office. His approach to leadership impressed me on one occasion. This was my first tour of duty as a married Marine, and "brown bagging" was new to me. I came down with a bad case of flu one night and the next morning early I called the captain at his home to tell him. I'll never forget his sound of concern and his insistence that I stay in bed, not to worry about a thing at the office, and when I got well in a few days—to then concern myself with coming in. What had I expected? Not what I got! I guess I expected something along the line of doubt and a run-around ending with something like "bring me a no-duty chit from a doctor." How many of us are too quick to lump everyone into the whole and not consider the merit of each Marine individually?

How about keeping all hands in the office during normal working hours for the sake of appearance, regardless of special situations? Example: working hours are from 0800 to 1630 (maybe I should mention the normal daily 0730 show and the 1700 to 1800 wrap-up of the day's work). The tactics section ran the night attack field problem, and the student company performed the night attack well. All instructors were finished by 2400 and sent on their way home with: "If you don't have anything pressing in the morning, have a late breakfast with your wife and come in at 1300." This has the makings of a true professional atmosphere and one that will have Marines feeling like it is all worthwhile. How many chief instructors would give that kind of thought to the Marines who work for them? Not many! The first thought is in the other direction; someone who counts might come around the office or need something. The chief could come in after giving his men the morning off and cover the office himself. Then if his boss comes around, the chief gets an "atta-boy" for showing concern for his Marines and at the same time proves that he is a workaholic. Another way would be to work up a duty list for the office watch and spread the load. Give your Marines due concern; if they have something that needs doing, they will do it.

Here is an example of negative Marine leadership that happened back in the mid-sixties and in one of our more glamorous, gung ho units and, I suspect, in many others as well. Time came around for the physical fitness test and the officers and staff NCOs took their test on one day and then supervised the sergeants and below on another. Weak! Where is the "doing things together"? Where are the leaders? In this case, the sergeants were the leaders; they were the ones who were involved with their Marines. The higher rank had cut themselves out of the unit. If we are not watchful, we do that in many ways.

Do we have a leadership problem today in retaining our best Marines? Who are our best Marines? They are our educated, motivated, young men who have a purpose in life; they are responsible and seek the same personal satisfactions in their lifetimes and their careers as the other members of our society. Half of these young men are married by the time they are promoted to sergeant and why not? Marriage is the natural outcome of maturity.

Here we have a change in the needs of today's Marines from those of the Old Corps. Yesterday's Marine was easier satisfied with a simple barracks life, day in and day out. This life consisted of long working hours and the evenings spent in the "slop-chute" dulling the awareness of any need. The loss in quality of life didn't matter much as everyone was in for his enlistment, and he hadn't enlisted for a rose garden. After discharge would come wife, family, responsibility, job position, and monetary reward, those normal things responsible young Americans seek in life.

The profile of our Marine has changed, but the biggest change is in our reenlistment goals. We are no longer contented to let the great majority of our best young men go back to civilian life. Problem! The job atmosphere has not changed in our Corps. How do young Marines view a career or life in our Corps? Maybe more importantly, how does his wife perceive their future together as a Marine family? The answer is a matter of their perception, and they don't get much encouragement.

I assumed command of an infantry battalion and learned that our work day started at 0600. The division's day officially started at 0800, although most, if not all, offices were fully manned by or shortly after 0700. All officers and staff NCOs were in their units within my battalion by 0600 and most were around by 1800 that evening. (This is not field time, I am referring to those few days that we would be in the barracks area.) It goes without saying, all sergeants and below were in from reveille at 0500. What time does one get up to be in by 0500? If no leader in the chain of command had demands on their time, the rank and file might be secured somewhere around 1700.

It is easy to see that family life suffers and for what gain? To come in at 0500, make a formation, smoke and joke and drink coffee for several hours—maybe all day? What about field day nights when all hands come in to clean up the barracks whether they live there or not. On top of this, the unit is in the field for days almost every week, on deployment away from base for weeks almost every quarter, and deployed overseas for six months almost every eight months. Doesn't sound like the kind of thing that strengthens young marriages or encourages reenlistment among our best Marines.

The field training and deployments are facts of life for Marines, and they—for the most part—welcome them. That is what being a Marine is all about. The wear and tear, and the "separator" are those areas that happen because "we have always done it that way" even though there is no purpose or gain from it now.

In the fifties I would hold a formation immediately after reveille and expect to see and count all hands in my unit. That formation was the basis for my morning report. I have been in other units where the first formation was held at a later time, as late as 0800, and that worked just as well; the living areas got cleaned and the Marines were just as squared away. When Marines have work to do, they will do it and on their own time if need be. We do not need to have them on hand just for drill; they have better things to do.

I learned many things while serving with my last battalion, but one stands out overall. I have always believed that if a leader personally tells his Marines what he expects of them, tells them "how it is" and how it is going to be, then his Marines will always come through for him and the Corps. I found it just that way in practice with today's Marines. I will use unauthorized absence as an example.

While other battalions were having up into the two digit figures, I all but eliminated unauthorized absence simply by talking to my Marines. Other than for the few misfits and malcontents—and the Corps did have more than its share this past decade—there is no reason to have unauthorized absence. If a Marine has or he perceives that he has a personal problem big enough for him to hurt himself by "going over the hill," then he has a reason to take leave. Short of a national emergency, why not let him go and keep him productive? With that understanding through all leaders right down to the squad and the individual, you don't have unauthorized absences. To my knowledge, no one abused the policy; after all, we all rate thirty days of leave each year. Most Fleet Marine Force Marines don't get to take half of that amount annually. And as for the effectiveness of the unit, our battalion never seemed to be more depleted of personnel than any other unit.

The same approach applies to the elimination of all disciplinary problems, drugs, drunkenness, drunk driving, or whatever. The leader demonstrates concern for his Marines, he lets them know that he cares about them and simply tells them that they will not do this thing. A six month deployment in WestPac with only thirty-three office hours and one court-martial (the offense of half of these charges occurred earlier while stateside) may not be a disciplinary record, but it is a record of a battalion of Marines who care about themselves, their future, their battalion, and their commanders. It all started with and was maintained by leaders at all levels. A leader doesn't threaten Marines with "what will happen if," but he does make sure that they understand the Corps' position and the importance to them personally in not getting themselves in trouble with it.

I have found the best way to approach the task of keeping our young Marines out of trouble is by helping them plan their life. I talk about personal goals—near, intermediate, and long-term goals. It is somewhat surprising to learn the number of young men who haven't thought about what they really want out of life and where they want to go. With no plans or goals to work toward, it is easy to fall by the wayside of life. A suggested near-term goal is the rank of an NCO, which is a launch pad for anything else he might want later. And the immediate payoff is that if a Marine really wants to become an NCO, he is not knowingly going to do anything to jeopardize his chances.

As leaders, we need to check ourselves now and then to determine if we are a help or a hindrance to our Marines in performance of their duties. The leader selects a Marine for the job or he is inherited along with the job, it doesn't matter, he is responsible to the leader for the work. A leader must give his Marine the necessary guidance and then move on and let him do it. My battalion enjoyed a highly rated success in several major operations, and I, of course, received the credit for that success. The one sure thing that I did to cause that success was to recognize that my Marines in key positions knew their business, and I stayed out of their way while they did their work.

One irritation that Marines have always had to live with is the "change of the word." How that works against good morale! Seldom if ever does an event come off without major changes causing Marines extra work and hardship. Right next to "changing the word" on my list of irritants is the man in charge who can't make a decision. These two irritants are closely related as I found after a short time in command. How? I would be approached by a well-meaning junior leader with a recommendation for an action or a change that made good sense to me. His idea would be sound; in appearance, all personnel involved would stand to gain. Being a man of action who can make decisions (as was my intent), I would decree his recommendation so. Invariably, the leader with the recommendation would be hardly out of my sight before I would be approached with a different slant on the subject as to why the change should not have been made. Sometimes I would have to back up, restore, or modify. That is "changing the word," not once but twice.

The answer is simple—get all the facts on which to base your decision before you make it. But, some of the important facts are not always readily available. How long do you wait before you get in the arena of not being able to make a decision? In some instances, by the time a leader has all of the facts at hand, it is too late to act on any worthwhile decision. A mix somewhere in the middle is no doubt the answer. For sure, the more a leader is in tune with his Marines, his unit's capability, and his mission requirements, and the more he is abreast of what is going on, then the more facts he will already have on which to base a quick decision. Rapid, sound decisions that stand help to hold down the "change of the word."

Some Thoughts

How well have you done your job? An evaluation could be made and based upon how much time you spend out of your office. Do you have junior leaders who know what to do and who can take over and run your unit? Seniors don't seem to exercise their junior leaders enough because the seniors are always on hand. Juniors need the experience of higher leadership and the workload needs to be adjusted so as to allow them the opportunity.

I honestly believe that officers have more work today than their equal rank did thirty years ago. Rank and position then seemed to have their own working hours; officers came in later and left sooner, and I appreciated that as a sergeant. That time was mine to get the things done that sergeants have to do. I really don't see how a platoon sergeant gets any troop time today. But in spite of the workload, I have seen officers read newspapers and do other things only to fill in the time rather than get away. If it is the workload, take it home with you now and then, just so you can give your young leaders some growing room. If it is your concern for the boss, let him know your aim and purpose; he already knows whether or not the job is getting done. And if you just plain don't have anything to do, pay a call on a fellow commander. Too much leader time around the command post is as bad for the leader as it is for the junior leaders.

Fortified with a good cause, men make good soldiers and will fight courageously even in the face of certain death. The young men of America had a worthy cause in our national situation during World War II. The "All-American Boy" fights readily for God, Country, and Mom's apple pie. What happens then when something like Vietnam comes along and there is no obvious national cause? Without strong, positive leadership, realistic and sound training, and esprit de corps, troops are not going to conduct themselves well in combat.

I haven't seen much written on the subject of why Marines performed in their expected manner during the Korean and Vietnamese Wars, but it is no secret that the above three elements are the underlying reasons. I am aware of something that lives within the breast of Marines that causes them to do things in the heat of battle, which other men probably would not have done if caught in the same situation. I won't attempt to put a name on this unique power, but it begins with the joining of the ranks of Marines. This power is nurtured along with the Marine's graduation from boot camp, and it matures among the expressions, the largesses, and the deeds of other Marines— juniors, peers, and seniors alike. Marines care what others, especially other Marines, think of them. Pride in oneself and his unit are part of this power, and pride itself goes a long way. Marines are so proud of their Corps that the more sentimental sea soldiers choke up just talking about it or hearing the band strike up the "Marine Hymn."

Marines might join the Corps for God, Country, and Mom's apple pie, and truthfully, this cause is never far in the background, but it is not the first call up for support when the going gets rough. A Marine's buddies and his unit (which to him are the Corps and rightfully so) quickly take the forefront. Even though the price in doing what has to be done sometimes is death, Marines don't brood over this fact or make a fuss over the probable outcome. I have never known a Marine to worry much about what he will or will not do in a firefight. Certain things have to be accomplished, and with Marines on your right and left, things get done. Your buddies will do most of it, but your mind has long since accepted the fact that you are going to do at least your share.

Wars without a clear national cause, to include special operations, are taken in stride by Marines. With their brand of leadership, training, and esprit de corps, Marines understand that the going just never gets too rough.

There is nothing better than a long, forced march to show you how your leaders operate, as well as to give you a "down to earth" chance of leading. Marines as a whole, to include infantry battalions, don't hike much anymore. True, most infantry units walk several miles almost daily to nearby training areas. This is good, except that it gets logged as condition hikes and replaces long distance movements in short periods of time with full combat gear to include battalion crew-served weapons.

Hurting together molds togetherness. Marines like to see their leader in front of them, making them put out and hurt. Good leaders want to exercise their units at a level that is beneficial to the strong majority. Let the weak fall out; hikes should be at a rate and distance that is a challenge to all. The more you hike, the stronger your weak become.

Many Marines have a good running program. Don't let the fact that you are in good running shape fool you when it comes to hiking with full combat gear. A person uses different muscles and his feet take more of a beating in boots at a fast walk with a load. A 12-mile individual run in 1½ hours with running shoes and jock gear is far easier than moving with a unit in full combat gear for the same distance in 3½ hours. Further, the run does little to prepare a Marine for the hike except for respiration and cardio benefits.

On the hike, observe who is helping the weaker Marines when they start to fall back. Who carries the extra load when the end is yet a long way off? During the breaks, all leaders from squad leader on up should move back through their unit. Squad leaders check each of their men, platoon commanders pay close attention to individuals, and higher commanders move through their respective columns and talk with their Marines. That is leadership to me, but when I first started hiking my battalion, there were very few leaders moving during the breaks. The leader's movement during breaks should be automatic because he is concerned about his Marines. The best way to find out how they are doing is to look at them and ask them. They like to see their leader among them, showing concern. Hiking has many basic benefits and all units, to include garrison types, ought to schedule periodic hikes. I found every Saturday morning in the 3d Marine Division ideal for forced marches, while in the 2d Marine Division, Friday was a better day but couldn't be scheduled every week because of other priorities. Take them when you can get them; hikes are good leadership tools. Hikes put the leader up front where his Marines should always know to look for him. Marines expect their leader to set the pace and the direction on a hike. That is what leadership is all about.

I have already given some observations of the things we do to make Marine life discordant with family life. Does it have to be that way? Can a young man be an effective Marine and at the same time have a complete family life? Our recruiting effort says that we can, our career retention goals say that we must, and if there is to remain a capable Corps of Marines in today's world, commanders had better believe it. Believing it means doing something about it. Having a family day now and then is only a token effort in that direction. What is needed is an awareness of the problems brought on by the way we want routine things done and an elimination of those things that serve no useful purpose. Remember, we still do most things around the barracks the way we did when all Marines lived in the barracks. The Fleet Marine Force will never have a standard eight to four work day, but on days that your unit is in the barracks area, you can do a little toward making up for all the time spent in the field. At least let your young Marine know that his wife might plan dinner for a time that he can make a couple of times each week. Spend some effort on getting that young wife informed on her husband's job and his unit; but more importantly, get her involved in the Marine Corps community. To reenlist that Marine, you will also have to sell his wife on a life in the Corps. Meals and nights alone, week after week, wondering where he is and what he is doing, is not a life that she or anyone else will choose. She has to see the big picture and know that there are better times ahead.

My aim is not to take anything away from the single Marine, he is still our majority. His numbers are declining, however, and while we gear everything to him, we must make allowance for his family, which is just a short time away.

The old way of leadership was good, and it served its purpose well. But just as weapons of today are different from those used in the Old Corps, leadership today has its modern requirements. Some things have not changed they are the need to lead from the front, show the way, and tell it like it is. When the leader stands tall in front of his Marines, they are with him all the way.

In spite of my comments that today's leader needs a different approach in his technique, the basics have not changed over the centuries. Sun Tzu's writing in his *Art of War* is as true for our Marines today as it has been for soldiers down through the ages. He wrote:

Regard your soldiers as your children, and they will follow you into the deepest valleys; look upon them as your own beloved sons, and they will stand by you even unto death. If, however, you are indulgent, but unable to make your authority felt, kind hearted but unable to enforce your commands; and incapable, moreover, of quelling disorder, then your soldiers must be likened to spoiled children; they are useless for any practical purpose.

A Philosophy of Leadership

Brig. Gen. Paul K. Van Riper, USMC

Marine Corps Gazette
January 1992

Preparing for the responsibility of command is a task that confronts nearly every officer sooner or later. Part of that preparation involves expressing a personal philosophy of leadership in a way that provides subordinates with a clear understanding "of their new commander's goals and priorities." Several Marines have brought the following material to our attention as a fine example of one such effort. We are pleased to reprint it here for a wider audience.

Memorandum #1-9111 July 1991
From: Commanding General, 2d Marine Division
To: Division Staff/Regimental/Separate Battalions
Subject: A PHILOSOPHY OF LEADERSHIP

1. Introduction:

This paper describes my philosophy of leadership. I am concerned with how the 2d Marine Division is to be led by its officers and noncommissioned officers in the coming months, for as in the past, we face challenging times.

You will find much of the philosophy that I describe to be very familiar, since many elements of it have been used by Marine Corps leaders for generations with great success. I am certain we will continue to rely upon these same elements in the future. They have served us well.

2. The Environment:

a. My first and most important charge to you is to maintain an environment which allows our officers and noncommissioned officers to lead properly. This environment has and must remain one in which all have a strong sense that being a Marine is a special calling, not an occupation or a job. I urge you to be wary of those false prophets who would have us believe that our destiny lies in accepting the values of the market place. Nothing could be further from the truth. The ability and readiness to engage in combat is our Corps' and thus our Division's reason for existence. This creates an obligation that every Marine carries with full knowledge of the great personal risks. No economic model could ever produce the devotion to duty and courage required to close with an enemy on the battlefield. Neither could it produce the genuine human concern each of our leaders must have for his or her Marines as individuals. I find it extremely appalling that one could ever look upon Marines as employees or workers. You will see that it does not happen!

b. For my part, I pledge to you that in all my contacts with those inside and outside the Division, I will stress our determination to adhere to traditional military ideals in both organization and functioning. Similarly, I will emphasize that we truly are a band of brothers. No one will be allowed to confuse our part of the Marine Corps with any business or industry.

c. Equally important to maintaining the environment in which our Marines must function is the unbending requirement that officers and noncommissioned officers focus their efforts on the welfare of the Corps, not their careers. We cannot tolerate those whose personal goals run counter to our organizational values. The first loyalty of every leader must be to the Corps. You are to take action to eliminate from our ranks those whose self-seeking ways would undermine the higher good we are committed to achieving.

I will only support the advancement of those Marines who have demonstrated competence in all billets, not those who have attempted to follow a stylized career pattern of "ticket punching." We want our leaders to seek the tough assignments; we want even more for them to dedicate themselves to professional efforts in every assignment.

3. The Task:
a. No one likes to fight, but someone has to know how to if our nation is to be protected. This is the task of the Marine Corps and obviously the 2d Marine Division—to be able to fight and win in an amphibious or expeditionary operation. Such a task calls for leaders who are competent in the profession of arms. Some would have us believe that our leaders, particularly officers, should be well versed in international relations or in managing large organizations. Others maintain that military leaders need to be adept at solving societal problems. Though such knowledge or abilities may on occasion be of value to Marine Corps leaders, it is of secondary importance. In fact, it can prove costly when if interferes with the development of our primary warfighting skills. For this reason, those of us responsible for training must examine our programs carefully to ensure that we provide every opportunity possible for our leaders and their Marines to develop and hone such skills. Marines have been known for professional competence throughout our history. This is to continue to be our hallmark in the future.

b. You have my promise that I will vigorously resist all attempts by anyone to saddle us with requirements or programs that in any way detract from the Division's ability to accomplish its basic mission. We must not be made a laboratory for fashionable social, educational, or managerial experiments.

4. The Chain of Command:

Though our structure may change in the months ahead to accommodate the introduction of new doctrine and equipment or to achieve greater efficiency, it will continue, as always, to be based on the chain of command. No committees, councils, ad hoc groups, or other organizations for which we are responsible, nor the Division Headquarters itself, will be allowed to circumvent this chain. Commanding officers remain one hundred percent in charge—and responsible—for "all they survey." Under no circumstances will I permit anyone to reach down into regiments and separate battalions in a directive manner, except through the formal structure. The Division Headquarters will exercise its staff responsibilities through subordinate staffs; command responsibilities will obviously remain with me and commanders throughout the Division.

5. Leadership:

a. I am going to turn now to an extremely important subject, the leadership of Marines. As each of us is well aware, leadership is more than giving orders. For Marines, it has traditionally been a way of life. We have always known that the best way to lead is to *live* leadership. The concept of "living" leadership is described in the worlds of Maj. Gen. Commandant John A. Lejeune as they appeared in the 1921 edition of the *Marine Corps Manual*.

The relation between officers [and noncommissioned officers] and enlisted men should in no sense be that of superior and inferior nor that of master and servant, but rather that of teacher and scholar. In fact it should partake of the nature of the relation between father and son, to the extent that officers [and noncommissioned officers] are responsible for the physical, mental, and moral welfare, as well as the discipline and military training of men under them. . . .

The Manual continues:

Individual responsibilities of leadership are not dependent upon authority. Each Marine is expected to exert proper influence upon his comrades by setting the example. . . .

Each officer [and noncommissioned officer] must endeavor by all means in his power to develop within himself those qualities of leadership . . . which will fit him to be a real leader of men.

b. Crucial to the philosophy of "living leadership" is the knowledge that military leadership must be considered as the means to an end—a means of carrying out the mission. In peacetime this means achieving the necessary operational ability and high state of readiness. In combat, it is to take the objective in the shortest possible time with the minimum loss of men and equipment. There is more, however, for in the final analysis the essence of Marine Corps leadership is the concern of each leader for his or her Marines as individuals. Their welfare is his or her preoccupation. If one Marine is let down, the entire Corps is let down. General Lejeune also reminded us in 1922 that:

You should never forget the power of example. The young men serving as enlisted men take their cue from you. If you conduct yourselves at all times as officers and gentlemen should conduct themselves, the moral tone of the whole Corps will be raised, its reputation, which is most precious to all of us, will be enhanced, and the esteem and affection in which the Corps is held by the American people will be increased.

c. The one trait that I believe every Marine leader must possess in full measure is *integrity*. I will be uncompromising towards those who are found deficient in this vital ingredient. A single incident of dishonesty in word or deed will be grounds to initiate actions for immediate separation from our Corps. It can be no other way if we are to live up to the trust our nation has placed in us.

d. The strength of our Corps depends greatly upon the *courage* of our leaders. Thucydides observed that, "The secret of happiness is freedom and the secret of freedom is courage." No officer or noncommissioned officer can expect to be a leader if he or she does not have physical and moral courage, in fact he or she is not worthy to bear the name Marine. Courage comes largely from the confidence derived out of being professionally competent and from one's integrity. Thus, I remind you again of the necessity to ensure we are not lacking in either area.

e. The final trait I want to emphasize is that of *sobriety*. Abuse of alcoholic beverages and use of illegal drugs will not be tolerated. You are enjoined to act against violators in the following manner. Marines who become dependent on alcohol yet have demonstrated potential will receive one opportunity to complete a rehabilitation program. Those who are not subsequently successful in tempering their use of alcohol will be discharged. I absolutely will not tolerate the use of illegal drugs. Those who cannot abide by the law will be disciplined in accordance with regulations.

f. I want to assure you that I am convinced that the Corps' officers and noncommissioned officers have always provided, and will continue to provide, the most direct and personal leadership found anywhere in the world. They do it today in peacetime as they have before in both peace and war. No better example could be given from our past than that of Gunnery Sgt. Jimmie Howard who led his reconnaissance platoon in Vietnam in a fierce all-night fire fight though outnumbered twenty to one. The citation for his Medal of Honor states, "His valiant leadership and courageous fighting spirit served to inspire the men of his platoon to heroic endeavors in the face of overwhelming odds." He led by example. Though Gunnery Sergeant Howard's actions "above and beyond the call of duty" were exceptional, his relationship with his Marines was traditional. This is best evidenced in a United Press International report of his award ceremony in August 1967.

As he stood in the East Room of the White House, far from the steaming battle-fields of Vietnam, Gunnery Sgt. Jimmie Howard's thoughts were for his men. "I don't know how to speak, gentlemen," said the nation's newest Medal of Honor winner, "but I want to say in all sincerity . . ." here his voice seemed to break for a second, but with a wave of his hand toward his Marine buddies, Gunnery Sergeant Howard said quickly, "That's the guys who did it right there." They were all younger, more like his sons than his subordinates. He was their "gunnie"—strong, broad shouldered, ready to take them through anything.

Gunnery Sergeant Jimmie Howard *lived* leadership. He set the example. He carried out the mission, yet, his concern was for his Marines as human beings—"more like his sons."

6. In the Marine Corps leadership is a way of life! We must see to it that it remains so, always. With this as your guideline, I charge you to "continue to march." Semper Fidelis!

Paul K. Van Riper

Memorandum #2-91 11 July 1991
From: Commanding General, 2d Marine Division
To: Division Staff/Regimental/Separate Battalions
Subject: WORDS OF ADVICE TO SUBORDINATES

1. *Take a larger, wider view of what is "good for the Marine Corps."* Far too many of us cannot see beyond our own unit, be it a section, company, battalion, or the Division. Moreover, "today" for many has far more importance than "tomorrow," the future. Is it in the Corps' best interest to deny Sergeant Jones the opportunity to attend NCO school so that he will be available for a particular section requirement? In most cases I think not. Many of us are far too concerned about making ourselves and our units look good in the present and consequently fail to consider how the Corps can get to where it needs to be next year or five years from now. We and our Marines *are* the future. We must lead with that thought in mind. We will accept short-term loss for long-term gain.

2. *Work in a positive mode; don't advance on the troubles or problems of others.* We are all too quick to lend an ear to listen to the latest scoop on another Marine's or unit's foul ups. Subconsciously, we increase our own or our unit's status in relation to the person or organization with the problem. It's a flawed yardstick. We haven't improved one iota, but a fellow Marine or Marine unit has dropped a notch. Make your yardstick a set of objectives which can be measured, and strive to achieve them. Take pride when you do, redouble your efforts when you don't. Extend a hand to your fellow Marines when they hit a rough spot in the road. Measuring "success" against others' failures is futile.

3. *Be inquisitive, assume nothing, keep your eves and ears open, and ask questions.* The Marine Corps is a large and complex organization. No Marine can ever understand all of its elements in detail. Yet, many of us act as if we should, refusing to admit in public our lack of knowledge when an unfamiliar subject is broached. We assume that somehow we have been uniquely deprived of instruction on the subject, so we remain silent now with the intention to later break out the manuals (or take a correspondence course, or get to an appropriate school, etc.) and "come up to speed." Seldom is our secret promise made good and the ignorance remains. Soon this approach becomes habit and we lose our natural inquisitiveness. Before long we can even rationalize away the need to keep up our basic skills. How many of us know how to adjust battle sights on an M16A2? How many of us can discuss in any detail the concepts of employing combined arms within a MAGTF? Next time you are in a meeting or conference and hear something unfamiliar being discussed, ask some questions. The chorus of, "Yes, explain that, I don't understand it either!" may surprise you.

4. *Have a reading program—even more importantly your own "clip-and-save" service.*
   a. Professional reading is constantly touted these days as a good thing. Seniors routinely tell juniors how important it is to read. Probably not one out of ten Marines, however, has anything akin to a serious reading program. Don't believe it? Ask your compatriots to tell you about the latest book they've *read*. Not just the *title* of some book currently in vogue. Was it really a professional book or the newest novel on Vietnam, or a questionable "expose" on the Defense Department dashed off for the general public's consumption? If professional reading is as important as advertised, and I believe it is, then set some of your duty hours aside to engage in this worthwhile activity. My own rule of thumb is that an officer should make every effort to read one book a month and review about a half-dozen periodicals.
   b. Most of us start to save professional reading materials early in our careers. Unfortunately, the stacks of paper, manuals, magazines, etc., get out of hand in

a few years—and we discard the whole mess. The answer: develop a file system early on. Get in the habit of reproducing the important articles you read and placing them in the appropriate file. It beats going through indexes trying to find the dimly remembered feature covering the subject you want to instruct on next week.

5. *Professional Responsibilities*
    a. Marines, particularly leaders, should view their responsibilities in the following manner:
        - Know the way things should be done.
        - Recognize when they are not being done the right way or up to standards.
        - Provide instruction to subordinates to enable them to make corrections.
        - Supervise.
    b. Younger Marines should concentrate on the basics. The focus of their responsibilities is as follows:
        - Discipline
        - Weapon
        - Uniform and equipment
        - Living and working spaces
        - MOS skill
    c. Noncommissioned Officers and Staff Noncommissioned Officers should:
        - Supervise and inspect Marines
        - Train and correct Marines
    d. Officers should:
        - Provide general supervision
        - Plan (for next month, not tomorrow)
        - Think

6. *Personal Values.* Despite what some so-called modern thinkers would have us believe, values are important. We should be proud to have and to profess our moral and spiritual beliefs and, most importantly, to live by them. In this regard, I offer the following for your consideration:
    a. A Marines most sacred value should be his or her faith in God. Those who have experienced combat know all too well that there are no atheists on the battlefield. In tough times when human will alone is not enough, faith in one's religious beliefs will often be the only sustaining power a Marine can depend upon. Our macho images should not cause us to ignore this reality. We must support every Marine's right to practice his or her chosen religion.

b. Enjoy life in all its aspects, especially family and friends. It has been my observation over the years that Marines who literally "live, eat, and sleep the Marine Corps" to the exclusion of all else are, ironically, after the early stages of their careers, poorer performers than those who have wider interests. Part of the reason can be attributed to "burn-out," however, the more important factor is the absence of any frame of reference upon which to base their everyday Marine Corps activities. Their vision is narrow and their answers stereotyped and predictable; they can handle the routine staff assignments, but lack the innovativeness and flexibility required of the more difficult assignments, particularly command. The Greeks were right—all things in moderation. Show you value family and friends—spend more time with them.

c. We should remind ourselves and those in our charge frequently that upon entering the Corps we each took a solemn oath to " . . . support and defend the Constitution of the United States against all enemies, foreign and domestic . . . " Unlike the members of many armed forces throughout the world, we do not serve to protect an individual or small group of rulers, a political party, a flag, or even a cause, but an idea—the freedoms guaranteed by our Constitution through the rule of law. We should also be reminded of and remind others that we swore to " . . . bear true faith and allegiance to . . . " that same document. That is, we promise to demonstrate a loyalty and fidelity of the highest order in support and defense of the Constitution. We have, in effect, agreed to an "unlimited liability" contract with our nation—we are prepared to die in its defense! Value that oath.

d. Finally there is the Corps, an organization whose hold on all who pass through its ranks is almost mystical. Early on there is a bonding where we forever become a part of the Corps, and the Corps forever becomes a part of us. We are bound to uphold its honor, traditions and glory for all time. In return we retain the privilege of bearing the name Marine.

e. For most of us these four values will normally be in balance and we need make no decisions in regard to their priority. Occasionally, however, conflict can arise. If it does, use the order in which I have presented them to make a judgment. For example, if our Corps asks you to do something that would violate your oath to support and defend the Constitution *don't* do it. Or if the nation asks you to act in a manner which violates your faith, *don't* do it. Those who live by their faith, remember family and friends, defend our nation, and honor the Corps will be a source of pride to all who stand with and behind them on the frontiers of freedom.

The Art of Command

Gen. A. M. Gray, USMC

Marine Corps Gazette
October 1987

The following extracts from recent speeches given by Gen. A. M. Gray reflect his views on leadership and the art of command—a subject area of great importance to the Corps and one the 29th Commandant feels strongly about.

Leadership is the art of getting things done through people.

If you are to succeed as a commander, you must dedicate yourself to lifelong learning about your profession. You have to be a student—a student of people and what motivates them; of weapons and equipment; of strategy, operations, and military history. You've got to be able to do anything you ask others to do. You've got to remember it is no sin to learn from someone who's junior to you.

As a leader, you have to recognize that your people want to be taught. They want to do well and to be somebodies. You have to create an environment that fosters teaching, and you have to be both a teacher and a trainer all the time. You must be prepared to step up and teach at anytime, any place. You must train your service support and fighting elements to function as a team. You must train them how to communicate, how to maintain equipment, how to do whatever it takes to get the job done. The effective commander—the effective leader—is always a student, always a teacher, always a trainer.

Beyond all these things, you must remember you live in a fishbowl. You must set an example. If you don't show the way, if you don't do the right things, your people won't do them.

Leaders should think more about others than themselves. I don't like creeping careerism. I tell my people I'm their career planner. We need more professionalism and less careerism. Being in the Service is not a job. We don't work; we're members of a profession. We serve.

We now, in the Marine Corps, have more dependents than Marines. About 205,000 dependents and 198,000 Marines. We have to take care of the families. But the most important thing we can do for the families is to "bring 'em back alive." And that means

Marines need good training. Time invested in operations and training is time well spent. The more you train in peace, the less you bleed in war.

I believe there will be war in the next decade. Probably some Third World scenario. The time to think about it is now. We need to be able to conduct low-intensity warfare. We need to be able to conduct revolutionary warfare and to defeat it. Sure, we have to be prepared for NATO contingencies, but we must not lose sight of the kind of conflict that's most apt to confront us. We must be effective at the low end of the warfare spectrum, in the protracted conflicts that so often occur in the Third World.

One of the key leadership challenges facing us is the need to learn to operate better in the joint and combined arena. Joint operations increase complexity. But they shouldn't become so complex that command and control becomes unworkable. We must remember that even minor contingencies require multi-Service support.

When it comes to training, I believe in having a campaign plan that is focused on warfighting. A campaign plan is really a thought process that integrates our efforts and gets everybody going down the trail together. Training and education programs have to dovetail. You need an annual training plan to be what you want to be. Without one, you won't get there.

Don't let the higher headquarters cause you to lose your focus. There are too many regulations and directives. We're trying to cut back on directives. We tend to lose sight of our priorities. If you can't tie something to operations, training, or warrior preparedness, then you'd better think twice before doing it.

The complexities of the modern, fast-moving battlefield will make it essential that leaders at all levels are prepared to think, able to anticipate what might happen, and prepared to act. Learn to use mission-type orders. They are essential in battle today. Everyone must understand the commander's intent—two echelons up and two down—whether in administration, logistics, or signal. In the "fog of war" there is chaos, and in that chaos opportunities present themselves. The first to see these opportunities are the people on the "tip of the spear." They must act, and their actions must be consistent with the commander's intent.

That's why critiques during training exercises are so important. The purpose of the critique should be not only to examine what people did, but also—primarily—*why* they did it. It's the thought process that's important. Almost anybody can run around and yell "Arrugha," but what counts is having people who can think.

A commander must let his people do things. You have to let 'em make mistakes—not dumb things that get them killed, but mistakes they can learn from. Marines care about their Corps. They want to be players in it. They want meaningful roles, and it is the job of all leaders to provide that opportunity for their subordinates. This is how you keep people challenged and committed.

We also have to recognize that today's Services—the Army, Navy, Air Force, Marines, and Coast Guard are thin—we lack numbers and depth; we're not as robust as we could be. To overcome that, you must make your organization and your people winners. You'll probably never have your full table of organization and equipment. So, you must instill in your people the idea that "you take what you get and make what you want."

It's going to take bold, innovative, and aggressive leadership to overcome the complexities of the modern battlefield. Only this kind of leadership, exercised by both the commander and his staff, will provide purpose, direction, and motivation in combat. At all levels of command, leaders must be men of character. They must know and understand their people and the physical tools of battle. They must act with courage and conviction. Their primary function is to inspire and motivate their people to do difficult things in trying circumstances.

Commandership: The Art of Command

Brig. Gen. F. P. Henderson, USMC (Ret.)

Marine Corps Gazette
January 1992

Having had the opportunity to command on many occasions throughout a lengthy career, and having observed many other commanders during that time, the author offers present and future Marines some sage advice on commandership.

In the "Focus on Leadership" section in the February 1991 *Gazette,* Capt. David Hickey, USA, opens his first paragraph with:

> Leadership is a tired, washed-out topic. It has infested classrooms and discussion panels
> for centuries, and it is rapidly becoming the scourge of military periodicals. . . . The last
> thing this world needs is another paper on leadership.

In his next paragraph he says, "But the truth is, it's not the topic that's bad, it's how we look at it." And he then goes on to write a very nice paper on the subject.

While it is possible to say, "Amen, brother!" to his challenging opening remarks, the truth is that the subject must always be a primary concern of military schools and journals for two reasons. The first is that good leadership at every echelon of command, and in every element of a command, is essential for success in an assigned mission. With it, good commanders can overcome deficiencies in organization, weapons, equipment, support, and inferior numbers. This is one of the enduring lessons of military history through the ages.

The second reason is that the criteria for, and demands of, leadership are not static, but are constantly in change, slowly in centuries past, much more rapidly now as the societal foundations of armies and the means for the conduct of war are continually changing. The leadership problems of a Marine commander today are in many respects much more difficult and complex than they were at Belleau Wood. The *Gazette* has published many fine articles on the subject in the past fifty years, but how many of them have been read by today's company grade officers?[1]

Every generation of Marine officers must think about the problem of command in their time and express their thoughts and beliefs in the *Gazette*.

Because every officer is a unique individual in his personality and capabilities, there can be no "one size fits all" in the practice of command. Instruction in the Corps' schools and articles in the *Gazette* are essential to focus each officer's thinking in developing his own concept and practice of command. But I agree with Captain Hickey—careful observation of other commanders ("The best way to learn how to lead is to watch leaders"), good and bad, throughout a career, is indispensable to being a good leader when one becomes a commander.

In this respect I was fortunate to have unparalleled opportunities to observe and judge commanders at all levels, from company grade to three star, in all types of ground units. I had two tours of Fleet Marine Force (FMF) duty in the pre-World War II Old Corps, five amphibious campaigns from Guadalcanal to Okinawa, the FMF again in the late forties and during the Korean War. I was privileged to command a Marine detachment on a heavy cruiser at the start of World War II, and later on an infantry battalion (2d Battalion, 5th Marines) an artillery regiment (11th Marines), a heavy artillery group in an Army corps artillery, and was director of a school at Quantico. My intervening duties also provided the opportunity to observe the exercise of command in non-FMF activities, which comprise much of an officer's service time. The following, then, are my conclusions, drawn from what I observed of those command practices that led to units being superior or above average in mission execution. How the commander carries out these practices will obviously vary in peace and war and with the size and type of unit he commands and his own personality, strengths, and weaknesses.

Also, partly in deference to Captain Hickey's wish, I have not used "leadership" in the title. But, more important, because that is not the true name of the subject. It is *commanders* that the talking and writing are about, and what differentiates between a good commander and a poor one. There are no "leader" officer billet titles in FMF tables of organization so far as I can determine. For every unit led by an officer, the title is "commander" and so specified in all official publications and correspondence. In dictionaries, thesauruses, and Heinl's *Dictionary of Military and Naval Quotations* you will find little difference between the entries on these headings; they could be exchanged in many cases. I do not consider this semantic quibbling, for we are talking about Marine *commanders,* and the ancient Chinese saying that "the first step to wisdom is to call things by their right names" should apply. Thus, "commandership" is the logical word to name the art by which a commander exercises command. To state that commandership of a military unit is an art is within the definitions of that word.

The Troops Know Him or Her[2]

Every Marine has the right to know the man who has authority over him twenty-four hours a day, every day in the year. He should know him by name and on sight and something about him. (Was he a star college athlete? Did he come up from the ranks? Is his son a second lieutenant in the Corps? Does he have the Navy Cross? What's his nickname? etc.) This is not a great problem at the company/squadron level, but it is increasingly difficult to achieve and sustain at each higher command level.

At these higher levels he makes every effort to show himself to his men as soon as possible on taking command in a manner that permits some personal contact. This is best done by seeing them in what a naturalist would call their natural habitat, in both their duty and off-duty hours, and not by formal, staged events. This should not be done by a published schedule but bypassing the word through his subordinate commanders that he could show up at any time to see and talk to his men.

On these visits he should be the center of attention and not be accompanied by an entourage of his staff. Often he is accompanied by his sergeant major, who should pass the word through noncommissioned officer (NCO) channels that the new commander would like to renew acquaintance with any Marines who have served with him before. If this introduction period in his new command is done with friendly informality and an obviously sincere wish to meet and know his men, all hands will soon know who the new "Old Man" is and form their opinion, hopefully favorable, about him.

To support this knowledge, all of his written orders and directives, as far as possible, are in the first person singular and signed by him so that the troops know it is his personal command. He avoids having his wishes written in bureaucratic, obscure language, published "By the order of . . . ," and signed by his executive officer or chief of staff.

He Commands Through His Subordinates, Not His Staff

He is meticulous in observing the difference between commanders and staff officers. He is a commander. His subordinates are also commanders and should receive their orders from him personally, by telephone, radio, or in writing. His staff is there to support him in reaching his decision, and then seeing that they are carried out by all subordinate elements. This does not prevent the desirable; interchange between the superior and subordinate similar staff sections concerning details of how to execute his orders.

His subordinate commanders must always feel that they have direct access to him without the approval of his executive officer or chief of staff. But the realities of military protocol and life make it advisable for subordinate commanders to inform these officers of their wishes and purpose. He should meet with his subordinate commanders as often as possible in an informal atmosphere to talk shop, exchange scuttlebutt, and discuss the present and foreseen problems they each face.

He Doesn't "Know It All"

The good commander is wise in admitting to his staff and his troops that he is not an authority on everything in his command. With the frequent changes in organization, doctrine, tactics, weapons, and equipment much could have changed since he was last in the FMF, probably on a lower command level.[3] He can both educate himself and gain the confidence of his men in his visits to them if he asks them to tell him about their weapons or equipment and how they do their jobs in achieving mission success for the whole unit. He will find his Marines anxious to tell him all about their unit, what they do, and how they do it. The commander of a Marine expeditionary unit or brigade has the opportunity to broaden his knowledge by doing this in those types of units he has not previously commanded within his own military specialty.

He Has a Close Relationship with Senior NCOs

As he has advanced in rank and level of command he has realized that NCOs, from the squad level on up, are the Corps' secret weapon. Under the guidance of their commanding officer (CO), they make his desires become accomplishments. While he cannot personally know every NCO in a large command, he can cultivate a relationship with those veteran staff grade NCOs who have served the Corps as long or longer than he has. He treats them as Marine Corps *officers,* as he is, except they do not have an officer's commission. He believes that they share the same goals, aspirations, and loyalty to the unit and the Corps that he has. There are many ways a commander can achieve this relationship in both a one-on-basis and as a group.

He should take advantage of opportunities to win their allegiance and support by his command actions. Here is an example from World War II and Korea when officers were entitled to have liquor but NCOs were not. (A bottle a week in the earlier war via the supply system, and later in Korea, by unit cash purchase through a British entrepreneur merchant in Inchon.) Many commanders felt it was not fair for a new second lieutenant with less than a year in the Corps to be able to have a bourbon and branch water now and then when a veteran gunnery sergeant or sergeant major with long service could not. So they established formal or informal ways, often under the control of the unit sergeant major, to rectify this. In every instance I knew of the NCOs were deeply grateful for being treated as members of the "band of brothers" and never violated the trust implicit in the CO's action.

Predictable and Consistent

All hands in his command know where he stands in discipline, training, and other matters so they can conduct themselves accordingly. He can be strict, permissive, or somewhere in between as a commander, but his subordinates and the troops must know how their actions will be judged. Troops never know where they stand under a commander who vacillates between being a flamethrower and an old softie. A strict commander makes sure that he never discourages initiative in his command when it may fall outside his guidelines if it was obviously well reasoned and intended for the good of the command. Also, to forgive an occasional sinner shows the command that he, too, is human and will not penalize a good Marine for a minor human frailty.

Teacher and Mentor of Officers

General Lejeune's famous 1920s injunction that a primary responsibility of an officer was to be a teacher to his enlisted men applies equally to the officers under him. This is especially true at the lower command levels in war when many young officers rise to responsible command and staff positions without the usual schooling and varied duty experience. In peace or war it is important that the commander pass on to his subordinates all that he has learned in his longer service and schooling and use this opportunity to know them and their abilities better. They will then be better qualified to both command their units and respond to his orders by knowing his beliefs on how to succeed in the unit's mission.

Unfortunately, this was a too infrequent practice in my time. This was especially true in the case of staff officers. For some unknown reason, neither the CO nor his executive officer nor chief of staff felt that officers assigned to the staff, often without previous staff experience, seemed to need any guidance on how to be a good staff officer—one who could both aid and support his CO in his decisions and plans and aid the subordinate commands in executing his orders. I have long felt that this was one of the reasons subordinate commands so often had such a dim view, often vehemently expressed, of their superior commander's staff.

The Use of Power

A commanding officer has complete authority (power) over the lives of all of the officers and men in his command. This has not changed since the dawn of military history. In the Bible, a Roman commander came to Jesus and asked him to heal his sick servant. In their dialog, the Roman said ". . . I have soldiers under me. I order this one 'Go,' and he goes; and I order that one 'Come,' and he comes. . . ."[4] This is still true in the Corps. But how it is exercised will often determine a unit's effectiveness in accomplishing its mission. Few, if any, officers will have had power of this nature before their first command and may be perplexed or troubled on how to use it, then, or in higher commands.

The most successful commanders I observed used the "iron hand in the velvet glove" approach. They made every effort to obtain willing compliance with their policies and directives, but if this did not succeed, they did not hesitate to use their disciplinary power, e.g., reprimands, courts martial, relief of subordinate commanders, etc.

He Knows the Limits of What His Command Can Do

A good commander never orders his command to do something he believes is beyond its capabilities unless ordered to do so by his superior—and over his protests. At Gettysburg, Gen. James Longstreet persistently objected to General Lee's plan to attack the center of the Union line on the third day. But when Lee insisted on it, Longstreet complied, with disastrous results for the Army of Northern Virginia.

Also, a good commander never hesitates to order his command to do something that seems impossible when he is certain that they can do it. When Gen. Gouverneur Kemble Warren discovered, on the second day of Gettysburg, that Little Round Top was undefended and the Confederates were moving to occupy it, he rushed units on the double to defend it. The 20th Maine Regiment was placed on the extreme left of that line, and of the whole Union Army, and ordered to hold the position at all costs. Its commander was Col. Joshua Chamberlain, a college professor before the war. In 1862, when the regiment was formed he received a commission and joined it. The week before Gettysburg, he was promoted to regimental commander. They arrived at Little Round Top just in time to repulse the first attack and then the subsequent attacks by superior numbers. Finally, with a third or more of the regiment casualties, the remainder out of ammunition, and the Confederates coming again, Chamberlain ordered his men to fix bayonets and charge at his command. This they did with a roar, and the startled attacking rebels broke and either surrendered or ran. Little Round Top and the Union Army were saved. Chamberlain knew what his men could do, and they had faith in him and did it.

This knowledge of what his command (of any size or type) can or cannot do does not come from schools or writings, but from within himself and from being totally immersed in the life of his command. The best commanders I observed were so immersed and used their own variations of the command practices previously discussed. They know the operational capabilities and limitations of every element of their command, the unique character and talents of each of their subordinate commanders, and the esprit of their men and how they would respond to challenge or adversity. They would never knowingly order them to do anything that would lower this esprit, which should be, "We're Number 1!" (The famous Union Iron Brigade was the 1st Brigade of the 1st Division of I Corps in the Army of the Potomac. They let everyone know they were Number 1—and then repeatedly proved it in battle.)

---

1 Probably the finest exposition on leadership I ever read was a research paper by Capt. John H. Burns, USA. "Psychology & Leadership," written as a student in the 1931–33 class at the Army C & GS School and published by the school in 1934. Has any Marine today read it?

2 For brevity, the masculine only is used hereafter.

3 Compare today's infantry battalion with that of 1918. Then it had 1,036 officers and men, 900 bolt action rifles, 64 automatic rifles, and 328 pistols. No mortars, machineguns, antitank weapons, radios, vehicles, computes, etc. However, it did have two horses, one for the commander and one for the exec, whose care and feeding are not a problem today.

4 Matthew 8:9.

Are You Ready to Disobey?

Capt. John D. Kuntz, USMC

Marine Corps Gazette
October 1986

It was late, but the sergeant was fully awake as he stared out across the wire into the jungle. The dark humidity smothered his skin and drops of sweat dripped from his armpits. As each drip fell, lie shivered. He watched and he waited. It was Guadalcanal, October 24, 1942, and the sergeant was "Manila" John Basilone. That night, in the battle for Henderson Field, Basilone and his machinegun cut down wave after wave of Japanese. He killed so many that in the lulls between assaults he had to clear his fields of fire by pushing down the walls of stacked corpses.

During the long night, different Japanese officers led the assault waves, but each one blindly obeyed orders to assault straight ahead; each one was methodically cut down; and each one became a new layer in the grisly pile of death. Those Japanese officers gave their superiors obedience, but they did not give them what every officer must give: professional judgment. Those Japanese officers were nothing more than orders passers. They probably mumbled to themselves, "Why don't we envelop this crazy machine-gunner or probe for a weak spot farther down the line?" But, instead of doing something, they just passed the order on and went to their deaths.

Officers must give independent professional judgment. Very often that includes one of three types of disobedience, which from least to most severe shall be designated preemptive disobedience, moderate disobedience, and complete disobedience.

Let there be no mistake, this discussion includes only disobedience that occurs when an officer using professional judgment acts other than strictly obeying specific orders. Disobedience that results from caprice, insufficient perseverance, or intentional sabotage is excluded. There is a strong bias in the military for obedience and that is how it should be. All Marines have a duty to obey orders. Obviously, the Marine Corps could function in no other way. But Marine officers have a duty in addition to merely obeying orders: they must also exercise professional judgment. Officers must do more than merely pass orders from one hand to the other. There come times—not all that rarely—when an officer must use his professional judgment and disobey.

Of the three types of disobedience, preemptive disobedience is the least severe. Preemptive disobedience means acting in the absence of orders, refusing to wait for permission, refusing to be bound by inertia. Preemptive disobedience means acting in the absence of complete information in those sudden unclear, chaotic hours when timely action is often most valuable. In 1891, George Dewey, a man destined to become admiral of the Navy, had his ship off the coast of Chile as relations between the United States and Chile's new revolutionary government became strained. When two Americans died on shore, the U.S. undersecretary in Washington, D.C., and the U.S. minister to Chile in Santiago began the delicate process of politely badgering the Chilean government for an apology so that war could be averted. During this fragile period, Dewey, without orders, took on a load of coal (paid for with his own money), repositioned his ship, and went on battle alert. These preparations for war could have scuttled the negotiations. Dewey, however, refused to wait; he was preemptively disobedient. Because of his quick actions, no war broke out. While most men in his position would have seen the benefits of preparation, many would have waited for permission before acting. Dewey put his professional judgment into action—the essence of preemptive disobedience.

The second type of disobedience occurs when an officer receives an order and obeys it selectively rather than to the letter. During tile Korean War, Col. Lewis B. "Chesty" Puller, was in command of the 1st Marines, the rear guard for the 1st Marine Division as it moved out of the Chosin Reservoir. Puller received orders to destroy or abandon all equipment and vehicles and bring his men out. Puller selectively obeyed the order. He did bring his men out, but he refused to abandon vehicles and equipment. Not only did he bring out every working Marine vehicle, he also brought vehicles that the Army had previously abandoned. Puller brought out almost all his men, equipment, and vehicles, including his wounded and dead. He did it not because he had been ordered to do it—in some ways his orders were nearly the opposite—but because in his professional judgment that was the way it should be done. He obeyed part of his orders, part he did not; that is one example of moderate disobedience.

Another example of moderate disobedience occurred in 1898 during the Spanish-American War. A few days after Theodore Roosevelt led his Rough Riders up San Juan Hill, he came up against Army regulations. It seems that Roosevelt's regiment had had very little to eat other than hardtack and water for two or three days and, because of supply problems, little food was expected for another week. When Roosevelt unexpectedly heard that a supply of beans had come ashore, he marched down to claim the beans for his men. The quartermaster on duty, however, cited Army regulations chapter and verse clearly stating that beans could be used only for officers.

Roosevelt left the quartermaster's tent, turned immediately around, came back in and claimed all 1,100 pounds of beans for his officers' mess. The quartermaster said that if Roosevelt signed such a requisition he would be investigated in Washington. Roosevelt told the quartermaster to do whatever he needed, but hand over the beans.

While the story of Roosevelt and the beans may be humorous, it does make a serious point that at times an officer must be able to disobey official regulations when in his professional judgment it is necessary. Sometimes the spirit of a rule is best observed by breaking the rule. As Gen. Willard W. Scott the current commandant of West Point has said, "Any fool can keep a rule. God gave him a brain to know when to break the rule."

A final example of moderate disobedience occurred just before World War II when the commander of 1st Battalion, 1st Marines, 1st Marine Division was in the field on a training operation with his men. The commander again was Chesty Puller, never a stranger to disobedience based upon professional judgment. Puller, who was a major at the time, had recently returned from the Far East where he had been much impressed with tile oriental use of camouflage.

Puller had introduced camouflage to his battalion and thus his men went to the field covered with mud, leaves, and branches. One day, as Puller and his men were training, a staff car drove up and the 1st Marines' regimental commander looked at Puller's mud-encrusted men and ordered Puller to clean them up and stop using camouflage. Although Puller replied, "Yes, Sir," he did not clean up his men and he did not stop using camouflage. Instead, he delayed his obedience until he got a chance to speak with the commanding general about camouflage. The commanding general then introduced camouflage throughout the division. The courage to perform some type of professional disobedience in the proper situation is not a flaw, it is it great asset. In 1916, after Admiral Jellicoe had mixed success at the battle of Jutland, Lord Fisher said that Jellicoe had all the qualities of a great fleet admiral except one: "he has not learned to disobey."

Preemptive disobedience and moderate disobedience, while serious, are not as extreme as the third type of disobedience, complete disobedience. Complete disobedience occurs when an officer simply refuses to carry out an order. The officer evaluates the order and completely, fully, and absolutely refuses to obey. The German officers sentenced to death at the Nuremberg trials attempted to rely in part on the defense of superior orders. They said that when they performed various macabre duties, they were only obeying orders from superiors and thus should not be held personally responsible. While that defense may sound reasonable, the officers were hanged by the neck until dead. Those deaths so long ago should remind every officer today that an officer is responsible for his actions no matter what orders he receives.

This question of obedience and responsibility is not confined to theoretical discussions of World War II. In Vietnam during March, 1978, Lt. William Calley and his platoon entered the village of My Lai and killed more than 300 Vietnamese, mostly old men, women, children, and babies. At his trial, Calley said, among other things, that he was acting under orders and thus should not be held responsible. Although there is great doubt about what orders were issued, it was Calley's duty as an officer, even if orders to kill babies had been issued, to evaluate such orders and, if necessary, disobey. The idea is not radical. With Calley, on the very same operation, was a young pilot who was so shocked by what he saw that he continually landed his observation helicopter in and around My Lai so that he could rescue wounded Vietnamese.

Perhaps disobedience, whether preemptive, moderate, or complete, really is a simple matter of boldness. Officers must use their own independent professional judgment and then have the boldness to put their judgment in action. We must not be mere orders passers, doctrine passers, or policy passers. We must stimulate and reward judgment and boldness. To accomplish this, we must change ourselves and those around us. There has been too much talk about changing schools, doctrine, and institutions. The problem is not that some standing operating procedure is not written correctly, it is people; people are always both the problem and the solution. Each of us in our daily decisions must decide in favor of boldness. To complain about orders but pass them on while waiting for the policy or institution to change is to shirk our duty.

Next month or next year, it is at least possible that the Marine Corps will again find itself on the ground in a foreign country. If politicians, who are well meaning but without understanding, attempt to impose unreasonable restrictions on basic defensive measures, will we have a bold ground commander to resist those restrictions? If not, can we even find a captain or lieutenant to go to the commander and say, "Sir. I know you are really busy so I won't take up your time, but I've been thinking over and over again about the way we have all our men billeted so closely together and I just couldn't go any further unless I did something. I have my men outside, dispersed. and digging in." Ridiculous? Absurd? Maybe.

Perhaps such an officer would be relieved and perhaps his career would end. But what is wrong with that? Being an officer, particularly in the Marine Corps, should mean more than just staying off the skyline and passing orders. It means sacrifice, and there are all types. The bars, leaves, birds, and stars that mark an officer are not just to be worn, at times they must also be bet. Sometimes you win the bet, sometimes you lose. But that willingness to dare is the foundation of the Corps' great history. If we lose that boldness, the Corps will be asphyxiated by bureaucracy; its strength will ebb until all that remains is the polite scramble for promotion.

The story of President Lincoln's search for a general officer to lead the North in the Civil War has been told too often to be repeated in detail here. Suffice it to say that the first generals that Lincoln selected all had immaculate service records compared to the somewhat disreputable Grant. But Grant, despite his flaws, was willing to fight; he was willing to dare, to risk. In Grant's boldness, the Nation found victory.

Where will we find such boldness today? One thing is certain, we will never find it unless we search for it, nurture it, and reward it unceasingly. All officers must search, nurture, and reward boldness, creativity, and flexibility and give those same qualities to superiors—whether they want them or not. Your immediate boss may or may not welcome boldness, but the Marine Corps is desperate for it and we will perish without it. It simply means developing real professional judgment and having the courage to act on that judgment, even though it may involve some type of disobedience.

The Japanese officers of Guadalcanal were slaughtered because they could not bring themselves to disobey. Bureaucrats can follow rules, remain inconspicuous, and make no blatant mistakes. Such a policy, however, is not sufficient for the leadership cadre of an elite fighting force. Officers must be bold. In large measure, the United States depends upon the Marine Corps for its immediate military strength. When the Marine Corps fails to encourage and reward independent judgment, initiative, and even professional disobedience, it weakens the Corps and undermines those who trust its abilities. In every officer's career, there will come a time when some type of disobedience is necessary. Are you ready?

Lessons Learned in Leadership

Col. Bruce G. Brown, USMC (Ret.)

Marine Corps Gazette
June 1984

The ranks of field grade officers are filled with talented performers whose minds are fixed on their mission and their Marines.

This article presents five personal "lessons learned" in leadership. The lessons per se are not new or original. The presentation is designed to reflect on what is considered fundamental. It is an attempt to separate the "wheat from the chaff" amidst the proliferation of sophisticated leadership/management (and risk avoidance) theory. It is intended to provide some insight, particularly for relatively junior leaders who must exist and lead in a maze of conflicting priorities in the so-called "peacetime" Marine Corps.

Lesson 1: Leadership is Results

This lesson is first, primary, and overriding. It is the essence of combat leadership by definition. It is a simple, fundamental truth. However, it is also almost overwhelming to one who has never been in combat. One can argue that it implies that the end justifies the means—that is correct, in combat the end (results) justifies the means! Although this axiom appears contrary to a basic principle we have been taught as God-fearing Americans, it should be remembered that there is no second-place ribbon on a battlefield.

Does this then imply that illegal, immoral, or unethical methods can be justified? It does not, simply because clearly illegal, immoral, or unethical methods usually result in failure. However, I suggest that there is some gray in each of these areas—that it is useful to consider them as relative rather than absolute terms. Although we have a formalized legal code, we are often tempted to ignore the letter of the law or interpret it in a manner that fits the situational problem (e.g., "midnight requisition"). Neither morality nor ethics are formalized as specific codes of behavior. Therefore, our individual standards of behavior tend to be relative rather than absolute, constant, and shining examples for others to emulate. If you have ever condoned a midnight requisition, you have already established that your moral standards are relative not absolute.

I can illustrate the relative rather than absolute nature of my own ethical standards with a sea story. In 1968 I had the privilege of commanding the 1st Military Police Battalion in Da Nang. We were operating as a ground defense battalion and our mission did not actually involve any military police functions. One day a company commander came to me with a problem. One of his "good Marines" had totaled a jeep through admittedly reckless driving. No one was injured, and the good Marine claimed he could get the jeep completely repaired in less than twenty-four hours. Of course such repair could not be achieved within the system, and I suspected that only the Seabees were capable of doing it in that time frame. I also suspected that the cost was at least a case of good scotch and that some of the junior leaders in the company were prepared to help defray the expense.

Now, mister battalion commander, do you have the accident properly reported and investigated or do you "give the Marine a break" and see if he can get the jeep repaired in less than twenty-four hours? The first principle to remember when confronted with situations like this is contained in the leadership chapter of the *Guidebook For Marines.* The principle is "The leader, *alone,* is responsible for all that the unit does or fails to do."

In this case, it meant that if I gave the Marine "a break" I was also taking the company commander "off the hook" and that if such actions were ever discovered and investigated, I would have to assume total responsibility for the decision. The company commander either consciously or intuitively suspected that I would normally follow that principle rather religiously and that by presenting the problem to me it was no longer his problem or our problem, it was exclusively my problem. He also suspected that my code of ethics might permit giving the good Marine a break or he would not have bothered to present the problem in the first place.

I chose to leave the accident unreported and uninvestigated. The jeep was "repaired" in less than twenty-four hours. Officially there was no accident, and the Marine was not charged. Was that decision legal or illegal, moral or immoral, ethical or unethical? I submit that the answer is none of the above—not completely legal or illegal, not completely moral or immoral, not completely ethical or unethical. I believe it was a decision that Adm. Robert B. Carney once termed "the gray areas of command." Recalling his central theme as I understood it, I believe it can be summarized with these words: *All tough decisions (of a military commander) lie in the gray areas of command where absolutes do not apply.*

The sea story contains several additional teaching points. First, you get paid to make decisions not judge them. Both my decision and its alternatives are "OK"—neither good nor bad, neither right nor wrong. All commanding officers have the right to make what others might think of as bad or wrong decisions as long as they are willing to accept total responsibility for them. Second, you may have read or heard that a key to decisionmaking is to select the alternative you are "most comfortable with." In the gray areas of command that's not true. The alternatives, as the story illustrates, inherently include degrees of discomfort, not comfort. Understanding that makes the challenge less fun but more fascinating. Third, the objective of our leadership and decision-making, results, are not often measurable off the battlefield. Therefore, do not equate use of the term "results" with current Marine Corps standards embodied in MCCRES. My use of the word "results" is derived from the *Guidebook For Marines* in light of personal experience.

Lesson 2: Good Followership Produces Unity of Effort

This lesson has been expressed in a variety of ways by many leaders. It can best be summarized in these terms—*To be a good leader, you must first be a good follower! You "must first be. . . ."* Sound easy? This principle is easy to grasp—it is easy to accept its importance in combat—but for me it was most difficult to consistently practice. Why? My Marine ego of course! I am a leader—I don't want to first be a follower much less a good one. Now I want my juniors to be good followers; however, I want my seniors to accept all of my recommendations, give me my head, and let me do it my way. I'll accept the responsibility. If I must (on occasion) loyally execute an order I disagree with to achieve unity of effort, why do I have to issue that order as if it were my very own—as if I invented it? That's unfair! Why can't I grip about it a little? Why can't I say to my juniors "Gents, we are going to do this even if it's stupid"? Do you expect me to be inhuman?

I have no excuse for the degree to which I did not consistently apply this principle. As a second and first lieutenant serving in the 1st Battalion, 7th Marines during the Korean War, I was exposed to a master of the art in applying the principle. His name was James C. Short, and he served as both the S-3 and executive officer while a major and as battalion commander upon promotion to lieutenant colonel. In each of these billets he always issued every order as if he invented it. There was never any hint that he might have been in disagreement prior to the decision. On occasion, the junior officer grapevine in the regiment would subsequently reveal that he had been in disagreement, sometimes violent disagreement before the decision had been reached. We never told him we had found him out. Our respect for him and his ability to live by this principle was such that we intuitively knew he would have been disappointed to learn that we had heard of his disagreement—even after execution had been completed. If you ever serve with a senior who comes close to my description of Colonel Short, observe closely—you maybe at the feet of a master.

To place this lesson in context we need to add one more thought. Being a good follower implicitly includes presenting your views, including any dissent, to your seniors before the decision is reached (when possible). You are expected to do this. It is not simply a right or prerogative; you have a duty to do this in the context of good followership. Therefore, you are expected to present your ideas and views clearly and skillfully. Even when not invited or requested, you are expected to say what you think. The senior expects you to speak up—silence is consent. Then, of course, remember the bottom line of this lesson, the senior has the deciding (only) vote.

Lesson 3: Be Yourself; Remain a Good Student; Become a Good Teacher

This lesson is presented as a triad intended to illustrate the growth process of a good leader. The first pillar is well known so let's deal with it briefly. Man's basic imperfection means that there are no perfect role models to follow. Although we are influenced by many other leaders, the growth process takes place within the strengths and limitations of our individual personalities. Any effort to be something or someone we are not produces artificiality, which in turn produces insincerity and failure.

The second pillar, remain a good student, is designed to convey a perception of the lifelong learning process. The word "student" is used to illustrate the thirst for knowledge and understanding we feel when we are young and eager. It is used very deliberately because as we become older the thirst may become less eager, even become dormant. There is an additional danger of beginning to sound like we know it all or have heard it all. However, the primary danger is that we can grow older but not wiser if the thirst becomes dormant; therefore, let's try to remain good students. Also remember that a good student of the art of war and of leadership is never an expert; there is always more to learn.

You have noted by now I love the word "teacher." I believe it better describes our efforts to convey knowledge and understanding than the term "military instructor," which suggests a rigid and formal image typified by the platform lecture. All officers and NCOs teach regardless of their current billets because if you lead, you teach. Commanding officers spend most of their time teaching one way or another and it is not just platform limited.

In that context then, the last pillar, become a good teacher, implies that we are not necessarily good teachers just because we have achieved a rank associated with leadership. As we become more senior and, therefore, must spend more time teaching, it is healthy to think of the process of becoming a good teacher as a continuing, never-ending challenge.

Lesson 4: It Depends on the Situation and Terrain

Do you recall the first time you heard that? No matter what we thought of this adage at the time we first heard it, upon entering the FMF we find that it is the fundamental tactical lesson taught at the Basic School. It endures year after year, generation after generation, because it is basic to all tactical thought. As you know, good combat leadership is heavily dependent on sound and timely tactical decisions. That is the primary reason some thoughts on tactics are included to introduce this lesson. However, the focus here is not on tactics but on how the adage tends to operate in the tactical decisionmaking process and why it is so important.

First, let's look at the nature of the problem. In combat we are always attempting to apply the right tactics at the right time. In reality this is probably an impossible task, but because this business is so deadly we must try to find a near perfect solution. Unfortunately, there are no absolutes in tactics. Once the nature of the problem is understood, the true magnificence of the Basic School lesson becomes more apparent. It provides the focal point for our effort. It means we must focus on a keen awareness of both situation and terrain at all times. That awareness will guide (or drive) us toward sound and timely decisions.

The need for this keen awareness is what drives leaders forward in combat and is the basis of the principle "lead from the front." However, you cannot have your cake and eat it too. The need for keen awareness exists in all leaders including your senior commanders. Therefore, you will frequently find a senior commander at your side. Normally, he is not looking over your shoulder, *not* over-supervising; he is simply *sharing* an appreciation of the situation with you. Recall that the need for keen awareness is so great that both you and your senior must always be in a position or positions to influence the outcome. Frequently that involves face-to-face discussion or side-by-side perceptions.

How *far* forward? No one can answer this for you. "It depends..." you may have read or heard that leading from the front can be overdone and I am sure that's true. However, who is going to judge what is overdone and when? Consider these generals: (1) Jackson in the Civil War, (2) Patton in World War II, (3) Craig in the Pusan Perimeter, and (4) Walt in Vietnam. Who can say if any of these leaders ever went too far forward? Instinct and intelligent judgment probably combine to determine where you go and when. Remember that leading from the front is not a contest in bravery.

In attempting to apply the right tactic at the right time, we normally find that we run out of time before we have found the right tactic. If you are keenly aware of situation and terrain, you are probably holding the *high cards*—don't procrastinate, bet on them. Issue your orders and don't brood over them or second guess yourself. Recall the adage of Satchel Paige: "Don't look back, something may be gaining on you."

The Basic School principle serves to guide not just tactical thought but can be applied to a host of problems and activities outside of combat. Although one might have to use the term *terrain* loosely or figuratively, it should be easy to translate it to the word *environment*. The focal point then reads, "It depends on the situation and the environment." Add keen awareness and we have the key to finding good solutions to almost all problems. You may find yourself using many more complex and sophisticated tools, but never lose sight of the objective, which is to solve the problem or arrive at a decision. In that context the focal point remains basic.

Lesson 5: Fix Your Mind on Your Mission and Your Marines

This last lesson is a direct extract from the *Guidebook For Marines*. The sentence has remained virtually intact for more than twenty years. It serves as a fundamental guide or approach to all leadership billets, both command and staff. It endures because it is a powerful truth, simply expressed. In other leadership publications, it is expressed in more sophisticated terms but never better than in the guidebook.

Let me start by first illustrating the importance of mission focus with the story of the Marine and the jeep. You recall that the 1st MP battalion had no military police functions. Had our mission included military police functions, I would have had the accident reported and investigated simply because a good cop could not do otherwise. In other words, I would not have tempted my Marines to leave other accidents unreported in their execution of military police functions. Please try to understand that I am not implying that infantrymen can or should have lower moral or ethical standards than others. Nor am I attempting to rationalize my decision for you. All I am attempting to illustrate is the basic point: mission focus will always influence and sometimes drive or dictate your decisions.

Careerism and Personal Bias

To place this lesson in context, I believe we must consider, in some depth, the premise of "creeping careerism" to include the perception of "risk avoidance" and its effects on the officer corps. Be forewarned that I am quite biased on this subject, a bias derived from extensive personal experience and observation. Many articles in the *Gazette* have focused on the problem of creeping careerism. The idea of creeping careerism is founded on two basic perceptions that have been expressed both explicitly and implicitly: (1) that "careerists" advance faster and further than mission-oriented Marines, and (2) that the senior leadership of the Marine Corps today (i.e., the general officers) must be largely composed of careerists who have achieved senior rank by avoiding bureaucratic risks.

Let me set forth my bottom line first: I believe the basic perceptions to be inaccurate and the central premise to be a lesson in dialectics so skillfully articulate that the relative truth of the situation becomes obscure. I further believe that the additional perception that our senior leadership has been "captured" by the bureaucracy to be inaccurate. To say "victimized" by the bureaucracy may be accurate, but I never served with a general officer who was captive to it.

Careerism and the Senior Leadership

Now that my bias is obvious, permit me some personal observations offered as food-for-thought. First, by definition, a careerist as I understand it is an officer who is career motivated as opposed to mission motivated—one who thinks and acts in terms of his or her career before thinking and acting in terms of the mission and the Marines assigned to accomplish it. I do not contend that the Marine Corps was or is lily white. I have observed such officers, but in my experience they were (and are) very few and far between. Further, they did *not* commonly reach general officer rank. On the contrary, I served under many general officers and with many who later became general officers— they were all mission-oriented Marines. I contend that the senior leadership of the Marine Corps today is composed, as usual, of highly talented Marines who have proven to be outstanding leaders in combat. In forming your own opinion of today's senior leadership, consider these questions:

- Do personal decorations convey to you an image of a risk-avoiding careerist?
- In considering all of the decisions of general officers that you have been exposed to, how many decisions appear career motivated? How many involve risk avoidance and the absence of moral courage?
- Is their oath of office any different than yours?

Origin of Confusion: "The Fair-Haired Type"

My next observations deal with the officer selection process as related to the perception that careerists advance further and faster than promotion-poor, mission-oriented Marines. This perception stems from our informal classification of certain officers as "fair-haired boys." This classification is commonly used to describe an officer who has served in one or more high visibility billets and whose next promotion appears ensured. (Of course, appearances are often deceiving.) This classification is sometimes expressed with fondness and professional respect but more frequently with professional jealousy. In either case it exists and the allegations are that such "high vis" officers must be careerists and that they are continually selected over *equally qualified* officers who have not had the benefit of high vis billets.

The relative truth of the high visibility billets is that they are exceptionally demanding. There are highly talented officers who have been very successful in these billets; therefore, they are quite likely to be assigned to another high vis billet that is even more demanding. Do not be too quick to envy such officers, because for every "star" you see on the skyline there are several more "fallen stars." Also, please consider that it is only natural to select and assign the best talent to the so-called high vis billets. However, the bottom line here is that it is most unfair to equate those billets with the term *careerist* as defined—think again of the oath of office.

". . . selecting lieutenant colonels ranks equal in importance to selecting brigadier general. . . . in terms of our doctrine and fighting style it is difficult to imagine anything more important than the selection of our future battalion and squadron commanding officers."

Personal Experience and the Selection Process

My next observations are based on personal experience as a member of an officer selection board. I believe my experience to be typical. My first and most lasting impression of the process was its preeminent fairness. Just ask anyone who has served on such a board and whose opinion you value. Next, I believe that selecting lieutenant colonels ranks equal in importance to selecting brigadier generals. Many may disagree, but in terms of our doctrine and fighting style, it is difficult to imagine anything more important than the selection of our future battalion and squadron commanding officers. And that is the essence of the process I experienced: Do you want and trust this officer to *command* a battalion or squadron in the U.S. Marine Corps?

The fundamental problem, however, is that based on the records there are far more fully qualified majors than there are promotions available. The board process cannot focus on identification of the fully qualified; it must focus on the relative talent and potential among those fully qualified. We ended up voting for those we thought were more highly talented, not more fully qualified.

In the search for evidence of relative talent and potential, all billets provide some clues. In the process I experienced, there was no evidence of relative billet visibility tipping the scales in one direction or another. Talented performance in what could be described as "low vis" billets carried as much weight as talented performance in so-called "high vis" billets. That was true simply because of the nature of the search. Let me cite a couple of typical examples. First, take the Marine aviator. You know he had best be a damn good pilot, a good flight leader—if he is not a real good pilot, his selection probability is nil. However, cockpit skill alone is insufficient evidence of the leadership talent required to command a squadron—we need clues to relative leadership talent on the ground as well as in the air. Normally clues were found in what could be described as "low vis" billets including additional duty billets such as squadron maintenance officer. On the ground officer side of the house the problem was different, but the extent of the search was the same. All billets such as battalion S-4, headquarters, and service company commander, etc., shed insight into the question of relative talent and potential.

If relative billet visibility ever appeared "ready to drive" a selection board, it is conceivable that a "voting mafia" would silently but quickly form and would operate to the disadvantage of officers with high vis billet patterns in all close calls. No words would be needed to form this mafia, no glances exchanged. The composition of such a mafia would probably change or vary from one close vote to another, but every one in the room would know that a voting mafia was functioning.

Although we should not dwell on the selection process too long, I feel obligated to dispel another basic and persistent myth concerning promotion selections. The myth is that one bad or controversial (or even mediocre) fitness report will preclude your selection. That's not true. If my experience is typical, all major to lieutenant colonel boards select some officers (not many but some) with bad or controversial reports in their records. How does that happen? It's simple but not easy. The fact that it does happen is prima facie evidence of the preeminent fairness of the system.

Although the oath I took upon appointment to the board precludes a detailed discussion of exactly how such selections happen, I think it is ethical to share some insight on the nature of the process. The first clue is the statutory wording of the law that binds the board process. In over-simplistic terms, the law requires all eligible officers to be considered. Every single officer must be considered; therefore, his individual case or record must be reviewed, briefed, discussed as appropriate, and considered. The second clue is that the number of cases involving bad or controversial reports is such that each member of the board reviews and briefs one or more controversial cases. In other words, before the deliberations commence, each board member has had the personal experience of investigating and preparing such cases in order to present a fair and complete picture of the officer. The third and last clue lies in the nature of the beast itself, we remain a relatively small institution and with respect to fundamental obligations we tend to function as a social rather than bureaucratic organization.

If you understand this you can easily guess that all reporting seniors and reviewing officers involved in controversial reports are known by, or become known to, the board members—either personally or by professional reputation. Further, if you are not naive in regard to Marine senior officers, you can picture the deliberations of a board as it considers officers with controversial reports. For example, can you picture yourself as a board member withholding information or insight on a reporting senior or reviewing officer involved in a controversial report? I regret that I cannot take these clues any further but I hope you can accept the factual result: some officers with highly controversial reports do get selected.

Company Grade Eyes Only

These last paragraphs of what has become a rather lengthy lesson are exclusively addressed to company grade officers. I have "defended the system" long enough—worn the white hat too long. Now, let's suppose I am dead wrong. Let's assume that all of the allegations associated with creeping careerism are accurate and true in the contemporary Marine Corps. Does that assumption give you a choice between becoming a career-oriented Marine or remaining a mission-oriented Marine? I suggest that you have no choice, and I think I can prove it to your satisfaction. Having spent eight and a half years in the grade of captain, I hope to be able to prove it using a tone and perception that a company grade officer would truly appreciate.

First, there is no guidebook on how to become a successful careerist in the Marine Corps—no reference material of any kind, anywhere—not in your library, not in the Library of Congress. Second, unless you are currently serving as an aide to one of these careerist general officers, you are in no position to observe and learn the skills required to become a successful careerist. I remember who you are, what you are, where you are. You are in the trenches with the troops; you are the leadership "salamies" of the Marine Corps. The term is used here to convey the commonsense or blue collar approach that you employ in executing your daily leadership tasks. It is used with affection, respect, admiration, and envy—but not sympathy. I rejoice to see that you are in no position to observe the white collar leadership of the careerist generals.

Keep in mind that the goal is to become a *successful* careerist, not a failure that could be compared to the promotion-poor, mission-oriented Marine. Lacking a general officer model to emulate, you must select a nearby field grade officer to learn from—be sure of two things: (1) he is a careerist by definition, and (2) you know he is going to become a general officer. Now, if you can do that you have a start and I can offer some sage advice:

- Be very clever, because if you are not, one of your mission-oriented seniors will discover you and call an abrupt halt to your career.
- Be especially wary of your contemporaries—they are obvious enemies not friends. If you are now a captain you already fully understand that you might be clever enough to obscure your career motivation from your seniors but never clever enough to fool your contemporaries. You also understand that your contemporaries can stop your career clock faster than your seniors if they elect to do so.

Have I made my case? If so, be of good cheer, lesson five is a recipe for success not failure: "Fix your mind on your mission and your Marines." I predict that it will guide you to talented performance and promotion—promotion to the exalted ranks of the field grade officer. I further predict that some time during the period in which you are either a relatively senior major or junior lieutenant colonel you will make a very conscious decision about remaining with lesson five (and all that it implies) or becoming a careerist. I predict that you will decide to remain your own man or woman, lead on your own terms with your own style and all of the gusto you can muster. You will "go for the gusto" and willingly let the Marine Corps judge the results in any way it sees fit. My last prediction is that you will never regret the decision.

Summary

The five "lessons learned" can be reviewed in the sequence presented or in reverse order if you prefer. Therefore, a brief summary of the key words is presented in the following sequence:

- Fix—Mind—Mission—Marines
- Keen Awareness—Situation—Terrain
- You—Student—Teacher
- Follow—Lead
- Results

That's it—I have "shot my bolt" on the subject. The summary is left abrupt as an invitation to ponder what has been written. I leave you to form your own conclusions on the relative validity of the lessons. The germane basis of leadership in the Marine Corps today is already in your hands.

Noncommissioned Officers Will Win This War

The Battlefield May Change— But Our Values Are Timeless

Gen. James T. Conway, USMC

Leatherneck
November 2007

Our Corps faces challenges today that are unlike any in our past. Never before have battlefields been more decentralized, our enemy more ruthless, and never have we had more potential for our small unit leaders to determine our success as a Corps.

In Iraq and Afghanistan, the first battles of this Long War, we truly live in the era of the "strategic corporal"—where tactical action by a noncommissioned officer may have strategic consequences. To all our NCOs in the fight, make no mistake, your actions do have impact! You not only affect those serving on your left and right flank today, but also your fellow Marines who will follow you in future rotations.

Our NCO corps is the envy of professional militaries around the world; others can see the tremendous value of our small unit leadership in current operations. Whether fighting a complex insurgency, conducting major disaster relief, or rescuing noncombatants, the collective efforts of well-led Marine units have brought peace and stability to many regions during the opening battles of this Long War. That success will continue to rest on the shoulders of young men and women who wear corporal and sergeant chevrons—in the battles of today and the battles that will follow.

The challenges of combat demand strong leadership at all levels, but in particular where "the rubber meets the road." This is where the Corps has its greatest strength—the steadfast leadership of our NCOs. These small unit leaders reinforce our core values of honor, courage, and commitment—through example and action, and this value system is crucial to winning the Long War. While the battlefields may change, our values will not.

Leadership

The challenge to prepare our Marines for the complexities of a counterinsurgency battlefield, at its essence, is a leadership issue. Marine leaders must do what they have always done to coach, train, and inspire their Marines. Each level of leadership, if we are to function as a well-oiled machine, has a role in mission accomplishment.

Officers, particularly commanders, are responsible for leading their Marines with firmness, fairness, and dignity and creating a command climate that "powers down" responsibility to the lowest level. They must set a bold example for their Marines, particularly in combat. Officers must challenge their Marines to demonstrate moral and physical courage, and in the end, hold all accountable for their actions.

Staff noncommissioned officers provide the experience and mentorship that our Corps needs to maintain its high standards. Their toughness and determination form the bedrock of our combat formations. The genuine concern for Marines under their charge is frequently a reflection of leadership they received when they were young NCOs and pays huge dividends whether in training or in combat.

The NCOs have the toughest tasks of all. They are our 24/7 leadership. In garrison, they are tasked with the maintenance of good order and discipline. In combat, they make hard decisions at the point where strategy meets reality, linking commanders' intents to the actions of their Marines—often in a split second.

Noncommissioned Officers

Marine noncommissioned officers are the critical link in battlefield leadership, they close the final two hundred yards with the enemy—they make decisions where it counts. When I speak with our young second lieutenants at the Basic School at Quantico [VA], I advise them to listen to and learn from those combat-experienced NCOs in the units they will eventually join.

A brand-new platoon commander, by virtue of his rank and position, is indeed the recognized leadership and authority figure for that platoon. However, the battle-hardened corporals and sergeants are often the "informal leaders" within the unit. Frequently, they have one or two deployments to Iraq or Afghanistan under their belts. Many have scars from combat injuries; they have seen close friends killed or severely wounded, and they know the fears and harsh realities of war. In many cases, these NCOs have made life-or-death decisions, or decisions that have had strategic consequences. Marines will invariably look first to these leaders when their unit is in contact.

I am convinced that corporals and sergeants are the best instructors when it comes to rules of engagement and battlefield ethics. These combat-tested warriors have unique insights for young Marines going to the fight for the first time—they have "been there and done that." Of course, with that responsibility comes the need for thorough under-standing of the rules of engagement and an ability to teach them by the numbers. Examples and anecdotes are helpful for instructional purposes, but as a Corps, we must have unity of purpose and a common understanding of the overarching principles of something as important as the rules of engagement.

We all acknowledge that our NCOs have tremendous authority and responsibility in combat zones—our young leaders are literally responsible for the lives and well-being of our Marines. Yet, sometimes, when back in garrison, we strip them of that authority and responsibility, and fail to take full advantage of our NCO leadership. Good order and discipline, training, barracks life, and safety are just some examples of where I believe our corporals and sergeants can do even more than we presently ask.

The challenge for our officer and NCO leadership is to find and maintain that "sweet spot"—where we maximize the skill sets of our NCOs while staying personally and professionally involved in the development and preparation of our Marines for war. I encourage all to keep working at it—we're not there yet.

Challenges of the Counterinsurgency Environment

The Corps has a long history of successful operations in counterinsurgencies—the Banana Wars and our experience in Vietnam are the most notable—and our Corps rightfully takes pride in the innovation and aptitude we brought to these demanding and complex battlefields.

Our enemy on the contemporary battlefield is a cunning and remarkably adaptable foe whose courage at times borders on fanaticism. There is little else about him, however, that commands our respect. He employs vicious murder and intimidation campaigns against civilian communities—and then hides in their midst when we approach. He uses women and children indiscriminately to support his aims—then howls to the media if they are wounded or killed by our fires. He distorts an entire religion to match his own extremist ideologies. This enemy follows no rules of engagement, wears no uniform, and is answerable to no form of higher authority. He murders his prisoners.

Confronted with this despicable conduct on the battlefield, we are appalled by these acts. The worst thing we could do, however, would be to respond to his savagery with our own acts of brutality, because in a counterinsurgency, our enemy is fighting to win the support of the people—he wants to portray us as the bad guys. When we act with the discipline of a professional warrior, we advance our cause and defeat the enemy. Discipline is the hallmark of the professional warrior.

Ethical Mindset and Action

Our success today in Al Anbar province comes as a result of many battalions and squadrons demonstrating, to a watchful population, our discipline and ethical conduct in a most difficult combat environment.

For us to succeed in this Long War, an ethical mindset is an absolute requirement. Success in a counterinsurgency comes from an ethical mindset in action—knowing right from wrong and having a firm moral compass that guides your actions as a Marine.

This mindset cannot—will not—be developed at the moment of action in combat; it must be ingrained beforehand by mature leaders, realistic training, and the steady resolve of a principled warrior. Marines must possess an "ethical muscle memory" to make instinctive decisions when rounds are impacting nearby, it's 120 degrees, and your buddy is bleeding. An ethical mindset frames the problem—then it takes the moral and physical courage of a Marine to do the right thing!

Conclusion

The Marine Corps holds a special place in the heart of American society—and deservedly so. Our reputation is born of epic battles like Belleau Wood, Guadalcanal, and Hue City. Each of these battles occurred in vastly different terrain against skilled and resourceful enemies. Yet, one thing was constant: our young leaders—corporals and sergeants—took the fight to the enemy. In these battles, and others, Marines fought with professionalism and discipline.

I am certain our reliance on our noncommissioned officers will lead to success—they are our strategic center. I challenge NCOs throughout the Corps to carry forward this noble tradition—established by Marines of years past and still alive in the men and women who proudly fight today. Your Corps depends on it!

> *The time always comes in battle when the decisions of Statesmen and of Generals can no longer affect the issue and when it is not within the power of our national wealth to change the balance decisively. Victory is never achieved prior to that point; it can be won only after the battle has been delivered into the hands of men who move in imminent danger of death.* —S. L. A. Marshall

> *We have good Corporals and Sergeants and some good lieutenants and Captains, and those are far more important than good Generals.*—General of the Army William T. Sherman

PART IV

Marines on War

As part of the Navy/Marine Corps team, the Corps deploys "from the sea." However, the understanding of this relationship between the Navy and Marine Corps, while mostly harmonious, has not been without some disagreement. Following the end of the Spanish American War, as the United States emerged as a global power with global responsibilities, there were many, including the president of the United States, Theodore Roosevelt, who believed that the Marines were possibly a thing of the past. Historians Jack Shulimson and Graham Cosmas recounted Theodore Roosevelt's attempt, supported by key U.S. Navy officers, to remove Marines from their traditional place on U.S. Navy warships.

Next is an article by Col. Robert Heinl expressing his concern that the Navy in the modern era is moving away from its ability to support an amphibious assault in favor of other missions.

By all accounts the Marines are a unique and highly capable addition to the national defense force structure. In this regard an outstanding article is once again provided by Gen. Charles C. Krulak. From his perspective as commandant, he notes that Marine forces in partnership with the U.S. Navy provide the nation with a force in readiness that can be "used like a rheostat for the National Command Authorities (NCA) and CinCs—a combined force potency that can be adjusted up or down to meet any mission." In fact, modern day commandants like General Krulak and others have come to see the Marine Air/Ground Task Force as the Marine Corps' premier contribution to the nation's defense force structure.

During the late 1970s and early 1980s, the Marine Corps strongly embraced a concept known as "maneuver warfare." The lethality of modern weaponry and the advent of new technologies caused the Corps to reconsider how it might be employed coming "from the sea" in the future. Lieutenant Colonel E. J. Robeson IV wrote a prize-winning essay that recognized the efficacy of both firepower and maneuver but also the need to effectively combine the two in order to achieve maximum effectiveness on the battlefield.

An Army officer, Col. Douglas A. Macgregor follows up with an outstanding article on initiative in battle. He forcefully argues that blindly following orders of higher headquarters cannot be the guiding principles of small unit leadership in future war. However, Macgregor anticipates, thanks to better and more pervasive telecommunication capabilities, there will be a struggle for dominance between commanders on the scene and higher headquarters and that the only way to overcome this tension is to build trust among the echelons of command.

Colonel E. F. Riley next takes a close look at how the MAGTF is organized for combat. While the details of MAGTF organization have changed over the years, this article is a good resource for readers to gain a basic understanding of exactly what a MAGTF is and what it is capable of doing.

Three Marine Corps generals follow up with a view of twenty-first-century Marines and again reinforce the idea that the Corps provides a capability that is not duplicated by any other force.

The final article in this section was written by Gen. Lewis W. Walt as he prepared to retire from an extraordinarily long and distinguished career with the Marine Corps in 1971. General Walt's message to his Marines remains timeless and powerfully sums up why, despite a number of serious challenges that cropped up in the U.S. military as the Vietnam War drew to a close, the values and military attributes espoused by the Corps transcend changes in ships, weapons, and even personnel.

Teddy Roosevelt and the Corps' Sea-Going Mission

Jack Shulimson and Graham A. Cosmas

Marine Corps Gazette
November 1981

Seagoing Marines owed their salvation at least as much to the cross-purposes of their enemies as to the efforts of their friends.

President Theodore Roosevelt's attempt in November 1908 to remove Marine guards from the warships of the U.S. Navy resulted in a noisy congressional and public controversy. This episode is often depicted as a simple melodrama in which Marines heroically and effectively rose to save their Corps from a cabal of naval officers bent on its destruction. In fact, the issues were more complex and were related to the effort to redefine Marine Corps roles and missions in the twentieth century steam-and-steel Navy. In the larger context, the controversy illustrates both the complex bureaucratic infighting that shaped so much of Progressive Era reform and the growing estrangement between the lame-duck Roosevelt and the Old Guard Republican congressional leadership.

In November 1908, the Marine Corps consisted of 267 officers and 9,100 enlisted men. Approximately one-third of this force was stationed afloat, mostly as guard detachments on warships. Another third was on shore duty outside the continental United States with the largest contingent in the Philippines. The remaining third served within the United States as navy yard guards and constituted a reserve from which expeditionary forces could be organized. Since the Spanish American War, Marine Corps strength had expanded threefold. In the latest increase, in 1908, Congress had added almost 800 officers and men and had advanced the commandant of the Corps to the rank of major general.

While operating under the Navy Department, the Marine Corps enjoyed the legal status of a separate Service. Its staff in Washington, headed by the commandant, was closely allied with the powerful Navy Department bureaus and had a reputation for skillful and effective congressional lobbying. Despite this reputation, Headquarters Marine Corps, in the words of one Marine officer, was "not altogether a happy family." Major General Commandant George F. Elliott, known for his blunt and often hasty speech, was partially deaf and rumored to be overly fond of the bottle. His staff was riddled with intrigue as ambitious, politically connected officers pursued their own bureaucratic aggrandizement. Field Marines often regarded the Washington staff with suspicion. Lieutenant Colonel John A. Lejeune denounced "the politicians stationed at Headquarters" and declared, "Fortunately the real Marine Corps is elsewhere and consists of the 10,000 officers and men who are scattered around the world."

Within the Navy, sharp divisions had emerged between the so-called progressive reformers and the largely conservative bureau chiefs. The reformers, mostly young commanders and captains, favored establishing a Navy general staff, modeled on that recently created for the Army. President Roosevelt generally sympathized with the reformers and had as his personal naval aide one of the most aggressive of them, Cmdr. William S. Sims, yet the reformers usually met frustration at the hands of the bureau chiefs who enjoyed strong congressional support. The reformers generally viewed the Marine Corps, or at least its Washington headquarters, which usually sided with the bureau chiefs, as an obstacle to their plans. One of the more vociferous Navy progressives, Cmdr. William F. Fullam, claimed that "the Marines and the bureau system are twins. Both must go before our Navy . . . can be properly prepared for war."

Since the early 1890s, Fullam had been in the forefront of a movement among naval officers to take Marine guard detachments off the Navy's fighting ships. Fullam and his cohorts especially objected to the use of Marines as ships' policemen, on the grounds that it was an anachronistic holdover from the days of the press gang and was detrimental to the training, discipline, and status of the modern bluejacket.

The Fullamites envisioned a new mission for the Marine Corps within the Navy, once the Corps was freed from its obsolete tasks and was properly organized. The reformers urged that the Marines be formed into permanent battalions and given their own transports, so that they could accompany the fleet either as an expeditionary force or to seize and fortify advance bases. While many Marine officers eagerly embraced the advance base mission, all Marines insisted that the ships' guards be retained. They claimed that service on board warships kept Marines in close day-to-day association with the Navy and provided them with many of the skills needed for expeditionary and advance base duty. By 1908, Fullam's position had gained many adherents among Navy line officers, but Headquarters Marine Corps, with its allies in Congress and the bureaus, had defeated repeated efforts to remove the detachments from capital ships.

By mid-1908, naval reform was in the air. The reformers proposed to a sympathetic President Roosevelt the formation of an independent civilian-military commission to study Navy Department reorganization, specifically the breakup of the bureau system. As key instigators of the commission proposal, Fullam, in command of the Navy training station at Newport, and Commander Sims tried to use Sims' influence with the

President to have the Marines removed from ships. Fullam saw success on the Marine question as "an entering wedge" to break the power of the bureaus. "No legislation and no Congressional action are needed," he told Sims, "but it prepares the way for the new gospel—that the men and officers who go to sea and make the ship, the Navy, efficient must control."

On September 16, Sims, in a long memorandum to the President, outlined the case against the Marines. He reviewed the twenty year history of the issue, emphasizing Fullam's arguments that the use of Marines as ships' policemen undermined the discipline and morale of the bluejackets. Sims cited the fact that the Bureau of Navigation had twice recommended the removal of the Marines, but that "General Elliott goes to the Secretary and successfully combats the proposition." Sims urged Roosevelt to cut through this political tangle by using his executive authority to order the Marines off the ships. He stated, "The effect of removing the Marines from the ships would be electrical, because the demand is universal."

Besides Sims, Fullam used a number of other formal and informal channels to reach the president and secretary of the navy. On August 31, W. D. Walker, editor of *Army and Navy Life* and a close associate of the naval reformers, urged Roosevelt to remove the Marine guards, employing essentially the same arguments as Fullam and Sims. More important, a close Fullam associate, Cmdr. William R. Shoemaker, in the Bureau of Navigation, convinced the bureau chief, Rear Adm. John E. Pillsbury, to revive the Bureau's earlier removal recommendation. On October 16, Pillsbury wrote to Secretary of the Navy Victor H. Metcalf that "the time has arrived when all marine detachments should be removed from . . . naval vessels." Secretary Metcalf brought up the proposal at a Cabinet meeting, and President Roosevelt approved it. On October 23, Metcalf formally concurred in Pillsbury's recommendation and directed that it be carried out.

Up to this point, all those involved in making the decision had carefully avoided consulting or informing General Elliott. Elliott, however, had received hints that the Marines' shipboard position again was under attack. Earlier in October, Admiral Pillsbury had issued an order reducing the size of the Marine guard on one of the battleships. Although Elliott had persuaded Metcalf to rescind this order, he realized that the struggle was far from over. On October 30, he discussed the issue with Sims and stated that he planned to ask Roosevelt directly to "have the pressure stopped." Before Elliott could meet with the president, however, Secretary Metcalf informed the commandant that the Marines were to come off the ships. Elliot at once counterattacked. After an unsatisfactory meeting with Admiral Pillsbury, Elliott, on November 7, made a final appeal to Metcalf. He presented the secretary a long memorandum, prepared by his staff, which declared that:

the proposed removal of Marines from vessels of the Navy is . . . contrary to the long established and uninterrupted custom of the service, contrary to all precedents and rulings . . . contrary to the wishes of Congress, and is based upon no argument which is cogent or potent.

Metcalf rejected the Marine plea and informed the commandant that the president already had decided on removal. Elliott then requested permission to take his case directly to Roosevelt.

On November 9, in his meeting with the president, Elliott found Roosevelt sympathetic to the Marines but firmly committed to their removal. In the course of the conversation, Elliott emphasized that many Marine officers viewed abolition of the ships' guards as the "death knell" of the Corps. Roosevelt asked whether Elliott shared this opinion. Candidly, the commandant replied that he did not. Roosevelt then instructed the general to draw up a statement of the Marine Corps mission once the guards were removed from the ships.

Elliott entrusted the preparation of the proposed order to three officers of his personal staff: Lt. Col. James Mahoney, Lt. Col. Eli K. Cole, and Maj. Charles G. Long. All three were Naval Academy graduates who had been closely associated with the emerging advance base mission. Their draft order avoided mention of the ships' guards and provided that Marines were to garrison navy yards and naval stations within and beyond the continental limits of the United States. Marines were to "furnish the first line of . . . mobile defense" for overseas naval stations, and they were to help man the fortifications of such bases. The Corps was to garrison the Panama Canal Zone and furnish other such garrisons and expeditionary forces for duties beyond the seas as necessary. In an enclosure to the memorandum, the three officers recommended organization of the Marine Corps, once the ships' guards were withdrawn, into 9 permanent 1,100-man regiments. Elliott and his staff obviously were making a virtue out of necessity by trying to stake a firm claim to the advance base and expeditionary role, as well as making an expandable expeditionary organization, while conceding the loss of the ships' detachments.

On November 12, President Roosevelt incorporated the exact wording of Elliott's memorandum in his executive order. The order did not mention ships' guards or call for their removal, although all those concerned understood that to be its intent. During the next several months, the Bureau of Navigation gradually began the removal of the ships' detachments. By early 1909 about 800 of the 2,700 ships' guards had come off.

The immediate reaction to the executive order was predictable. Naval officers generally approved. Upon hearing the news of Roosevelt's decision, Fullam exclaimed,

"Hurrah for the President! God Bless him!" and compared the executive order to Lincoln's Emancipation Proclamation.

Marine officers looked upon the executive order with misgivings at best, and most saw it as a first step toward the elimination of their Corps. One Marine officer stated, "The President's order . . . in effect reduces the Marine Corps to the status of watchmen." Rumors circulated in Washington that Marine officers were organizing to lobby Congress for reversal of Roosevelt's decision. Despite the unhappiness among his officers, General Elliott loyally supported the executive order in public, claiming that it would be "the making of the Marine Corps." On November 16, in response to the reported Marine lobbying efforts, Elliott issued a special order forbidding such activity as "contrary to the motto of the Corps—for 'Semper Fidelis' would be but a meaningless term if it shone only on the sunny side of life or duty."

Even as Elliott publicly looked toward a new role for the Marine Corps within the Navy, Maj. Gen. Leonard Wood, a confidant of Roosevelt and a leading Army progressive, saw the removal of Marines from ships as an opportunity to incorporate the Corps into the Army. Wood and most other senior Army officers were looking for a way to expand the Army's infantry. The Marine Corps had a prominent place in Army proposals for achieving this objective. During 1907, Army Chief of Staff Lt. Gen. J. Franklin Bell floated as a trial balloon a plan to transfer the Army's large coast artillery corps to the Navy (and incorporate it in the Marine Corps). This would leave room in the Army for more infantry regiments. Wood, then commanding general, Division of the Philippines, offered as a counterproposal the simple incorporation of the Marines into the Army. Wood, who had a wide circle of acquaintances within the Navy and Marine Corps, respected Marine military efficiency but had gained the impression that the Navy no longer needed the Corps. Late in 1907, he wrote in a letter intended for Roosevelt's eye that the Marine Corps:

> is an able body, but its desire for enlargement is productive of unrest. A large portion of the Navy are in favor of dispensing with Marines on board ship, . . . their numbers are . . . far in excess of the actual needs of the Navy. We need them in the Army . . .

Neither of these plans had gone beyond the talking stage when Roosevelt's executive order reopened the entire issue of the Marines' future. Wood had just returned to the United States to take over the Department of the East. He was already regarded as the leading candidate to succeed Bell as Army chief of staff. At Roosevelt's invitation, Wood spent several days in mid-November as a house guest at the Executive Mansion. During this visit, Wood pressed upon Roosevelt his view that the Marines should be incorporated into the Army. He argued that Elliott, through the executive order, was aiming to establish an expanded Marine infantry under the Navy Department. Wood pointed out that the president, under his executive authority, could order the Marines to duty with the Army, as had been done temporarily several times in the past. Having established such a fait accompli, Roosevelt at a later time could work out with Congress and the Service Departments the legal details of the transfer. Roosevelt was receptive to Wood's proposal. Already irritated with Marine lobbying, he told his military aide, Capt. Archie Butt, that the Marines "should be absorbed into the Army, and no vestige of their organization should be allowed to remain."

While in Washington, Wood informally discussed his ideas with General Bell and other high-ranking Army officers. He also made an ill-fated overture to two key Marine Corps staff officers, Col. Frank L. Denny and Lt. Col. Charles L. McCawley. Both officers were well known in Washington social circles, and both had strong political connections. Denny, the son of a prominent Indiana Republican, had many Army acquaintances and nursed ambitions to become commandant of the Marine Corps. McCawley was the son of a former commandant and had been the military social aide to Presidents McKinley and Roosevelt. In a chance encounter with the two men on the street in front of the White House, Wood told them that he personally favored transfer of the Marine Corps to the Army and confided that the president was inclined to such a course of action. He asked Denny and McCawley to sound out Marine officer sentiment.

On November 23, Denny and McCawley told the commandant, who had just returned to Washington, about the proposed merger with the Army and the president's tentative support for the idea. Much to their surprise, General Elliott angrily denounced such a move. In a letter of protest to General Wood, Elliott claimed that neither he nor the secretary of the navy had been told of this proposal and declared, "I would as soon believe there was a lost chord in Heaven" as to believe the President, after redefining the Corps' mission, would contemplate separating the Marines from the Navy. Replying to Elliott, Wood reiterated his own support for Army-Marine amalgamation but denied that he spoke for the president.

In a further exchange of letters, Elliott declared that Wood, as an Army general, had no right to discuss disposition of the Marine Corps, which was a separate Service. The commandant insisted that "the entire Army and Marine Corps, with the exception of the general officers, would be bitterly opposed to such amalgamation." Wood apologized to Roosevelt for bringing his name into the discussion and forwarded all his correspondence on the subject. On November 28, Roosevelt, in a letter addressed "Dear Leonard," committed himself on the amalgamation issue. He wrote, "You are quite welcome to quote me on that matter. I think the Marines should be incorporated with the Army." Wood on December 2 flatly informed Elliott that the President supported the transfer. The entire incident convinced Elliott, who up to now had publicly defended removal of the Marine guards, that he and the Marine Corps were being double-crossed. As he later stated, "While we had been following quietly our duties, elimination and absorption were casting unknown to us their shadows at our heels."

Elliott was among the last to learn about Wood's scheme. Almost as soon as Wood had arrived in Washington, the future of the Marine Corps had become a matter of public and private speculation. Fairly accurate accounts of Wood's proposals and Roosevelt's reaction appeared in newspapers and journals. While few Marines expressed any enthusiasm about going into the Army, many thought such a course of action inevitable as a result of the removal of ships' guards. In an extreme expression of this point of view, one officer declared, "It is imperative that we immediately sever every possible connection with the Navy by transfer to some branch of the Army . . ."

The regular House Naval Affairs Committee hearings on the annual Navy Department appropriation provided the scene for the first political skirmish over both removal of the Marine detachments and the merger of the Marines with the Army. On December 9, in his testimony, Admiral Pillsbury flatly stated the Navy Department position: "I think that it will be a very great mistake to put them [the Marines] in the Army. We want them in the Navy. We do not want them on board ship." Although the Marine officers, including General Elliott, made no mention of the subject in their public testimony, Elliott informed the committee off the record that he now opposed removal of the ships' detachments. In perhaps the shrewdest maneuver of the hearing, Lt. Col. George E. Richards, assistant paymaster of the Corps, responding to a prearranged question from a committee member, presented a memorandum estimating that it would cost the Navy Department an additional $425,000 to replace Marines with sailors on board ships. At the end of the session, the committee voted to hold supplementary hearings by a subcommittee on the entire Marine issue.

In the period between the conclusion of the full House committee hearings in December and the opening of the subcommittee hearings in January, the Marine Corps and its allies mobilized for the struggle. Marine staff officers prepared several detailed memoranda supporting their position. On December 20, a group of Marine officers from several East Coast navy yards met privately at Boston to discuss "the new status of the Marine Corps." While they publicly denied that their meeting had anything to do with attempts to reverse the president's executive order, few observers believed they met for any other purpose. Sims and Fullam exchanged rumors and warnings about the Marines' organizing and lobbying efforts. The Army question, meanwhile, faded into the background. Although Wood continued to discuss the subject privately, neither he nor Roosevelt took any overt action. They and the War Department were apparently unwilling to challenge directly Navy control of the Marines if the Navy wanted to retain the Corps.

When the subcommittee began its hearings on January 9, 1909, it was obvious that pro-Marine forces were in control. Representative Thomas S. Butler, who presided over most of the sessions, had a son in the Marine Corps and was on the record as opposing Roosevelt's executive order. The clerk of the subcommittee was a former Marine officer. General Elliott and his staff attended almost the entire hearing, and the subcommittee permitted them to cross-examine witnesses. Commander Fullam described the atmosphere of the proceedings: "The Marine colonels were ever present. A stranger could not have distinguished them from members of the Committee. They rose at will to exhort, object, and cross-examine." Although one-sided, Fullam's observations were in the main correct. He and the other reformers faced a rigged jury and a hanging judge.

Before the hearings ended on January 15, a parade of thirty-four witnesses testified. All of the Marines opposed withdrawal of the guard detachments from ships, while the Navy officers split evenly for and against. Both sides reiterated their traditional arguments for and against keeping Marines on warships. Using rudimentary cost-effectiveness analysis, they presented conflicting estimates of the expense involved in replacing Marines with sailors.

While the subcommittee focused on the cost issue, the question of transferring the Marine Corps to the Army was never far from the surface. Several Marine and Navy opponents of the executive order warned that removal of the guard detachments might lead to the Navy losing the Marine Corps, while supporters of the order affirmed their desire to keep the Marines in the Navy. Fullam, for example, declared, "If I were king here tomorrow, I would preserve the Marine Corps . . . as a splendidly organized mobile force, to serve with the Navy . . ." Secretary Newberry testified that if it were a choice between losing the Marines and putting them back on ship, "I would rather put them back aboard ship." The prospect of absorption of the Marines by the Army was also a stumbling block to congressional supporters of Roosevelt. Representative John W. Weeks, wrote to Fullam: "My mind now inclines to leave in the hands of the Executive the question of where the Marines shall serve, but takes a positive stand against action which will tend to amalgamate the Corps with the Army."

When the full Naval Affairs Committee reported the naval appropriation bill to the House on January 16, it was clear that the Marine point of view had prevailed. The committee recommended insertion in the bill of a provision that: "hereafter officers and enlisted men of the Marine Corps shall serve . . . on board all battleships and armored cruisers, . . . in detachments of not less than eight per centum of the strength of the enlisted men of the Navy on said vessels."

When the appropriation bill came up for consideration before the House, administration forces, assisted by vigorous Navy Department and White House lobbying, turned the tables on the Marines. On January 21 the House passed the bill without the proposed amendment to keep Marines on board ships.

The fight now shifted to the Senate Naval Affairs Committee, where the Marine Corps could depend on the support of the powerful chairman, Sen. Eugene Hale of Maine. Hale, a staunch Roosevelt opponent, was at loggerheads with the president over Navy Department reorganization in general and specifically had come out against taking the Marines off ships. Without bothering to hold hearings on the question of Marine removal, Hale's committee on February 10 reported the appropriation bill to the Senate with numerous amendments, including reinsertion of the House committee's original provision overturning Roosevelt's executive order.

On the Senate floor, the administration made a major effort to defeat the amendment. Massachusetts Senator Henry Cabot Lodge, a personal friend of Roosevelt and long-time supporter of a big Navy, led the fight, liberally supplied with argument and documents by Sims and Fullam. During the Senate debate on February 16 and 17, Lodge restated the reformers' arguments about the need to restructure the Marine Corps, but significantly disavowed any intention to put the Marines into the Army and stated that he himself would oppose any such effort. Senator Hale, on the other hand, kept hammering at the point that Congress had equal authority with the president over the Navy Department and warned that "the underlying purpose [of removal] is to take these people away from the Navy and in the end turn them over to the Army." When the amendment came up for final approval on the 17th, it passed by a vote of 51 to 12. This result reflected more personal and political hostility to Roosevelt than conviction about the status of the Marine Corps. Among the supporters of the amendment were most of the Democrats and a strong contingent of conservative Republicans. All of the opponents of the amendment were either Roosevelt loyalists, such as Lodge, or Republican progressives, including William E. Borah and Robert M. LaFollette.

After Senate passage of the entire bill on the 17th, the legislation went to a conference committee headed by Senator Hale and Rep. George E. Foss, chairman of the House Naval Affairs Committee. As part of the complex bargaining over dozens of amendments, the House initially refused to accept the Senate provision on the Marines. Roosevelt, however, now was willing to surrender on the Marine issue in order to obtain favorable consideration on the other naval issues. On February 18, he wrote to Representative Foss: "The bill as it passed the Senate will, as regards this point, do a little damage [but] it does not do very much." Roosevelt made no mention of putting the Marines in the Army and declared that he had issued his executive order "with the explicit object of retaining the Marines for the purpose of an expeditionary force . . ." With this signal from the president, the House conferees gave way on the

Marine issue. On March 1, both houses passed the naval appropriation bill with the amendment requiring return of the Marine guards to the ships of the fleet.

During the remaining days of his administration, Roosevelt and Secretary Newberry attempted to find loopholes in the language of the appropriation act, which would permit the president to keep the Marines off the ships. Newberry declared, "I have issued no orders about the return of Marines to the ships and will not do so."

The new president, William Howard Taft, was not about to challenge Congress and immediately took steps to reverse Roosevelt's final measures. As early as January 25, the president-elect had taken a conciliatory tone, writing to Senator Hale: "I intend, so far as possible, to do nothing without full consultation with you managers of the Senate, and while of course it is not expected that we may always agree, it may be asserted that we shall never surprise each other."

On April 5, Taft's attorney general, at the Navy Department's request, declared that in his opinion the congressional requirement that Marines make up 8 percent of a ship's crew was constitutional. Very soon thereafter, Marines began marching up the gang-planks of Navy warships, and the controversy was over.

The participants reacted predictably to the outcome. For the Army, it was a case of very little ventured and nothing gained, since Wood's negotiations had been entirely confidential and informal, although quite serious in intent. Some Army officers, never-theless, believed that "a great opportunity has been lost by the restoration of the Marines to the ships." Navy reformers such as Fullam railed against the decision, denouncing the "parlor and club colonels" of the Marine Corps and grumbling that the entire Navy was "at the mercy of the shore-staying staff and their political friends." More moderate reformers, for example the respected Rear Adm. Stephen B. Luce, founder of the Navy War College, warned that withdrawal of the ships' guards would have led to the "oblit-eration" of the Marine Corps. Taking Luce's lead, the Navy's general board in later years would refuse to support the Fullamites in their agitation for removal of the Marine guards on the grounds that such action would lead to the loss of the Corps to the Army. Marines breathed a sigh of relief over what they considered their narrow escape and would cling ever more tenaciously to what was in effect a relatively minor mission. They viewed Fullam and his henchmen with suspicion and often outright hostility and believed they were continually vulnerable to power grabs by ambitious Army and Navy officers. On the occasion of renewed agitation by Fullam in 1913, Maj. Smedley D. Butler exploded in a letter to his Quaker father, Rep. Thomas Butler, who had chaired the special subcommittee in 1909: "I wish somebody would beat the S.O.B. to death. Please try to help us, Father," he pleaded, "for the Lord only knows what will become of our little Corps."

Despite Butler's alone-against-the-world outlook, the Marines in 1908–9 owed their success against Roosevelt's executive order only partially to their own political action. The Marine Corps approached the removal issue with divided councils. General Elliott, obviously influenced by the advance base-oriented members of his informal staff, initially tried to trade acquiescence in the removal of the detachments for a reinforced and expanded. Corps designed around the advance base and expeditionary missions. There was much justice in the accusation, made by both Admiral Luce and General Wood, that the major general commandant was trying to take advantage of Roosevelt's order to establish an army of his own. Probably a majority of Marine officers in the field, as well as key members of the Headquarters staff, adamantly opposed removal of the guards from the beginning. Still other Marines, typified by Denny and McCawley, simply sought to turn the situation to their own personal advantage and flirted, more or less seriously, with amalgamation into the Army. Whether Elliott was simply swayed by the conflicting currents within the Corps or acting from firm conviction is not entirely clear from the evidence. What is certain is that he swung into active opposition to removal of the Marine guards only after becoming convinced that the president had betrayed him.

President Roosevelt did a great deal to frustrate his own order by, in effect, double-crossing both the Marine Corps and the Navy reformers through his dealings with Wood. Even these factors and the Marine lobbying would not have been enough to reverse Roosevelt's order, had it not been for the general anti-Roosevelt hostility of the conservative Republican Senate leadership and the particular enmity of Senator Hale for all manifestations of naval reform. Taft's retreat from Roosevelt's policy toward the Marines foreshadowed the new president's gradual drift into alliance with the conservative faction of the Republican party. In the end, then, the ships' detachments owed their salvation at least as much to the cross-purposes of their enemies as to the efforts of their friends. Perhaps a newspaper's amateur poet had the last word:

> The guard they stood at attention,
> Like they didn't give a damn,
> to hear the word of the Overlord,
> The original great I am.
> And he tells us that we ain't wanted,
> That the jackies will go it alone.
> But I thought I heard an under word
> From a power behind the throne.

The Gun Gap and How to Close It

Col. Robert D. Heinl Jr., USMC

U.S. Naval Institute *Proceedings*
November 1965

On assuming duty as chief of naval operations in August 1963, Adm. David L. McDonald said, "In many ways I believe that our Navy is in better shape today than it has ever been in times of peace."

But if we were to look at the reverse of the coin by asking in which ways our Navy is in *worse* shape today than it has ever been in the past two decades, naval gunfire support would quickly come to mind. Evidently, it has indeed come to the mind of Gen. W. M. Greene, Jr., commandant of the Marine Corps, who has drawn sharp attention to what he referred to as "the gun gap."

Sad but true, ships' gunfire support, now a professionally unfashionable backwater of naval capability, forced to the wall by more glamorous competing weapons and by shipbuilding and development programs preponderantly pointed toward general war, is one of the few significant areas of naval performance in which the Fleet of today (including the Fleet Marine Forces) could not hope to equal the standards of training, of shipboard skill, of planning expertise—let alone results against hard targets—that were commonplace in 1944–5.

The ability of the U.S. fleets to conduct successful opposed landing operations has been taken for granted since World War II. In 1945, a senior officer who should know, Lt. Gen. Tadamichi Kuribayashi, the tenacious and able Japanese commander on Iwo Jima, radioed back to Tokyo shortly before his death: "The firepower of the American warships and aircraft makes every landing possible."

And in 1964, Vice Adm. J. S. McCain, Jr., described amphibious warfare as "a unique means of carrying out our national objectives."

This vital and vaunted capability—that of forcing home any landing attack and of supporting it beyond any question of failure or fall-back—depends above all on firepower. Yet, today, it is at very least questionable, most certainly arguable, whether our active fleets embody the aggregate non-nuclear firepower—be it aviation, guns, or missiles—required to *assure* success in a seriously opposed assault landing.

The Dominant Arm

Among the agencies of amphibious fire support, naval gunfire has been the dominant arm in all past assaults. This dominance can be measured by various yardsticks such as weight of fire, rapidity of response, all-weather capability, economy, uninterrupted availability, and peak power during the beach assault itself. From records of past opposed landings, we know, for example, that the tonnage of ships' gunfire employed on D-Days has been on the order of five to six times that delivered by aviation; and that, even in prolonged, large-scale amphibious battles in which artillery and aviation have been well established ashore and used without stint, the tonnages of ships' gunfire delivered against shore targets have still generally exceeded those from the other arms.

It was Marshal Saxe who said, of weight of firepower, that it took a ton of lead for every enemy casualty. In the eighteenth century, this was probably so. Now the price has gone up. On Guam—a model operation in terms of coordinated employment of fire-power—1.76 tons of bombs or projectiles of all calibers were required to produce each enemy casualty, while, in the Italian campaign of World War II, it has been calculated that from 3.5 to 4 tons of projectile and bomb weight were expended for every casualty.[1] Whether, in future campaigns, the weight of metal necessary to inflict casualties will be that of Maurice de Saxe, that of Guam, that of Italy, or, as might be inferred from all three figures, something still higher, a tremendous bulk of firepower will be needed.

It will thus be clear from the foregoing statistics that the ability to deliver large tonnages of firepower onto any battlefield, especially the amphibious one, is crucial, and that, in the case of amphibious warfare, the means of delivery, which up to the present has consistently been the heavy hauler, is one that we overlook at considerable peril. Yet, this is just what we have been doing. While the nuclear stalemate continues, and with gunboat diplomacy very much alive these days, the most powerful conventional means of firepower should obviously be kept at full availability; but despite this evident fact, and despite an encouraging revival of conventional warfare capabilities in many other fields, our 1945 assets in the realm of naval gunfire support have eroded steadily, even in face of extensive use of ships' gunfire in Korea.[2]

Alternative Possibilities

It is often asserted, usually in general terms without supporting specifics, that air and missiles have largely taken over the role of naval gunfire in amphibious operations,[3] or that "new developments," either classified or unspecified, will do the job. These assertions remain to be proven and supported. So far as I know, there is no way, in a non-nuclear operation, to support an opposed landing today or in the foreseeable future without guns and bombardment rockets in a central role.

Support aircraft, especially of the Marine Corps and Navy, highly trained in precision attack, operating in a rational command framework based on years of combat experience and intended to be responsive to the needs of the landing force, are indispensable in an amphibious operation. However, any type of air support, even the best, is subject to difficulties of control, limited availability, and—if the air effort is joint or combined—inordinate delay and inacceptable response time (those with Korean service will remember that requests for urgent air attacks against fleeting targets or for vital tactical purposes, when processed through the Joint Operations Center, Eighth Army, sometimes involved anywhere from seven to twenty-four hours' delay in response).

In addition, the airplane and its pilot are an expensive team for the delivery of bulk ordnance onto enemy heads. The principle of economy of force, even that of cost-effectiveness, demands that air should be reserved for targets of high priority that cannot be attacked by any other means. Based on past experience, there will always be an ample supply of such targets, fully sufficient to occupy the strike-potential of available aircraft without trying to overextend the role of aviation into areas where less deluxe types of firepower will serve.

Many of the objections just raised against trying to substitute air for naval gunfire apply equally to surface-to-surface bombardment missiles (if any such actually exist in the here and now). But the missile is enormously more costly than the old-fashioned, immensely reliable, 16-inch, high-capacity projectile, whose range is not much less than that of battlefield missiles, whose conventional payload is comparable, and whose accuracy, certainly to date, is as good or better. In fact, at least so far as published reports shed light on the rather stately developmental progress of landing force support missiles, we read only of disappointments—Lance and Taurus, for example—and are left with a distinct impression that the current replacement for the 16-inch gun's proven ability to destroy hard precision-targets is a vacuum.

It has been calculated that within certain ranges it would cost as much as fifty times as many dollars to neutralize a given area using non-nuclear surface-to-surface missiles as it would to do the same job with naval guns and bombardment rockets now in existence.

The words "now in existence" have particular bearing on the possible substitution of bombardment missiles for naval guns. For it appears that, in order to save maintenance dollars, while we have scrapped or mothballed practically all our older ships with heavy (i.e., 8-inch–16-inch) gun power, we have as yet no missile in service, or anywhere near service, which, regardless of cost-effectiveness, is capable of pinpoint destruction of the hard targets that our old battleships and heavy cruisers of 1945 routinely blew sky high.

If our fleets were called on to execute an opposed amphibious operation next week, there would certainly be no doubt that, among the means presently and for some time at hand, the vanishing naval gun would be the most reliable, cheapest, all-weather weapon.

The Gunfire Support Problem

Up to this point, we have considered naval gunfire support almost entirely in terms of materiel, that is, as a problem of ships, guns, ammunition, and competing or alternative materiel systems. Because materiel is the most tangible and therefore readily grasped aspect of gunfire support, it is the portion of the iceberg that we usually see above water.

The truth is, however, that, like the ASW problem, the problem of naval gunfire support, cuts across many fields and extends far beyond questions of materiel. To obtain effective naval gunfire demands specialized personnel, continuous training of ships and landing force units, reliable communications, navigational virtuosity, capable staff and control organization, and considerably more developmental impetus than has apparently been devoted to the subject in some time.

To be more specific, the prime contributing elements of gunfire support are as follows:

Materiel—ships, number and calibers of available guns (i.e., Fleet gun-barrel population, or GBP), magazine capacities of ships suitable for shore bombardment, and ammunition reserves afloat or ashore.

Organization for command and control—a shore fire control and naval gunfire (NGF) liaison organization in the landing force, and full-time representation of the naval gunfire/amphibious gunnery specialty on all amphibious and Fleet Marine Force staffs, and—of special importance—in the headquarters of the chief of naval operations and the commandant of the Marine Corps.

Training—as always the key ingredient, but here more difficult—as in ASW—because of the wide and disparate range of participating agencies and detailed component techniques to be mastered.

Doctrine and development—adequate, up-to-date doctrine, publications and bombardment charts, and vigorous, imaginative developmental effort.

We might reduce the elements just given to a mathematical formula as follows:

$$NGF= (S+GBP+MC+R)+(SFC+LN +STF+HQ) +T+[D+(P+CH) +DVL]$$

Where We Stand

Ships. As noted before, we have scrapped or mothballed a preponderance of the conventionally armed, older heavy ships, which represented our conventional war capability as of 1945. All rocket ships and all ships with batteries heavier than 8-inch guns have either been broken up or are in reserve. As this is written, the major-caliber gun power of the active Navy is down to four heavy cruisers, two of which, the USS *Boston* (CAG-1) and the USS *Canberra* (CAG-2) have each had one of their three 8-inch turrets removed in favor of Terrier missiles. To make a bad situation worse insofar as gunfire support is concerned, the missile-equipped heavy cruisers will very likely be employed with fast carrier task forces or as Fleet command ships, and in either role their 8-inch batteries, so badly needed for bombardment duties, will be effectively lost. Planners, confronted with the necessity of stretching resources, especially in the paper phases of warfare, suggest that the missile-equipped heavy cruisers might well be assigned to provide missile defense of an amphibious objective area and thus be theoretically available for fire-support duties, too. But the whole weight of combat experience shows that whenever a fire-support ship has a second simultaneous mission, fire-support responsibilities tend to be slighted, usually at the worst possible time. Having learned this lesson at some cost during the Gilberts and Marshalls, do we have to re-learn it in the 1960s?

Harking back again to Korean War days, of 1952–3, it is still a painful memory that the only ship in the U.S. Navy then possessing a shore-bombardment fire-control system, USS *Salem* (CA-139), was so badly needed in the Mediterranean that she never got to the Far East, then the only place in the world where shore bombardment was being routinely conducted. Thus was lost an irretrievable opportunity for combat test at Wonsan, for example—of a highly interesting if not revolutionary development in the field of naval gunfire support. This system, incidentally, or its descendents, is now embodied in a few ships, but the majority of those still equipped with guns—and therefore the presumed basis of our remaining fire-support potential—do not have anything of the kind, and will not.

Fleet Gun-Barrel Population (GBP)

While the rapid trend toward a gunless, general-war-configured Navy seems to have been checked or at least slowed down, the net loss of gun-barrels on suitable platforms (i.e., destroyers, cruisers, battleships) is the basic phenomenon which has so gravely eroded the shore-bombardment capability of the Fleet today. Not only have guns given way to missiles on new construction, but also in modifications of existing ships, such as the FRAM program, which, while producing much more effective ASW ships, has, in the case of each 2,200-ton destroyer involved, reduced her trusty 5-inch/38 gun power by one-third (i.e., by removing two out of six guns).

While it is said to be theoretically true that, on a Fleet-wide basis, introduction of the new 5-inch/54 rapid-fire guns in new destroyers offsets the loss of 5-inch/38s in FRAM ships, an acceptable Fleet-wide balance will be small comfort to a hard-pressed battalion being supported by a four-gunned 5-inch/38 ship when the nearest

5-inch/54 is hundreds of miles away in a task force screen. And, in any case, it has been estimated that, if current building, disposal, and ship-modification programs continue as now planned, about three-quarters of even the remaining gun barrels of the combatant ships of the Fleet will be gone by 1975. Then, how do we propose to support amphibious assaults?

Magazine Capacities and Reserves

Obviously the ability to carry a given load of ammunition to the scene virtually determines the amount of gunfire support that can be fired in support of a given operation. Thus, the magazine capacities of the Fleet for gun ammunition imposes fixed limitations, which despite greatly improved techniques for underway replenishment, largely control the scope and tonnage of the naval gunfire bombardment effort. Behind the magazines afloat and the stocks in ammunition ships, lies the factor of national stocks in magazines ashore, and of production actions taken to maintain or augment such stocks. Here again the picture seems bleak. A hasty look at the fleets planned for the 1970s strongly suggests that, if we had to mount a major landing in that period, the then existing magazine capacity of the entire U.S. Navy would not be sufficient to meet the ammunition requirements for one single operation of this kind as supported in World War II. While I have no information on national gun-ammunition stocks or on plans for their maintenance, the structure of future fleets as now visualized hardly renders likely the continuing existence of ammunition stocks on anything like the scale that past experience in amphibious assault has shown will be required.

Command, Control, and Staff Organization

The organization for shore fire control and naval gunfire liaison exists and is in working order. One powerful factor in keeping this portion of the art alive has been the existence since 1949 of the Marine air and naval gunfire liaison company (ANGLICO), one of which is assigned to the Force Troops of the Atlantic and Pacific Fleet Marine Forces, respectively. This unit, composed entirely of naval gunfire and tactical air support teams, has been the principal reservoir of shore fire control skill for the Fleet Marine Forces, in fact for the Armed Forces as a whole. Additionally, of course, the Marine divisions have their own shore fire control and NGF liaison teams, but in 1952 the division ANGLICO was disbanded as an entity by land-minded thinkers who were fresh from Korea's largely non-amphibious war. The lack of an ANGLICO in the Marine division has unquestionably diluted our naval gunfire skills and capabilities and has frequently degraded the division's organic shore fire control parties into the status of "spare parts." Yet, what part of the Marine division, other than the shore party, is more distinctively and uniquely amphibious than its means of obtaining and using the fire support of the Fleet?

Above this level the condition is one of almost unrelieved decay and desuetude. The once active special staff function of the naval gunfire officer at Marine division and FMF headquarters has—even though still remaining in tables of organization—been downgraded in importance or allowed to lapse into the hands of a naval liaison officer. In the amphibious groups a fleet gunnery officer—once a highly trained amphibious gunnery specialist—is now usually just another body, while the gunfire support function has been merged into something called "fire support" or "weapons." The Marine gunfire support officer assigned to each amphibious group is now rarely used in this role, nor is he usually trained or qualified to be so used.

Worst of all, and undoubtedly a main reason for today's problem, gunfire support, as a staff function, was completely unrepresented, for nearly a decade, in the top echelons of the Navy Department. Neither Marine Corps Headquarters nor the Office of the Chief of Naval Operations had a full-time naval gunfire/amphibious gunnery officer billet for at least a decade (1954–1964), although the other supporting arms— aviation, missiles, artillery—had and, of course, have continuing staff representation and specialist advocacy in either or both headquarters. It is no accident that the sharpest period of decline in our naval gunfire support potential has coincided with a period in which this mode of fire support was seemingly not considered important enough to warrant a voice at the top.

(To do Marine Corps Headquarters justice, one of the first personnel actions of General Greene on becoming commandant in 1964 was to reinstate a naval gunfire officer billet in the G-3 Division, thus filling a gap which had existed since 1954. No comparable action has, at the time of writing, been taken in the Office of the Chief of Naval Operations.)

Training

Compared to the tempo of training, which produced the superb naval gunfire support of 1944–5, today's training is insufficiently exacting and insufficiently comprehensive. In many cases, ships have to rush through bombardment exercises as bottom priority items in already overcharged training programs. The exercises themselves, let alone standards of evaluation, do not approach the demands made on World War II fire support ships in the Pacific. Some ships, through combinations of favorable factors, still shoot beautifully and prove that there is no magic in shore bombardment; but, just as the Navy's shooting in Korea was generally poorer than 1945's, today's Navy shoots less and worse shore bombardment than it did in Korea, simply because of lack of training emphasis. Hopefully, however, one hears that the screws are being tightened with regard to bombardment training and that the forthcoming months will bring higher priority and, just as important, higher qualifying standards for ships. We shall see.

As for formal advanced training of amphibious gunnery officers or troop naval gunfire officers—the staff and planning backbone of the system—it simply ceased about ten years ago and has never been revived. The comprehensive naval gunfire officer course, given by Marine Corps Schools for some years, has not been held in almost a decade. This advanced course, attended by Marine, Army, and allied artillery officers, and by Navy amphibious gunnery officers, was the only one of its kind in the world.[4] When it stopped, the supply of professionally trained naval gunfire officers was cut off, and the decline of the art thereby virtually guaranteed.

Another area where effective training has simply stopped—and stopped long ago—is naval gunfire air spotting. Ships of course no longer carry float-planes whose pilots' main job was spotting, while cruiser helicopters find it dangerous indeed to brave today's flak with nothing below them but an auto-rotating descent to a hostile shore. In World War II, the Navy had two superbly trained carrier squadrons (VOF-1 and VOF-2) of high-performance air-spotters capable of surviving flak and fighters, adjusting gunfire and artillery, reading maps, finding and identifying targets. In 1946, this tested expedient was blandly junked.

Doctrine and Publications

Existing doctrines for naval gunfire support, which essentially represent careful distillation of World War II and Korean experience, are solid and tested, and are well stated in today's NWP-22, which owes so much to the unsung work, a few years ago, by Adm. Thomas S. Combs and Gen. Merrill B. Twining and their juniors.

Below the level of NWP-22, the quality of the implementing publications, both Marine and Navy, drops appreciably—sharply, some would say. One overlooked yet critical area of short-fall is that the large-scale charts that are mandatory for accurate naval gunfire support (the 1:25,000 chart, so-called NATO "amphibious chart") are no longer being produced. It is next to impossible to plot precision NGF fire missions with sufficient accuracy on a 1:50,000 chart, no matter how compellingly attractive this magic scale may be from the viewpoint of standardization, production, use by aviators, etc. Here is a problem, probably not unique to naval gunfire support, which has been swept under the carpet and ought to be rethought.

Development. A Navy *Times* article of January 6, 1965, shed presumably unintended light on the state of naval gunfire support development insofar as the needs of today are concerned. With italics supplied by me, here are excerpts from this article obviously intended by its source (described only as "a high ranking Naval officer") to convey the

impression that complaints about the gun gap are wide of the mark and that all's really
right with the world:

> The Navy has ordered full steam ahead on a many-pronged program that, *by the
> mid-1970s* not only will eliminate the "gun gap" but will actually exceed the firepower
> the Marines insist they need . . . a program calling for *development of surface-to-sur-
> face guided missiles* mounted on "super" landing force support ships. . . . Development
> of these ships, *scheduled to make their appearance in 1972–1975,* already has
> begun. Only the incorporation of the *missiles, which must be especially constructed
> and developed,* is holding up *drawing of blueprints. . . .*

This prediction can be translated to read as follows: "If you are prepared to wait ten
years during which we hope there will be no acute need for naval gunfire support, and
if we ever develop a practicable surface-to-surface bombardment missile, we can then
start drawing blueprints for a ship which, if ever funded and built, about 1975, will, we
imagine, have firepower enough to make these Marines stop complaining."

So far as today's—not 1975's—state of naval gunfire and shore bombardment development is concerned, it is difficult, without lifting the curtain of security, to evaluate
the progress of the effort, except to note that few if any major developments in this field
have become known to the Service during the past decade.

A good indicator of the moribund state of naval gunfire doctrine and development—and maybe an important cause of it—is that the once annual Naval Gunfire
Conferences convened in the 1950s under joint Navy/Marine sponsorship have not
been held in many years. Apparently the Navy and Marine Corps did not think they
were worth the per diem involved—or perhaps there are not enough qualified officers
left to attend such conferences.

Are We Fooling Ourselves?

The state of affairs described in the foregoing paragraphs is not an encouraging one.
From the materiel point of view (and here I include development as well) the root of
the problem is one of allocation of funds, effort, and manpower in competition with
the other pressing demands of the Navy. In making such allocations, however, the fact
ought to be faced—and I doubt that it has, or if so, only quite recently—that unless
the continuing degradation of once superlative gunfire support capabilities is not only
halted but reversed, our ability to ram home opposed landings will cease to exist. We
have taken this capability for granted since World War II, and our confidence was
renewed at Inchon, but are we fooling ourselves today?

Well, then—short of recreating and reactivating the 1945 surface Navy, what steps
should be taken to close the gun gap (which, as we have seen, involves so many things

other than guns), to close it now rather than in 1975, and thus revive our drooping amphibious fire support? To readers who have come this far, I hope several possibilities will suggest themselves.

An essential first step would be to halt all decommissionings, conversions, or ship alterations, which reduce the Fleet's gun-barrel population, its magazine-capacities, or other shore bombardment capabilities.

A second step—on which encouraging progress has been publicly reported—would be to recommission additional conventional heavy cruisers in both the Atlantic and Pacific Fleets. The question of reactivating a battleship—probably in the Pacific Fleet—ought to be carefully considered. According to press reports, we are now regularly conducting shore bombardment in Vietnam, using 5-inch and 6-inch guns. Think how much greater return we could realize from the virtually doubled range inland and enormously multiplied hitting power of 16-inch projectiles, and how much more economical such gun strikes would be than air attacks against the same targets.

If outright activation is too much for the present, why not raise at least one reserve fleet battleship to readiness for recommissioning in thirty to forty-five days? And, while we are talking about recommissioning, it seems little short of foolhardy that not one rocket ship remains active. For the state of the art alone, the single IFS ought to be recommissioned; for the state of our amphibious capabilities, it would be better to have one active rocket division, even at reduced strength, on each coast.[5] It would also be good to have a shore bombardment computer and fire control system in every ship—*destroyers especially and particularly*—mounting guns that might be used in gunfire support.

Obviously, another step should be to reinvigorate and add thrust to research and development projects dealing with amphibious fire support. If cruisers and battleships—our only present means of destroying hard targets—are too expensive, then we should be thinking of alternatives, such as the "super landing force support ship" bruited earlier. Maybe the monitor concept, which the British used, with considerable technical ingenuity, even in World War II, deserves examination as a source of heavy, long-range naval gunfire on the cheap. (However, we should be wary of creating single-purpose ships unless very clear and special superiority is shown; much of the Navy's genius and capability stems from the all-around flexibility and usefulness of ships in many different roles.) And what about Admiral McCain's imaginative proposals for "commando ship" conversion of existing battleships?

Hand-in-hand with the moves just proposed are required a number of less obvious but equally important actions in the interlocking fields of people and training. Among these, the unquestionable top-priority step would be to add a full-time amphibious gunnery billet to the CNO's staff just as a full-time naval gunfire officer has recently been detailed to Marine Corps Headquarters. Such a step, which would cost so little

compared to the big materiel actions, would exert a healthy influence out of any proportion to the weight of the billet.

Annual Naval Gunfire Conferences should be recommenced at Quantico without
delay; this is something that could be done in the summer of 1966—but will it?
Advanced-level naval gunfire schooling is direly needed. This deficiency could quickly
be met by reconvening Quantico's naval gunfire officer course with an input of mid-
rank Marine and Navy officers of suitable background.

Assuredly, the air and naval gunfire people within the Marine division should be
regrouped into a reconstituted division ANGLICO; until we do so, can we honestly
describe a Marine division as amphibious? Training requirements for fire-support ships
should be given higher priority, shore-bombardment qualification standards should
be raised, and existing bombardment exercises ought to be continually reviewed for
possible improvement.

A long bill of particulars and an expensive list of recommended actions, you say?

True enough.

But if we are not prepared to pay for fire support on a scale, which is adequate to
underwrite success in opposed landings, then we should accept squarely that, whatever
amphibious capability we now possess, it will soon no longer be one of assault.

---

1. World War II records kept by the Naval Gunfire Section, FMF Pacific, indicate that some 172,000 tons of
   naval gunfire support projectiles were fired in landings during the Central Pacific Campaign.
2. During a ten-month sample period in Korea, in 1951–2, the Navy fired 24,820 naval gunfire missions,
   approximating 1,500 tons of projectiles, against shore targets.
3. An example of such claims was that of the Eighth Air Force during the fire-support planning for Normandy
   (Omaha Beach) in 1944. Air planners, claiming an all-weather precision bombing capability, took on the
   massive "beach-drenching" role normal to ships' guns. On the night before D-Day, when heavy overcast
   was predicted, and without informing the landing force, the air commander ordered a one-minute delay
   in dropping bombs, so as to ensure troop safety. As a result, the thousands of tons of bombs, which the
   troops expected to plaster the formidable German beach defenses, fell three to five miles inland on French
   pastures. The fearful—and largely unnecessary—casualties on Omaha Beach are a matter of record.
4. As a matter of historical interest, the lone British graduate of this course was abruptly ordered home from
   Hong Kong in 1956 to prepare the fire plan and act as force naval gunfire officer for the Suez landing, a role
   which he filled with distinction.
5. As this article goes to press, information has been received that four rocket ships, including the one IFS, are
   to be reactivated during the forthcoming fiscal year. If correct, this is a highly encouraging development.

The United States Marine Corps

Our Nation's Force-in-Readiness for the 21st Century

Gen. Charles C. Krulak, USMC

Marine Corps Gazette
April 1998

In 1952, the 82d Congress, armed with fresh memories of near disaster in the opening days of the Korean War, engaged in a spirited debate over the readiness posture of the U.S. military. Vowing that the Nation would never again be put in the position we were in during June, 1950, the Congress called upon the Marine Corps to fulfill the following special role.

> . . . American history, recent as well as remote, has fully demonstrated the vital need for the existence of a strong force-in-readiness. Such a force, versatile, fast-moving, and hard-hitting . . . can prevent the growth of potentially large conflagrations by prompt and vigorous action during their incipient stages. The nation's shock troops must be the most ready when the nation is least ready . . . to provide a balanced force-in-readiness for a naval campaign and, at the same time, a ground and air striking force ready to suppress or contain international disturbances short of large scale war. . . .

For the past fourty-six years, the Marine Corps has provided that force-in-readiness in both peace and in war. Today, as we stand on the brink of the twenty-first century, the strategic landscape unfolding before us appears vastly different than it did during the Cold War. The vacuum created by the demise of the Soviet Union has created new challenges for the United States, forcing us once again to analyze and debate our national security requirements.

U.S. Defense Strategy Reviews

Two comprehensive and far reaching studies concerning future U.S. military requirements were successfully completed in 1997. These efforts, the Quadrennial Defense

Review (QDR), and the National Defense Panel (NDP), were chartered to ensure that the United States remains capable of shaping the future security environment, instead of merely reacting after the fact. Significantly, both the QDR and NDP validated the traditional role of the Marines and pointed out that the Corps, as one would expect from the nation's force-in-readiness, was already developing the capabilities needed to prevail in the next century.

The QDR and NDP both characterize the next century as one of crisis, conflict, and chaos in the littorals brought on by rapid economic growth, increased competition for limited resources, terrorism, technological diffusion, exponential growth in urban populations, nationalism, ethnic and religious strife, and increasing access to modern conventional weaponry and weapons of mass destruction. The Marine Corps is in complete agreement with those assessments and has been actively preparing for just such an operating environment for some time. As our nation's force-in-readiness, we must be prepared for the dangers inherent in the age of uncertainty that is forecast by these projections.

The QDR faced the difficult challenge of constructing a strategy that could simultaneously shape the current security environment, respond rapidly to emerging threats, and prepare the Department of Defense (DoD) for the long term. The QDR calls for "flexible and multimission capable" forces to respond to the full range of crises, not just the high end of the conflict spectrum. Furthermore, it stresses the need for forces that can address multiple small-scale contingency operations and are able to transition rapidly from one end of the spectrum of conflict to the other. Naval forces are ideally suited for this purpose, based on their flexible, multimission characteristics. Additionally, naval forces require no permission to enter an area of impending crisis. There are no issues of sovereignty involved with the deployment of naval forces, and they can be sustained in the area for extended periods of time. Furthermore, mobile sea-based forces are far less vulnerable than land-based forces.

As the element of naval power that operates along and across the interface between land and sea, Marine forces complete that multidimensional aspect of presence needed by the regional/unified commanders (CinCs) for effective crisis resolution. From various types of military-to-military contact to simply signaling resolve, and from disaster relief to high-intensity combat operations, Marine forces provide the range of capabilities that allows a sea power to compensate effectively for the absence of permanent overseas bases.

The United States has been, and will continue to be, the world's critical guarantor of stability through its forward deployments of credible combat power. At the same time, we cannot assume that we can continue to conduct business as we have in the past. The methods and strategies by which we established presence during the twentieth century may no longer suffice in the future. While our allies rely on us to provide military forces to maintain stability and security, they are coming under increasing pressure to reduce the numbers of American land-based personnel and their supporting infrastructure. We have seen this in the Middle East, Panama, the Philippines, Japan, and throughout Europe.

Regional stability requires the United States to maintain a credible presence, but political dynamics may not allow us access to, or the use of, the traditional land bases and facilities to which we have become accustomed. If U.S. military presence is critical to stability, then we must ensure we have the flexibility and the means to project decisive military force across the range of operational situations, with a force whose basing posture is acceptable to our allies. The forces best suited to provide this flexibility and acceptability are sea-based forces.

Why? Traditionally, sea-based forces have been looked on as politically and culturally acceptable because they are viewed as transitory in nature and have a lighter political footprint. Furthermore, such forces are free to deploy rapidly to situations elsewhere in a region and are not formally tied to a single mission. Designed to operate from both land and sea bases, Marine forces, in concert with the Navy, provide a tailorable, on-scene team that can deter a threat to stability, conduct assistance operations, or participate in a major theater war. In many ways, Navy and Marine air, land, and sea forces can be used like a rheostat for the National Command Authorities (NCA) and CinCs—a combined force potency that can easily be adjusted up or down to meet any mission.

An Operational Concept for the 21st Century

In recognition of this changing security environment, the Navy and Marine Corps revised our strategic direction with the publication of ". . . From the Sea" in 1992, and "Forward . . . From the Sea" in 1994. These two documents frame the Navy-Marine Corps vision. The Marine Corps will execute this vision using the operational concept, operational maneuver from the sea (OMFTS), published in January 1996. The heart of OMFTS is the maneuver of naval expeditionary forces at the operational level of warfare to exploit enemy weakness and deliver a decisive blow. It combines high technology with maneuver warfare and is enabled by the advantages of sea-basing. These forward-looking responses to evolving world events are designed to ensure naval forces maintain superior capabilities in the projection from the sea of decisive power and influence ashore across the spectrum of peace, crisis, and war expected in the century ahead.

Joint Vision (JV) 2010 was issued in 1996 to provide the chairman of the joint chiefs of staff's (CJCS) strategic direction for the Armed Forces to achieve new levels of effectiveness through joint warfighting. The U.S. military's overall strength as a fighting force is ultimately a function of Service competencies, each reflecting distinctive capabilities, cultures, and traditions. Additionally, these core competencies offer a diverse set of options to the NCA and the CinCs. In this regard, the operational themes called for in JV 2010 are entirely compatible with OMFTS. The operational pillars explicit to JV 2010 (dominant maneuver, precision engagement, focused logistics, and force protection) are all embedded within OMFTS. By using the sea as a maneuver space, both dominant maneuver and force protection are enhanced. The use of over-the-horizon sea bases to minimize the logistics buildup ashore during power projection operations also enhances force protection, while relying upon focused logistics to sustain the maneuver force from its secure sea base. Additionally, OMFTS will use weapons with significantly improved range, accuracy, and lethality for precision engagement.

Core Capabilities

Articulating what the Marine Corps does to support our national security strategy and how we operate is best accomplished by examining our core competencies. With over 222 years of expeditionary experience, including the last 46 as the nation's legislated force-in-readiness, these six core competencies define the essence of our unique institutional culture and role within the National Military Establishment:

Expeditionary Readiness: This quality stems from an institutional mindset and organization that holds itself ready to respond at once to any worldwide crisis, 365 days a year. This expeditionary mindset implies a Spartan attitude—an expectation and a willingness to endure, in fact a certain pride in enduring hardship and austere conditions. As an example of this attitude, in most Marine Corps units, embarkation boxes substitute for bookcases, locker boxes are packed, and our packs are filled and at the ready. In essence—as an organization—we are ready to go at a moment's notice. To Marines, this orientation is characterized by three things. First, it means being ever ready to transition from peace to war without Reserve augmentation and ready to win our nation's first battles. Second, it means being committed to innovation, continuously anticipating evolving strategic challenges, and preparing to defeat the "opponent after next." Third, it means being an adaptive force with leadership that is trained to improvise and capable of flourishing under conditions of extreme uncertainty.

Combined Arms Operations: The nation's premier crisis response force must be capable of acting on short notice and without immediate support from other warfighting forces. While we are fully capable of, and frequently practice, operating as part of a joint force, many times we arrive at the scene of a crisis before the rest of the joint force can arrive. It is for this reason that the Marine Corps requires an organic, balanced combined arms capability. Marine air-ground task forces (MAGTFs) have trained for more than a half century so that their ground combat, air combat, and combat service support capabilities are cohesively led by a single commander. Because MAGTFs operate as a joint force in microcosm as part of their everyday operations, it allows them to seamlessly integrate into the combined arms nature of joint force operations when required.

Expeditionary Operations: The key to achieving success on foreign soil is the ability to sustain combat and noncombat operations without host nation assistance. This ability to rapidly project force requires a special mindset, one that is continuously prepared for immediate deployment into an austere environment. Marine forces arrive at the scene of a crisis with what they need to get the job done. Any resources available from the host nation are considered a luxury. This mindset drives the design, development, and acquisition of everything from individual equipment to expeditionary airfields and hospitals—of everything necessary to accomplish a wide variety of missions.

Sea-Based Operations: Unlike any military force in the world, the naval character of the Navy-Marine Corps Team singularly gives our nation an enduring means to shape and influence global events. Sea-based operations provide extraordinary strategic reach to shape events and provide units with a large measure of inherent force protection. A highly ready, combined arms MAGTF, operating from mobile sea bases provides the NCA with politically unencumbered access to global trouble spots.

Forcible Entry from the Sea: Ultimately, a global superpower must possess the ability for unilateral action. A key requirement is the capability to project power ashore in the face of armed opposition. In the past, forcible entry from the sea was defined by amphibious assaults that focused on establishing lodgments on the beach and then building up combat power for subsequent operations. Forcible entry is now defined as the uninterrupted movement of forces from ships located far over the horizon directly to decisive objectives, whenever and wherever we desire.

Reserve Integration: Although a force-in-readiness cannot pause to call up its Reserves during an emerging crisis, Marine Reserves have continuously met the challenge of quickly integrating into the MAGTF team. As a part of the Total Marine Force, our Reserves have also recently assisted and augmented our forward presence around the globe. Marine Reserves routinely practice carefully crafted Reserve integration plans to augment or reinforce crisis response missions and add vital combat power, especially at the high end of the conflict spectrum. With common training, standard equipment, and identical combat readiness criteria, Marine Reserves represent a highly professional force multiplier for the NCA to call upon.

Navy and Marine forces provide self-contained and self-sustained air, land, and sea forces capable of operating from a protected sea base. We are structured to meet a range of contingencies including presence, humanitarian operations, evacuation of noncombatants, peacekeeping, and warfighting. We are compact enough to respond rapidly and yet heavy enough to get the job done. Most important in this increasingly uncertain world, the combined Navy-Marine team provides the NCA with enormous flexibility in their pursuit of national security interests.

First to Fight in the 21st Century

The words from the 82d Congress remain as sound and relevant today, as they did in 1952. The Marine Corps has always had a global outlook that transcended any particular scenario or threat. Instead, we have steadfastly focused on our statutory role to serve as the nation's premier crisis response force. Our role is to be prepared to be the first on the scene, first to fight, first to quell disturbances, and first to help, both in the United States and abroad. Our experience has taught us that the only common denominator for the types of missions expected of a force-in-readiness is an immutable commitment to be ready for worldwide commitment 365 days a year. Anything less is inconsistent with our ethos, our core capabilities, and the expectations of the American people. The Marine Corps has not failed them in the past—and it will not fail them in the future. The United States Marine Corps is, and will remain, our nation's premier force-in-readiness.

Forrest War: Putting the Fight Back...

Lt. Col. E. J. Robeson IV

Marine Corps Gazette
August 1986

War is far more complex than either the firepower-attrition or maneuver warfare models suggest. The campaigns of Maj. Gen. Nathan B. Forrest illustrate a third model that could prove devastating on the modern battlefield if we master the characteristics that made him successful.

The debate over the conflict in Indochina has prompted a renaissance in American military studies and has yielded essentially two schools of thought on how wars have been successfully fought throughout history; they are popularly known as maneuver warfare and firepower-attrition warfare.

The maneuver warfare school has been particularly vocal in advocating its position and in castigating firepower-attritionists. In fact, the debate has been singularly one-sided. Few strategists would openly advocate pure firepower-attrition (although several prominent leaders have come close in practice). Moreover, the skeptic must ask whether the firepower-attrition school is really nothing more than a "straw man" alternative developed by the maneuverists, for it has many detractors and no known champions.

I believe that warfare is much more complex than either of these two models suggests, and we should actually be striving to implement a third alternative. Let's call it "Forrest war," in honor of one of its foremost practitioners, Maj. Gen. Nathan Bedford Forrest, Confederate States Army (CSA).

Forrest war recognizes that both firepower and maneuver are essential components of warfare and that they must be integrated to obtain maximum effectiveness. Certainly, no one in the maneuver warfare school would argue with that; but there is a funda-mental difference. Forrest war also postulates that firepower is not only essential, but that it must always come first. This is true because of the realities of war, especially at the level of the individual combatant. For the infantryman on the ground, every attack is a frontal assault. Here, weapons are for killing, wounding, or causing the enemy to cower. Assertions that a rifle is not for killing, but should be principally regarded as a means to maneuver are simply ludicrous. (Only when the rifle butt is placed under the arm and used as a crutch could a rifle be considered as a means to maneuver.) In truth, it is only after the enemy has been dominated by aggressiveness and firepower that maneuver can become an effective option at all. Educating the enemy to the consequences of firepower can be a brutal, personal struggle; but, if it is successful, it will make him susceptible to maneuver. General Forrest understood this very well and knew how to fully implement this third style of warfare to which we have attached his name.

Six characteristics quickly become apparent in an analysis of the art of Forrest war. These are: l) fearsome reputation, 2) preparation and positioning, 3) surprise, 4) physical dominance through firepower, 5) moral dominance through maneuver, and 6) pursuit. Let's look at each of these in turn.

General Forrest initially gained reputation during the fight for Ft. Donelson, where Union forces captured the Confederate garrison with one notable exception: Forrest's command, which was then a Tennessee cavalry regiment. Here, in February, 1862, strong winds, sleet, and snow brutalized the Confederate garrison trapped inside the fort by superior Union forces. Forrest and other junior commanders advocated a breakout attempt, but the senior leadership faltered, even after the initial Confederate attacks were successful, and decided the garrison should be surrendered. As R. U. Johnson writes in his history of the Civil War:

> Colonel Forrest promptly announced that he neither could nor would surrender his command. He requested permission from General Pillow to cut his way out. He assembled his men, all as hardy as himself, . . . moved out and plunged into a slough formed by backwater from the river. An icy crust covered the surface, the wind blew fiercely, and the darkness was unrelieved by a star. There was fearful floundering as the command followed him. At length he struck dry land, and was safe. He was next heard of at Nashville.

Brice's Crossroads, 10 June 1864

The movement of Union troops southward from Tennessee, resulting in the battle of Brice's Crossroads, was ordered by Maj. Gen. William T. Sherman, USA, who hoped to trap Maj. Gen. Nathan B. Forrest in the reaches of Mississippi and thus prevent him from interfering with his campaign in Georgia. Sherman feared that Forrest would attack key rail lines in central Tennessee with the disastrous effect of disrupting main supply routes supporting his advance into Georgia. He, therefore, directed Brig. Gen. Samuel D. Sturgis to lead his troops from an attack and hold Forrest in Mississippi. Sturgis' efforts were unsuccessful, as were subsequent missions under the command of Maj. Gen. Andrew J. Smith, whose infantry column was repeatedly rebuffed by Forrest until it was recalled in late August 1864, Forrest's advances in northern Mississippi, western Tennessee, and northwestern Alabama continued with relative impunity throughout the remainder of 1864. But Sherman, too, succeeded with his plans, having marched through Georgia and occupied Atlanta by 1 September 1864.

It is from such character and stamina that the first requirement for successful prosecution of Forrest war is derived—the establishment of a fearsome reputation.

Cultivating this irreplaceable commodity is also essential. It can only be done through demonstrated excellence in the performance of duties in the field. Forrest accomplished this at the end of the Battle of Shiloh in April 1862. Forrest's cavalry regiment was assigned to cover the Confederate retreat, but even here, he was a dangerous opponent. When Forrest noticed momentary confusion in Sherman's pursuing infantry, he ordered an immediate charge. Firing their double-barreled shotguns, Forrest's men rode over their opponents, shooting down men by the score. Sherman himself, says W. Sword in *Shiloh: Bloody April:*

... was caught in the tumult and nearly killed. He said "My aide-de-camp was knocked down, horse and rider, into the mud, and I and the rest of my staff ingloriously fled pell mell ... closely followed by Forrest and his men. . . ."

It was for actions such as these that Sylvanus Cadwallader in *Three Years with Grant* observed:

Forrest was the only one whom Grant sincerely dreaded, largely because he was amenable to no known rules of procedure, was law to himself for all military acts, and was constantly doing the unexpected, at all times and places.

An excellent case study that clearly demonstrates all six tenets of Forrest war can be found in the Battle of Brice's Crossroads, MS, which took place from June 10–12, 1864, between the forces of Maj. Gen. Nathan Bedford Forrest, CSA, and Maj. Gen. Samuel Davis Sturgis, USA.

By May 1864, Sherman had advanced deeply into the South and was becoming increasingly concerned over the vulnerability of his lines of communication to Forrest's predations. Having previously met him at Shiloh, Sherman wrote to Sturgis, "I expect to hear every day of Forrest breaking into Tennessee from some quarter." Forrest's reputation had not been lost on General Sturgis either. When ordered to tie up Forrest in Mississippi, he reported:

The force sent out was in complete order and consisted of some of our best troops. . .
I saw to it personally that they lacked nothing to insure a successful campaign. The
number of troops deemed necessary by General Sherman, as he telegraphed me, was
6,000, but I sent 8,000.

In fact, Sturgis sent 8,300—3 brigades of infantry, 2 of cavalry with the latest
repeating carbines ("which would give them a big advantage in firepower over their
butternut opponents") and 22 field artillery pieces.

This force left Memphis on June 1 in an unrelenting rainstorm that soaked the
men and flooded fields and roads, and began to slowly move south toward Tupelo,
Mississippi.

At Tupelo, Forrest made known his presence in the area (characteristic 1), permitting his previously established reputation to begin to prepare the terms of the battle. He
then demonstrated the second characteristic preparation and positioning by collecting
his 4,800-man division for the fight.

A study of the terrain, possible Union objectives, and the axis of advance of the
Union troops provided Forrest the intelligence he needed to complete his prepara-
tions and position his force. He chose his battlefield just south of Tishomingo Creek,
Mississippi, now flooded by a week of rain, at Brice's Crossroads.

Meanwhile, Sturgis' forces continued to crawl along through the nonstop deluge
and muddy roads. Discouraged by his progress, as well as by the thought of all the
Confederate troops gathering ahead, Sturgis remarked in his official report that his
delay could provide time needed by the rebels to "concentrate an overwhelming force
against us." Like Sturgis, Forrest was also having thoughts about the comparative force
ratio. Even though Sturgis would have almost a two-to-one advantage in men, and
three times as many artillery pieces, Forrest believed that boldness and the nature of the
terrain, which he knew well, would make up for the numerical odds he faced. He said:

> I know they greatly outnumber the troops I have at hand, but the road along which they
> will march is narrow and muddy; they will make slow progress. The country is densely
> wooded and the undergrowth so heavy that when we strike them they will not know
> how few men we have. . . . Their cavalry will move out ahead of their infantry and should
> reach the crossroads three hours in advance. We can whip their cavalry in that time. As
> soon as the fight opens, they will send back to have the infantry hurried in. It is going to
> be hot as hell, and coming on the run for five or six miles, their infantry will be so tired
> out we will ride right over them.

Forrest's sensitivity to weather and terrain is clearly seen in this analysis. He had selected a battleground to which the enemy had only one avenue of approach, the narrow, muddy Guntown Road that crossed the flooded Tishomingo Creek bottom on an elevated dirt causeway before climbing for about one-half mile in a southerly direction to Brice's Crossroads. It was near this intersection that Forrest intended to meet the enemy, but from an easterly direction, requiring the Union forces to make a 90 degree turn as they entered the battle area. This radical change of direction would most assuredly create problems of command and control. Next day, as the rising sun began to bake steam out of the muddy fields and roads, Union cavalry moved up the hill to the crossroads to find a sense of foreboding in the air.

Forrest's march to this same location had begun well before dawn in the cooler hours of the day and on as many parallel routes as were available, for he had over twice as far to come.

Forrest initially had few forces available, but he opened his attack suddenly with lines of dismounted gray soldiers moving rapidly forward and fixing the lead Union cavalry units in position. These vicious frontal assaults were merely designed to buy time for his units to close and force General Sturgis to commit his entire force. In this, he was eminently successful. The Union cavalry brigade commanders were soon desperately crying for reinforcement or relief, and Gen. Benjamin H. Grierson even asked that his division be withdrawn, as it was being "overwhelmed by numbers" and was "exhausted and well nigh out of ammunition for its rapid-firing carbines." In fact, however, the Confederate "desperate charges" were being successfully conducted against Union forces that were much larger and that overlapped the Confederates on both flanks; the Union forces had six cannons in action and four more in reserve, while Forrest's guns had not yet arrived.

Meanwhile, on Guntown Road, the Union infantry brigades were marching to the sound of the guns. They were being hurried along by their officers and staff noncommissioned officers through the Mississippi summer heat. General McMillian was among the first to arrive at the crossroads, leading his infantry brigades and finding:

> . . . everything was going to the devil as fast as it possibly could, he [McMillian] threw caution to the winds. Though many of his troops had already collapsed from heat exhaustion on the hurried approach march, and though all were blown and in great distress from the savage midday, mid-June Mississippi sun, he sent preemptory orders for his two front brigades to come up on the double quick and restore the crumbling cavalry line before the rebels overran it.

With these actions, Forrest had achieved the third important characteristic of surprise.

Physical dominance through firepower had become the key concern. Forrest had closed all his units on the battlefield, and he rode along putting the fire of battle into his lines of soldiers lying on the line of departure. At the bugle call, he had them up and surging forward. It was a brutal frontal assault, and everywhere "there was a grim struggle, much of it hand to hand, before the contest reached the climactic point and the time came to hit 'em on the ee-end." The stage was set for the fifth characteristic—moral dominance through maneuver.

Forrest committed his final reserves, small units who were sent simultaneously around the right and left flanks of the Union lines to gain their rear. Because of the carnage occurring to their front, even veteran Union brigades were now susceptible to dislocation, and these actions ". . . made the whole line waver and cave in, first slowly, then with a rush." As General Sturgis related in his official report:

> Order gave way to confusion and confusion to panic. . . . Everywhere the army now drifted toward the rear, and was soon altogether beyond control.

The Confederate battery along with a captured Union cannon were now playing with deadly effect along the Union escape route, and the closely pursuing Confederates ensured ". . . that every attempt to make a stand only brought on a new stampede."

As General Sturgis related to Col. Edward Bouton during this retreat, ". . . for God's sake, if Mr. Forrest will let me alone, I will let him alone." Forrest, however, had other ideas. He directed his commanders to "keep the skeer on 'em," and they did just that, past sunset and on into twilight and full night. Forrest later reported that after 8 PM:

> It being dark and my men and horses requiring rest, . . . I threw out an advance to follow . . . after the enemy, and ordered the command to halt, feed and rest.

Pursuit was now in full operation, and unlike his contemporaries of that era, he did not see darkness as an insurmountable obstacle to further combat operations. By 1 AM, Forrest had his troopers back in the saddle and hard on the equipment-littered trail.

By dawn, Forrest caught up with the last Federal rear guard about four miles south of Ripley, Mississippi, and smashed it. His official report stated:

> From this place, the enemy offered no further organized resistance, but retreated in the most complete disorder, throwing away guns, clothing, and everything calculated to impede his flight.

One Union commander described it thusly:

On we went, and ever on, marching all that day and that interminable second night . . .
we marched, marched, marched, without rest, without sleep, without food.

An Ohio regimental commander reported that his troops became so stiffened they needed assistance to walk. Some of them crawled upon their hands and knees. These accounts are starkly indicative of the dangers that come when units are both physically and morally beaten.

As one Union cavalry major put it:

> . . . it is the fate of war that one or the other side should suffer defeat, but here there was more. The men were cowed, and there pressed upon them a sense of bitter humiliation, which rankles after nearly a quarter of a century has passed. . . Just over 8,000 troops had been thrown into a rout and driven headlong for nearly a hundred miles by just under 5,000.

What can we learn today from this exhilarating victory and tragic defeat?

First, success in combat requires all excellent professional reputation that is only obtained in peacetime through hard, uncompromising training. Secondly, preparation and positioning of friendly forces for battle must ensure that they will end the initial engagement where they are advantageously deployed for the next event. (Every billiards player understands this instinctively as he lines up his "next" shot with his current one.) This, of course, often requires modification of the open-ended mission-type orders that the maneuver school advocates. Stipulating the commander's intent for the current battle is important, but ensuring that subunits are properly positioned for the next sequence of engagements is essential. This often requires specific instructions that detract from the freedom of subordinates. Maneuver warfare extremists decry such "how-to" instructions, but a Forrest war proponent would counter that there is a middle ground between chaos caused by subunit "free play" and rigidity caused by instructions that are unnecessarily restrictive. When Forrest chose Brice's Crossroads as his battleground, he positioned his brigades so that he could meet the enemy there or respond to enemy initiatives elsewhere. He also enhanced the effectiveness of his surprise by permitting the enemy to extend before he struck at an unlikely time and place.

Achieving physical dominance through firepower is perhaps the single greatest difference between the contemporary definition of maneuver warfare and the tenets of Forrest war. General Forrest stated when describing his thirtieth victim in personal hand-to-hand saber/pistol combat: "You know, if that young fellow had had sense enough to give me the point, I wouldn't be here right now; but he tried to slash, which was his last mistake."

Military commanders today should recognize Forrest's symbolic intent: sophisticated movement will never compensate for failure to give the enemy "the point."

War is a grim and bloody business. Maneuverists seem to forget this fundamental fact. Clever schemes to gain the enemy's flanks or rear may appear eloquent and even delay the day of reckoning, but sooner or later the shooting must begin. As the Germans discovered again and again during Operation Barbarossa in Russia during World War II, bold maneuvers did not disconcert Soviet soldiers. In fact, the Red Army continued to resist even when surrounded and often succeeded in getting out large bodies of troops. Soviet soldiers, cut off in severe weather for days at a time, lay without shelter on the frozen ground in defensive positions until a breakout or exfiltration could be successfully accomplished.

Failure to recognize this hardiness and professionalism in our most dangerous adversary and his relative immunity to being "dislocated" by flank attack or even encirclement is the maneuver school's greatest error. Only after the shooting is well underway can the door to maneuver be opened with any guarantee of success against a competent adversary.

However, "giving 'em the point" through vicious application of firepower can unhinge even professional soldiers from their organizational security and ensure the disintegration that is required for total victory. Tough, not fancy, infantrymen are required for this task. Demonstration of physical dominance through firepower sets the stage for moral dominance through maneuver—and successful maneuver produces the conditions required for the culminating phase of Forrest war—the pursuit.

In summary, Gen. Nathan Bedford Forrest's campaigns stand as fine examples of how inferior forces led by hardened commanders with proven character and reputation can dominate a larger enemy. The six characteristics or phases of Forrest warfare form a pattern of building blocks that prove devastating when properly woven together on the battlefield.

So, while maneuver warfare advocates continue to press the Marine Corps to radically change its traditional mode of operations, perhaps the more prudent action would be to have confidence and believe in ourselves, to resist the current vogue, and to remember that at the core of every conflict is a rifleman, whose every attack will be frontal and brutal, and whose weapon is for killing, not for maneuver. The more effectively we institutionalize this truth in the souls of all Marines, the better able we will be to fight, maneuver, and pursue on the battlefields of tomorrow.

Initiative in Battle: Past and Future

Col. Douglas A. Macgregor, USA

Marine Corps Gazette
August 1997

It is the capacity for constructive initiative in battle that gives a force irresistible fighting power. Cultivating that capacity should be a primary peacetime goal.

Serious students of modern warfare understand that a host of factors contribute to success in battle. Focusing on only one aspect of effective warfighting—in this case the exercise of initiative in battle—potentially risks skewing the analysis and missing other factors of equal or greater importance.[1] Yet, initiative is a recurring theme in military literature. In the U.S. Army's doctrinal writings, initiative is defined as action that sets or changes the terms of battle.[2] In the U.S. Marine Corps' warfighting doctrine, junior officers are encouraged to make decisions on their own initiative based on their understanding of their senior's intent.[3] In the Army and the Marine Corps, initiative requires the decentralization of decision authority in combat to the lowest practical level. In offensive operations, initiative entails never allowing the enemy to recover from the initial shock of the attack. In the defense, initiative implies an offensive spirit in the conduct of all operations while negating the attacking enemy's initial advantages.

Without oversimplifying the problems associated with the exercise of initiative in battle, this essay argues that while it may not be possible to win wars at the company or battalion level, it has always been and will continue to be possible to lose them there. This is, in part, because the successful exercise of initiative in battle is inseparable from the adaptation of methods and tactics to the chaotic and rapidly changing nature of warfare.

Blindly following the orders of higher headquarters cannot be the guiding principle of platoons or teams, let alone battalion task forces, in future war.

In fact, new weapons and digitized communications technology will not fulfill their promise of shaping the future battlefield to American advantage if everyone in the chain of command waits passively for orders and is not trained to take the initiative—to

notice, to anticipate, and to exploit opportunities. As long as warfare remains explor-
atory in character, it will never be possible to foresee all contingencies, nor will the planning structures abstracted from the battlespace ever coincide precisely with conditions
in combat.[4]

For realtime information and intelligence to be of any value in future battle, tactical
leaders will have to be trained to exercise their initiative, to act decisively and often
without orders or permission from higher headquarters. Just as it is necessary to move
beyond deliberate planning to rapid decisionmaking based on limited and time-sensi-
tive information in the training of military leaders, it is equally important to develop
the capacity of junior officers and noncommissioned officers to act independently
and frequently without orders, but within a known tactical and operational mission
framework.

To some readers in the U.S. Army and the U.S. Marine Corps, these observations
will seem dated. Instantaneous communications are becoming so responsive and the
faith in the infallibility of surveillance technology and precision-guided weapons so
widespread that many contemporary military leaders are concluding that the responsive, but unimaginative military technician is all that will be needed in future war.[5] With
the ability to control from afar in realtime, the inclination among many senior military leaders will be to do so constantly. This is, of course, an oversimplification of the
problem. However, it is against this background that a discussion of initiative in battle
must begin.

Old Concerns, Current Realities

In theory, military leaders who exhibit initiative are much sought after commodities. In
practice, this is rarely the case. This is because initiative is, for the most part, only evident
in action when there is little or no time to seek and receive guidance from higher headquarters. In fact, it is always the absence of time that compels the responsible military
leader to act, and to act immediately when information or plans are overtaken by events.
However, without the opportunity to exercise initiative in training, the possibility that
officers, noncommissioned officers, and soldiers will do so in combat when initiative is
essential is always remote.

Today, advances in microcircuitry, directed energy, and materials are creating a new
dilemma for the Army's senior leaders. A brief look at what current observers inside
the Army say about initiative in training is illuminating. One former senior observer/
controller (OC) at the National Training Center (NTC) stated recently that:

Commanders are not taking risks. We continue to see cookie-cutter approaches with regard to tactics, like keeping two up and one back ... that generally results in frontal attacks instead of any really innovative or risk-taking effort on the part of unit commanders.[6]

In an article published in the *Washington Times* on May 30, 1996, Lt. Gen. Theodore G. Stroup, USA, assistant chief of staff for personnel, referred to anecdotal accounts from the field of "stifled initiative, lack of trust of subordinates, and a culture that overemphasizes perfection."[7] It is clear that inhibiting initiative and innovation at lower levels is not a uniquely Russian problem.

To combat the obstacles that traditionally obstruct the development of initiative in the Army's officers, noncommissioned officers, and soldiers requires an understanding of the many reasons for the apparent gap between the theory and practice of exercising initiative. First, given the opportunity to remain quiet as opposed to taking a risk and being wrong, most American military leaders prefer to keep a low profile. Officers and noncommissioned officers learn early that to raise one's profile in training by doing things successfully in a new way or to question the plans or views of a superior is always hazardous. Why? Displaying initiative is a risk, because if a decision to act differently from the norm is incorrect, liability is placed immediately on the person who made the decision, and as Lieutenant General Stroup implied earlier, the sanctions for doing things differently or making a mistake are likely to be hard on a soldier's career. In other words, when rewards in terms of promotion are structured to emphasize efficiency and control in a centralized decisionmaking environment, it is difficult to avoid imposing sanctions for violating established norms in what is really a low-risk situation.

Second, military leaders who do not display initiative are frequently a comfort to their commanders. Contrary to popular belief, military leaders in war or peace who are willing to risk action—the essence of initiative—are viewed with considerable apprehension. In contrast, military leaders who urge caution and conservatism are always welcome additions to any planning meeting or counsel of war.

Third, military leaders who display initiative are usually a mixed blessing for large military organizations that thrive on stability. Given the choice before the outbreak of the Civil War of serving with George McClellan, who exemplified the qualities of caution and conservatism, or Thomas Jonathan (Stonewall) Jackson, almost nobody in the U.S. Army's high command would have chosen Jackson over McClellan. Although Jackson possessed considerable originality, energy, intelligence, determination, and tenacity, those very traits that made him a gifted soldier and commander ensured that he would be, at the same time, a demanding leader and a difficult man for superiors to work with. The same would be said later of Gen. George S. Patton, Jr.

These points not withstanding, when professional understanding, intelligence, self-confidence, and a strong will are united in one person, the exercise of initiative in battle produces stupendous results. As the word is applied in this context, however, initiative is not the result of an untutored individual response based on a sudden, creative impulse. Rather the successful exercise of initiative in battle involves recognizing the relationship of an individual's personality attributes—physical and moral courage, intelligence, and character—to developed professional expertise and making decisions under the adverse conditions of combat that will contribute to mission success. In this sense, the exercise of initiative presupposes a concrete knowledge of the higher commander's intent, tactics and weaponry, extraordinary self-confidence, and a willingness to accept responsibility for taking actions that were neither planned in advance nor ordered by higher headquarters.[8]

Developing the Capacity for Initiative

Communications is at the heart of command and control in modern warfare. Advances in communications technology continue to extend the range of coverage, the reliability, and speed of modern communications. The U.S. Army is nearing the point when a digitized shared situation map at every level—battalion, brigade, division, and corps—will fuse near realtime intelligence with near perfect friendly situational awareness.[9] At the same time, the greater the ability to control, the greater the desire to do so at every echelon of command and control. In fact, the emphasis in contemporary Army training on the leading role of the commander in all activities makes it very likely that commanders at every echelon will seek to carefully plan and control the actions of their subordinates. It is safe to assume that the struggle for dominance between the commander on the scene and the responsible higher command authority remote from the scene of conflict will remain a significant source of conflict within all future military organizations. But to believe that the wars of the future, thanks to dramatic advances in such fields as computers, microwave transmission, and remotely controlled sensors will be less opaque and therefore more easily conducted by remote control is sheer delusion.[10] In the course of describing the chaotic nature of warfare to his readers, SLA. Marshall explains why:

In combat almost nothing has the appearance of juncture and of hanging together. Viewed from above, an attack would appear not unlike the disparate movements of a colony of water bugs. The first effect of fire is to dissolve all appearance of order. This is the most shocking surprise to troops who are experiencing combat for the first time. They cannot anticipate the speed with which their own forces become fractionalized or the extent to which the fractions will become physically divorced from each other as the movement is extended and enemy resistance stiffens.[11]

Today, the situation is not much better. Although the effects of fire on armored and air mobile forces may or may not be as great in the future as the effects of fire on dismounted light infantry in 1944, the probability that combat will be sudden, swift, and unpredictable makes the half-life of useful information and intelligence on the tactical and operational levels potentially quite short. More simply stated, if people are not prepared to exploit tactical opportunities based on realtime information without first gaining permission from some higher headquarters, realtime information probably won't make much difference. General Bruce Clarke, commander of Combat Command A, 4th Armored Division, during World War II, made the point directly: "That's why you've got to get your senior ground force commander to give you his final goal, not a bunch of phase lines. Once you're rolling, any break in the game may give you the opportunity to go all the way. In three, four, or five hours, you may be able to grab off what he has scheduled for three days. So make him tell you the final goal. Saves lives and a lot of grief and bloodshed." [12]

Far from determining the outcome of future battles, sophisticated communications and information processing will only shape the environment in which decisions involving the exercise of initiative will have to be made. Martin van Creveld argues in his work *Command in War* that transcending the limitations of new communications and weapons technology will necessitate rather than obviate the need for initiative in battle:

> In war, given any one state of technological development, to raise decision thresholds and reduce the initiative and self-containment of subordinate units is to limit the latter's ability to cope on their own and thus increase the immediate risk with which they are faced; in other words, greater certainty at the top (more reserves, superior control) is only bought at the expense of less certainty at the bottom.[13]

These points suggest that while a brigade or battalion task force commander can create the conditions conducive to victory in battle through leadership and training, once the battle begins, the commander's ability to influence the critical events that will determine the eventual outcome will be quite limited. No commander is capable of leading an entire unit in combat whether it is a company or a division. More important, modern technology is pushing the human mind to and beyond its normal limits of comprehension. Computers, satellites, signal intelligence of all forms, and instantaneous communications already create a situation in which far more information is available to a unit commander at any level than he can possibly digest in the time available. And this situation will not improve in the future. This is a fact of life in combat that was well-known to the Germans in the interwar period and which supported a training doctrine that relied for its success more on the quality of its junior officers, noncommissioned officers, and soldiers than on any particular weapons technology.

Anyone who had the privilege of leading American combat soldiers under fire during Desert Storm will attest to the high quality of American manpower in Army and Marine combat units. Is there any reason why a philosophy combining new technology with high-quality American manpower cannot also shape the structure and content of contemporary training in the Army and the Marine Corps?

Ready for Change?

In order to obtain a more initiating training structure and command climate, it is necessary to give soldiers at the lowest level more decisionmaking authority and much broader input into the command and control of their units on a regular basis than is presently the case in most American military formations. As the following example will illustrate, when American combat soldiers' freedom of action is less restricted, their performance is impressive. Consider this example:

> Task Force (TF) 1-77 Armor rotated to the NTC for the first time in March 1983. Initially, the unit's performance against the opposing force (OpFor) was poor. One of the TF's elements, Company C, participated in two successive operations that resulted in dramatic defeats for the Task Force. Although they played a minor part in these actions, Company C's troops and its commander were notably depressed by the events. When the third mission order was received for a deliberate defense, Company C was positioned in a traditional "goose egg" battle position near an outpost in the NTC's southern corridor. A mechanized infantry platoon was supposed to join them, but maintenance difficulties prevented it. Preparations for the defense went ahead without them. A few hours after preparation for the defense had already begun, a private from the third platoon showed his platoon sergeant a dry stream bed on the extreme flank of the battle position along an old impact area that allowed for the concealed approach of enemy armor. The platoon sergeant promptly called the tank company commander and urged him to look at the stream bed. On seeing the stream bed, the company commander thanked the soldiers for their suggestions and changed the disposition of Company C's 16 tanks. Instead of occupying the battle position on the overlay, the company commander extended his line of defense for nearly 2,000 meters to cover the approach on the right flank. The commander and his dismounted tankers then physically placed 600 mines in an angular

belt nearly 700 meters in length designed to drive attacking forces from the stream bed into the center of Company C's engagement area. When the tank company commander informed his TF commander of what he had done without consulting him, the TF commander grudgingly approved the change saying that he was prepared to try anything after the last two mission failures. The next morning, 123 OpFor vehicles were destroyed in less than 38 minutes in front of Company C's unorthodox position.[14]

At first glance, initiative in battle seems to be in conflict with the interests of synchronization and control. Yet, without the opportunity to develop a working relationship inside the organization that welcomes broad input and independent action to cope with changing circumstances, synchronization and the technical expertise to engage and destroy the enemy would have made no difference to the outcome in this example. Today, however far reaching the influence of information age technology may be, the assumption that technology will always work in anyone's hands or substitute for human judgment and intelligence is a prescription for failure.

But the major obstacle to exploiting the initiative of subordinates is not information age technology! It is more likely to be the absence of trust between echelons of command arising from a sense of discomfort in senior commanders with independent subordinates. Instead of trusting subordinates to exercise judgment and exploit opportunities, many of history's unsuccessful wartime commanders simply preferred to hold subordinates "liable" for their actions. Only repetitive training that emphasizes improvisation on the basis of known human and technological capabilities in the face of the unexpected can instill the initiative that frequently lies dormant in today's American soldiers. Without oversimplifying the issue, a possible formula far developing the capacity for initiative in battle that embraces the elements outlined in this essay might look like the following:

Computer simulations and field training exercises can all be structured and exploited in conformity with this equation to produce constructive initiative in battle. Commanders can create opportunities in training for subordinate initiative or they can exclude it from the menu. Opportunistic situations can supplant "no win" scenarios. Near realtime intelligence can be provided and commanders can practice exploiting it. Emphasizing the skilled employment of fires and forces to ensure that every enemy is attacked from at least two directions simultaneously and compelling subordinates to break the rules in order to win are additional ways for today's combat troops to avoid the "cookie cutter solution" mentioned earlier. A deliberate training approach to develop soldier initiative can result in constructive initiative based on trust in the chain of command, in new technology, and in greater individual self-confidence.

Concluding Thoughts

In the words of Frederick the Great: "To advance is to conquer!" Blind indeed is the commander who fails to understand this simple formula for victory and who suppresses rather than develops subordinates who seek to advance! Almost always, the pivots of strength in combat are those with the skills, intelligence, character, and physical courage to exercise initiative. Today initiative on the tactical level is still vital because modern firepower compels ground forces to disperse as well as to accomplish a multitude of complex tasks within a given mission.

To dismiss the emphasis on initiative in training risks reducing future joint task forces to inert masses; paralyzed, rather than empowered by new communications technologies and access to realtime information and surveillance. "Digitized communications" has the potential to magnify the problem of over-elaboration of detail in excessively long orders with the result that subordinate leaders enjoy little freedom of action or decision. Or digital communications technology, such as the commander's digitized, shared situation map, can potentially facilitate the swift changes in position and tactics at the lowest level that will support dexterity on the operational level. Still, this involves subordinate initiative "pulling" combat forces into action at the point of the sword, rather than fighting the detailed plan provided by higher headquarters at the expense of battlefield opportunism on the tactical level.

And while initiative in battle will never be enough to win wars on its own, without initiative in battle, victory is unlikely. Nothing contained in the record concerning the true performance and impact of surveillance technology and precision guided weapons in Desert Storm suggests that greater reliance on these capabilities in the future to substitute for initiative in battle will work in the future.[15] As the U.S. Armed Forces discovered in Vietnam, an increase in the responsiveness of applied firepower through digitized communications will not translate automatically into positional advantage in a tactically rigid and centralized command climate. Information age technology can augment, but not replace the American soldier's capacity for initiative in battle. This problem manifested itself when a container ship, the SS *Mayaguez*, was seized by armed forces of Cambodia's Khmer Rouge Government in May 1975.

In 1975, recently developed global communications structures in the Department of Defense created the notion that higher commanders who were remote from the scene of the action could exert the synchronizing influence on the conduct of Marine operations to liberate the SS *Mayaguez* from Cambodian control. The airborne command and control platforms jammed with sophisticated communications technology that orbited in the skies over the Cambodian coast convinced senior Navy and Marine officers that they could coordinate Marine combat actions on the ground, direct accurate fire support, and impose order on the untidy combat operations below them.

The opposite turned out to be the case. As noted by John F. Guilmartin in his excellent study of the action, instantaneous communications that are exploited for the purpose of micromanaging tactical operations from operational headquarters do not result in more effective command in battle or a more precise application of force: "No amount of communications can replace a competent and responsible commander on scene. To attempt to do so is to invite disaster."[16] Contrary to expectations at the time, it turned out to be Marine initiative in battle that averted disaster and rescued the *Mayaguez*.

Having said this, American fighting forces will only do in war what they have learned in prewar training. And while there is plenty of confirmation in the historical record that American enlisted men, noncommissioned officers, and junior officers can exercise initiative and make good decisions under the pressure of combat, there is also a lot of evidence to suggest that they will only make the right decisions if they are trained and encouraged to do so before the war begins.[17] This is because action without specific orders from higher authority requires independent judgment. But it is unrealistic to expect that American military leaders will demonstrate the requisite physical energy, mental agility and moral courage to inspire subordinates to enthusiastically cooperate and exercise initiative in battle if they have never been allowed to do so in training.

To achieve the aim of developing leaders in training who will exercise initiative in battle, American military leaders at every echelon must (as always) be prepared to share the danger and discomfort of close combat with their soldiers, support and promote unconventional and often difficult subordinates that accept danger, demonstrate initiative, take risks and devise new ways of accomplishing assigned missions. These are not easy tasks for today's senior military leaders, but the benefit to the combat troops in the Army and the Marine Corps will be a degree of internal simplicity that permits rapid adaptability in the face of constant change.[18] And, most important, the capacity for constructive initiative in battle at every level, as well as across Service lines, will guarantee that future joint task forces will be living organisms, endowed with irresistible fighting power.

---

1. Robert M. Epstein, *Napoleon's Last Victory and the Emergence of Modern War*, (Lawrence, KS: University Press of Kansas, 1994), p. 183.

2. U.S. Army Training and Doctrine Command, *FM 100-5*, (Washington, DC: U.S. Government Printing Office, 1994), p. 2–6.

3. *FMFM 1, Warfighting*, (Department of the Navy, Hqtrs USMC, Washington, DC: U.S. Government Printing Office, 1989), p. 62.

4. The author is indebted to Dr. Fred Kagan, assistant professor of military history at the U.S. Military Academy for his suggestions contained in this paragraph.

5. Thomas L. Friedman, "The No-Dead War," *New York Times*, 23 August 1995, p. 21.

6 Lt. Col. G. Chesley Harris, IN, "Topic: Battle Staff Proficiency," in "Notes from the Box: A Directed Study Project of the Army War College, Senior O/C's Observations and Comments on Training for Success," *CTC Quarterly Bulletin,* 4th Qtr, FY95, No. 95-11, September 1995, p. II–20.

7 "Report Shows Distrust Prevalent Within Army," *Washington Times,* 30 May 1996, p. 4. Also see Patrick Paxton's "You Will Not Fail: Fear of Mistakes Throttles Initiative in the Ranks," *Army Times,* 12 February 1996, pp. 12–15.

8 Mary Zey-Ferrell, Arlene Parchman, and Jerry Gaston, *Initiative and Innovation in the Soviet Military,* (College Station, TX: Center for Strategic Technology, The Texas Engineering Experiment Station of the Texas A&M University System, 1984), p. 7.

9 Col. Patrick Lamar, USA, Lt. Col. Billy McCollum, USA, Lt. Col. John A. Collier, Jr., USA, Maj. Edwin Kuster, Jr., USA, "Battle Command Battle Laboratories: Where Tomorrow's Victories Begin," *Military Review,* May–June 1996, pp. 58–59.

10 Martin Van Creveld, *Command in War,* (Cambridge, MA: Harvard University Press, 1985), p. 266.

11 SLA. Marshall, *Men Against Fire: The Problem of Battle Command in Future War,* (Gloucester, MA: Peter Smith, 122978), p. 90.

12 William Donohue Ellis and Col. Thomas J. Cunningham, Jr., *Clarke of St. Vith: The Sergeants' General,* (Cleveland, OH: Dillon/Liederbach Inc., 1974), p. 166.

13 Martin van Creveld, *Command in War,* p. 274.

14 The author was the company commander in this incident.

15 See Tim Weiner's article: "Smart Weapons Were Overrated, Study Concludes: War Boasts Were Wrong, Review of Persian Gulf Combat Questions Priorities of Pentagon's Arms Policy," *New York Times,* 6 July 1996, p. A1 and A14.

16 John F. Guilmartin, *A Very Short War: The Mayaguez and the Battle of Koh Tang,* (College Station, TX: Texas A&M University Press, 1995).

17 Hirsh Goodman and W. Seth Carus, *The Future Battlefield and the Arab-Israeli Conflict,* (New Brunswick, NJ: Transaction Publishers, 1990), p. 141.

18 Gen. Hermann Balck, "Observations Related to Moral Conflict," quoted by Col. John R. Boyd, USAF, in an unpublished manuscript entitled: "A Discourse on Winning and Losing," August 1987.

Command Relationships in the MAGTF

Col. E. F. Riley, USMC

Marine Corps Gazette
July 1985

A close look at the MAGTFs organization reveals disparate command entities that need to be more closely bound if the Marine Corps hopes to fight as an effective combined arms force.

Marine forces are formed into Marine air-ground task forces (MAGTFs) for combat operations. A MAGTF consists of a command element (CE), a ground combat element (GCE), an aviation combat element (ACE), and a combat service support element (CSSE).

Three sizes of MAGTF may be formed: a Marine amphibious force (MAF), Marine amphibious brigade (MAB), or Marine amphibious unit (MAU). This article will focus on the MAF, the largest of the MAGTFs. Similar organizational concepts are embodied in all three MAGTFs. Changes identified for the MAF would be equally adaptable in other MAGTFs. Matters uniquely affecting the MAB or MAU will be addressed by exception.

The MAGTF, a MAF in this instance, is created to form a combined arms team (i.e., to optimize the combatant power of the force by combining its elements in a way that provides an exponential enhancement to the capabilities of the force as a whole). Stated simply, this has been termed the synergistic effect, meaning that the whole—the combat power of the combined arms force—becomes greater than the sum of its parts.

The Problem

It requires but a cursory review of the MAF organizational diagram to sense that its elements are not organized in combination, but rather as distinctly separate entities, albeit under a common commander. Also, since each of its elements (division, etc.) is commanded by an officer directly concerned with but one characteristic of the force (i.e., ground maneuver, aviation, combat support, etc.), the MAF commander, organization- ally, is largely a mediator of competing interests. In the vernacular of management, it is a "dysfunctional" organization. As shall be seen, there are processes at work in the MAF, formal and informal, that help to overcome these otherwise awkward relationships; but other more fundamental changes are needed.

The purpose of this article is to analyze the form and processes of the MAGTF and to propose changes that will make it a more efficient and combat effective organization. The principal concern throughout is with relationships between the ground and aviation combat elements of the MAGTF. These relationships have been a longstanding contentious issue in the Marine Corps, but they have rarely been discussed in open dialog.

The institution of Marine aviation has, for much of its history, resisted any command relationships that would subordinate aviation to the ground commander. The present MAGTF structure is a concession to these sensitivities and exists as it is in order that the aviation combat element under "normal" circumstances will be insulated from the decisions of the maneuver (infantry) commander. The roots of these differences have been amply recorded by Lt. Gen. Vernon E. Megee, a retired Marine aviator. Two examples should suffice. Writing on air-ground relationships before Korea he notes:

> There also appeared an alarming tendency (to the aviators) to treat helicopter squadrons as attached aerial motor transport units, with little consideration for the element in which they operated or the problems of maintenance entailed.

And, discussing differences between Army and Marine helicopter pilots flying in Korea, and the latter's superior training for all-weather operations:

> Strangely enough, there were ground officers who failed to appreciate this significant difference, and there was some advocacy of making helicopter units an integral part of a Marine division, to be flown by hastily trained aerial truck drivers.

Interestingly enough, some five years after those words were written, and twenty years after the attitudes they describe, a group of thirteen field-grade officer students of the Marine Corps Command and Staff College published their proposed revisions to Fleet Marine Force (FMF) structure. Among their observations:

> The current Marine command organization reflects a long-standing compromise which appears to violate the principle of unity of command. . . . Air and ground elements remain divided into distinct commands controlled by ad hoc headquarters . . . [which] . . . control only one ground maneuver element, with staff duplication resulting at both levels.

Their resulting proposal was that " . . . certain air assets, particularly helicopters, [be] . . . assigned directly to the division commander" as part of a division aviation command.

More recently, a group of twelve company-grade officer-students from the Marine Corps Amphibious Warfare School and Communications Officers School, studying the topic of force structure, proposed that each MAF have a smaller combined arms force organized within it, with the aircraft wing providing helicopters in direct support of the force.

My point in straying to these examples is first to illustrate that these are disagreements of long standing and, second, to provide some measure of support for my contention that a change is needed in MAGTF relationships to bring aviation into the fold. I will now return to the topic of aberrations in doctrine.

The Present MAGTF Structure

The purpose of this section is to examine the current MAGTF structure and highlight just a few of the aberrations in doctrine that flow from the traditional MAGTF structure.

Roles of MAGTF Elements

The GCE is the ground-gaining instrument of the MAGTF commander. In the case of the MAF, this element will usually be a single division. But in that instance, since there is only one maneuver element available to the MAF commander, he is limited to giving broad mission-type directives to his subordinate ground and air commanders. It is the division commander who provides the concept of operations and does the detailed maneuvering of subordinate ground elements. Similarly, the MAF is without the means to constitute a reserve without robbing from the maneuver elements of the division. Consequently, the division reserve is routinely referred to as the MAF or landing force reserve as well. This is but a cosmetic repair to a serious flaw in organization, for the reserve, as with the other maneuver elements, can only be responsive to one commander.

The ACE of the MAF is a Marine aircraft wing (MAW). It performs six functions, to include antiair warfare, assault support, electronic warfare, reconnaissance, etc. Each function has its own character, ranging from combat (as in the case of fighters) to CSS (as in the case of photo recce squadrons). The generic term most applicable to the role of the MAW as an entity, however, is "combat support." This view is reflected in doctrinal publications as well. FMFM 0-1, *Marine Air-Ground Task Force Doctrine* (pp. 1–2), for example, discusses ". . . Fleet Marine Forces of combined arms, with supporting air components. . . ." The term appears again in FMFM 5-1, *Marine Aviation* (p. 5), which states, "The primary mission of Marine Corps aviation is to participate as the supporting air component of the FMF. . . ." The point is more than semantical, since at issue is the proper relationships among elements of the MAGTF. It will be noted that the present term, "aviation combat element," connotes a distinctly separate and co-equal entity, in partnership with the GCE and dedicated to combat in a different medium. It is a term that is at odds with operational reality.

The CSSE performs supply, maintenance, and service (e.g., laundry, medical, etc.) type functions for all elements of the MAGTF, including itself. There is no unmanageable problem with the relationship of this element to others, except that the MAGTF commander, to whom this element and the others are subordinate, is not now the supported commander, a significant flaw in the existing MAGTF organization.

The supported commander is the principal recipient, or user, of combat support and combat service support. The supported commander owns the forces that require support (as opposed to the supporting commander who, obviously perhaps, owns the means of providing the support). The supported commander is best qualified to prioritize available support where there is a shortfall in meeting all requirements since, as operational commander, he can best assess support requirements. It is an unfortunate feature of the present MAGTF structure that the lines of authority are vertical—MAGTF commander to three separate elements—while the lines of support are horizontal, i.e., element to element. It is for this reason that our doctrinal publications are replete with emphasis on the need for cooperation among the elements. However important cooperation might be in any organization, it is a term better applied to interpersonal relationships than command arrangements for combat, where unity of command is the preferred axiom.

Supporting Fires

Fire support for the MAFs maneuver element is provided by the division's organic artillery regiment and by the aircraft wing of the MAF. Here is another aberration. On the one hand, the maneuver commander owns his support, on the other he does not. Fire support coordination centers (FSCCs) are created at battalion, regiment, and division levels to integrate indirect fires and air support of all types. The direct air support center (DASC), a control agency of the MAW, is collocated with the division FSCC to manage air support of the GCE. The system is time-tested and can work quite well, but it is not without flaws:

The MAF commander, lacking the means to establish an FSCC, is reliant on the division to coordinate supporting fires. While provision is made, doctrinally, for the division FSCC to function concurrently as the MAF FSCC, this arrangement, like the matter of the MAF/division reserve, is unworkable since the FSCC can be responsive to but one commander.

In the amphibious operation the commander amphibious task force (CATF) coordinates supporting fires via his supporting arms coordination center (SACC). Prior to passage of control to the commander landing force (CLF) ashore (the MAF commander in this example), the SACC is augmented by Marine personnel of the "landing force" FSCC. As previously noted, however, this center is in reality an agency of the GCE (division) commander. Thus, the MAF commander has relegated a measure of his coordination responsibilities to a subordinate, while CATF, his superior in the operation, can exercise effective oversight through his own SACC. Recognizing this shortcoming, the Marine Corps in recent years has devised yet another patch-job called a fire support information center (FSIC), which as the name implies enables the MAF (landing force) commander only to monitor the status of fire support but still denying him any effective means to control/coordinate it. I would maintain that these arrangements, afloat and ashore, fail to provide the MAF commander the degree of control necessary to exercise the responsibilities implicit in his charter, which as noted in LFM O-1, *Doctrine for Amphibious Operations*, pp. 7–4, states:

> Establishing at the beginning of planning, at each appropriate level of the landing force, a fire support agency for the discharge and implementation of landing force coordination responsibilities throughout the planning phase and execution of the operation . . . [and for] coordinating the requests for artillery, naval gunfire, and air support for the landing force.

MAGTF Headquarters Functioning

Doctrinal publications devote many words to defending the rather odd relationships that flow from the current MAGTF structure. FMFM O-1, *Marine Air-Ground Task Force Doctrine*, for example, states:

> The MAGTF staff extends and complements the capabilities of the headquarters of the major elements of the MAGTF, but should not duplicate them under any circumstances... [no FSCC, etc.]. . . . As the senior Marine commander . . . [in an area of operations] . . . the MAGTF commander has responsibilities in the areas of civil affairs, combined, and joint operations. . . . The establishment of separate air-ground headquarters permits subordinate commanders to direct their attention primarily to the command of their respective elements. . . .

The suggestion here is evident, perhaps, but deserves some restatement for clarity. Between the lines, it is saying: (1) The MAGTF commander should not meddle in affairs better left to his subordinate commanders, and (2) he has sufficient external responsibilities to otherwise busy his headquarters, thereby relieving his subordinate commanders of such distractions to their combat operations. These notions appear with different shadings throughout our doctrinal publications.

It should now be noted that MAGTF doctrine also provides for the assignment of more than one GCE to the MAGTF, i.e., two or more divisions and two or more MAWs to a MAF. When these additional assignments are made, doctrine acknowledges that the MAF commander becomes the maneuver commander, establishes an FSCC in his own headquarters, and must be prepared to assume broader responsibilities. There is an implicit contradiction in logic here. That is to say, if the MAF commander's external responsibilities in the first instance are so great as to become the focus of his concern and to have justified the establishment of his separate air-ground headquarters to deal with them, how is it that the commander of a MAF that is two or three times larger can accept the additional burden of more direct control over maneuver, combat support, and combat service support?

Limitations of the Staff

In concept, a MAGTF headquarters contains the MAGTF general/executive/special staff, service elements, and communications assets to enable its commander to meet his responsibilities for command, control, and coordination of integrated air-ground operations; coordination with higher, adjacent, and supporting commands; and logistic/CSS of the MAGTF.

In addition to the staff's limitation in the area of fire support coordination during operations previously discussed, a second major limitation is the area of planning. Since the MAGTF is austerely staffed and functions as an extension or complement to subordinate element staffs, there is much duplication of effort in the planning process for an operation. Fire support planning provides but one example.

The fire support coordinator (FSC) heads the fire support planning and coordinating agency, the MAGTF FSCC. As I have discussed earlier, this agency in fact is an organ of the GCE, not the MAGTF headquarters. But, since the MAGTF commander is responsible to the CATF for planning fires in support of the landing force, the FSC must sell his fire support plan to two commanders, the division commander (in our MAF example), and the MAF commander (or CLF), and to a third, CATF, if his needed concurrence is considered. It is important to note too that air-delivered fires must first be incorporated into the plan through negotiation with the MAW staff, a partner in the process rather than subordinate agency, by current relationships. The Education Center teaches a sixteen step process for use in developing the plan. This is far too cumbersome, but is representative of the ponderous staff procedures engendered by current MAGTF commander relationships.

Intelligence-Operations Mismatch

The overall intelligence effort is planned, coordinated, and directed at the MAGTF level. The G-2 will have available to him portions of every collection agency in the Marine Corps. The section will tend to be large. On the other hand, since primary responsibility for the conduct of ground operations in the MAGTF area rests with the GCE commander (the supported commander), it is the division's G-3 that must be, and is, best staffed and equipped for command and control. The MAGTF G-3 has but a limited capability for the planning and supervision of operations. What results is a mismatch of key functions: intelligence centralized at the supervisory level and its functional counterpart, operations, coordinated from a subordinate level.

Alternative to the Current MAGTF

What are the qualities that should be embodied in the organization of the MAGTF?

Above all, it must be made a true combined arms team. Brigadier General P. P. Henderson, in a visionary piece published in the *Marine Corps Gazette* in July 1971, coined the phrase, "tactical space of responsibility (TSOR)" as a substitute for the then in vogue, "tactical area of responsibility (TAOR)," observing that in future warfare:

> ... Traditional distinctions between ground and air functions, responsibilities and units will diminish and blur. What was once black and white will become gray. . . . In tri-dimensional warfare, the control and use of the airspace over a tactical unit is inseparable from the control and use of the "ground space" (terrain), and both must be the responsibility of commanders with tactical missions. . . . The range of options in an amalgam of ground and air elements is broad and the forces of inertia and status quo resisting such a union are strong.

The point is clear. Weapons systems of all platforms and media must be applied as one, in the measure and combination suitable to the threat, and as the extension of a tactical commander's will. The tri-dimensional concept is not new. The Marine Corps' airground forces exist because of it. What is new is the growing recognition that airground combat has long since evolved from a requirement for *complementarity* of force into a requirement for fusion of force.

A second essential characteristic, implicit in the first, is that the MAGTF must be organized for unity of command. It must function as an efficient entity—ideally, under proven vertical lines of authority to a single maneuver commander at the apex.

A third characteristic is that it should be organized for the efficient exercise of command, control, and support through a simple, unlayered staff organization responsive to but one commander, while supportive of others, and with assistants/selected staff principals empowered to direct action in the commander's name.

With these characteristics in mind, and recalling the command relationship depicted in Figure 1, which will not change, let us now discuss the elements of an alternative MAGTF, one that might function with greater effectiveness in future combat.

Maneuver Commander

A distinction must be made here in clarification of the term, "maneuver commander," which has come to be associated with bi-dimensional ground warfare, wherein a commander, through two or more subordinate commanders, moves ground-gaining forces in such a manner as to gain a tactical advantage over his enemy. In tri-dimensional warfare, warfare as it exists today, this perception of the maneuver commander must be expanded to include MAGTF aviation as a maneuver element, moving and fighting in the third dimension in support of ground maneuver. The MAGTF commander, therefore, is properly the maneuver commander in the tri-dimensional combined arms warfare. An ancillary, but equally vital benefit: he would thereby become the supported commander as well, since lines of support would turn from horizontal to vertical.

MAF Command Element

The MAF would be commanded by a lieutenant general temporarily dual-hatted as division commander during the life of the MAF. As it is a combined arms team, it could be commanded by either a ground officer or an aviator, but the present MAF and division headquarters' staffs would be integrated into a single MAF/division level staff to eliminate duplication of effort, pool resources, and enhance efficiency. Command of the ground combat would reside with the MAF commander (maneuver commander).

The division's administrative and logistical ties outside the operational chain, however, would remain undisturbed, and its history, traditions, and heraldry preserved. The MAF commander would command the maneuver regiments directly, perhaps utilizing his major general, assistant MAF commander (maneuver) (AMC(M)), to exercise close supervision over the GCE. The MAF commander would command air maneuver through the wing commander, who would, for reasons of centralized control, airspace management (not fire support coordination), and coordination of Marine aviation with other Services, remain the MAFs tactical air commander (TAC), exercising supervision over air maneuver for the MAF commander, while the latter retained responsibility and ultimate authority.

MAF GCE

The GCE would remain intact, but with the present intermediate level of command (division) removed and command consolidated in the person of the MAF commander. I would anticipate some anguish from span-of-control purists. My counterpoints to them would be: (1) MAGTF concepts of the 1960s and before employed air-ground teams-Marine expeditionary forces (MEFs), etc.—without a separate common head-quarters being superimposed over the two elements, but with the command element of one exercising operational control of the other element and coordinating the command effort; (2) span of control challenges would be further reduced with the MAFs task organizing for amphibious operations, e.g., regimental landing teams (RLTs) would absorb a large measure of the assets of the separate battalions and the artillery regiment; (3) Sun Tzu said, "... Generally, management of many is the same as management of few. It is a matter of organization." Therefore, the AMC(M) will have full time employment, just as the wing commander remains the TAC.

MAF Aviation CSE

Command relationships are changed in that the MAW is permanently organized under MAGTF configuration, responsive to the maneuver commander for operations and combined training, while retaining administrative and logistical ties as they existed previously. Note that the name would be changed from ACE to ACSE (aviation combat support element) to more accurately depict the functional relationships within the MAGTF and to the supported commander.

MAF CSSE

Command relationships are changed in the same sense as with the ACSE.

Marine Amphibious Corps

With reorganization of the MAF as described, a fourth-type MAGTF would need to be devised in the remote likelihood of a requirement for an organization of two or more division/wing teams. It could best be referred to as a Marine amphibious corps (MAC) per World War II terminology. Its structure would be somewhat more scenario-dependent than other MAGTFs in that the proximity of its MAFs' areas of operations would drive its configuration (e.g., centralized or decentralized control of aviation being but one key decision). In most conceivable instances, its command element would probably be a FMF headquarters.

Alternative MAB

Current peacetime concepts of the centralized management of like assets below the division/wing level are probably the preferred arrangement prior to receipt of a mission requiring organization for combat. That is to say, there seems to be no compelling advantage to permanently organized MABs, when weighed against the disadvantages. I do, however, advocate there being at least one permanently staffed MAB headquarters in each MAF.

The MAB is commanded by a brigadier general, temporarily dual-hatted as regimental commander during the life of the MAB. As maneuver commander, he exercises command over the three battalion landing teams (BLTs) and all other components of the GCE. The regimental commander serves as assistant brigade commander (maneuver) (ABC(M)) during the MABs existence. He and his former staff provide the necessary continuity in transitioning to a MAB headquarters. The headquarters staff is formed by synthesis of the regimental staff with the staff cadre of the MAB headquarters. Other aspects of the MAB concept parallel those of the MAF.

Alternative MAU

The MAU concept mirrors that of the MAB, except that permanently staffed command elements would be required for each forward-deployment commitment of the MAF.

The alternative MAGTF structures suggested here have promise in resolving some problems in fundamental command relationships among elements of the MAGTF. They have, in varying measure, all the characteristics deemed essential to the combat effectiveness of a combined arms team, while, in transitioning from the MAGTFs more familiar form, forfeiting none of its positive, combat-proven qualities.

Conclusions

It will be noted that, in the development of alternative MAGTFs, the requirements for assets held by separate units of the FMF (communications battalion, force reconnaissance company, etc.) have not been addressed. Certainly the MAF command element would require some slice of these units; I did not consider it essential to my purpose to treat the issue in that detail. The establishment of a permanent MAF headquarters in command of forces in garrison is but one of many matters bearing closer scrutiny. Since it is by present doctrine an operational headquarters in the Fleet commander's chain, possibly some roles and missions pitfalls would be encountered in its being superimposed over service-owned forces before their chop to the Fleet.

Readily admitting that I held a preconceived notion of the conclusion I would reach—a notion some twelve years in the making—I must quickly add that my research on the subject has only served to reinforce my belief that the Marine Corps must soon confront the air-ground issue head on. I recall that as a student at the U.S. Army Command and General Staff College some years ago, my section was undergoing instruction on the employment of FMFs. The instructor's wiring diagram of the MAF's organization had been on the screen for only seconds when the Army major next to me turned with a quizzical look and asked, "What does the MAF commander do?" I was hard pressed for an answer, and remain so after my research. Whatever the Army's shortcomings, they understand command relationships.

My conclusion is that the alternative MAGTF structure discussed in this paper has greater merit than the existing organization.

A final word drawn from Brigadier General Henderson's *Gazette* article seems in order:

> Faces change like men. Some cherished institutions and practices are inevitable casualties in the continual process of change that typifies any vigorous, self-renewing society. When fact and logic clearly show that the proper place of some things is not longer on the battlefield but in history books, send them there (with honors) to join the Roman Legion, the British thin red line, the cavalryman's lance and saber, and the aviator's leather helmet and goggles. For this often traumatic experience, draw both courage and consolation from St. Augustine's words, "Let those be angry with you who do not know with how much anguish truth is sought."

The initial draft of this article was written in 1981 when the author was stationed at the Naval War College. Colonel Riley died on August 14, 1984 while serving as G-4, 7th MAB at Twentynine Palms.

Marine Forces: Ready and Relevant For the 21st Century

Lt. Gen. Bruce B. Knutson Jr., Lt. Gen. Earl B. Hailston, and Maj. Gen. Emil R. Bedard

Marine Corps Gazette
July 2000

Our role is clear, our readiness is high, and we provide a capability that is not duplicated by any other force.

In recent months, there appeared in these pages a number of entries comparing the role of the Marine Corps in national security with the roles of the Army and the Air Force. In "Still the 9-1-1 Force?" (April 2000), Col. Mark F. Cancian speculates that our routine peacetime commitments exhaust our resources, leaving the Corps little to dedicate to larger scale contingency operations, thereby diminishing the value of our contributions. Also, in a two-part editorial entitled "Watching the Army" (March 2000 and April 2000), the editor of the *Marine Corps Gazette* expresses the view that the Army transformation will result in the creation of new power projection forces that will duplicate existing Marine Corps capabilities. We feel compelled to respond to these concerns.

The Army Transformation

Regarding the Army transformation, while it is true that the program is intended to bring improvements to the strategic mobility and mission flexibility of Army forces, this does not equate to an attempt to duplicate the capability of the Marine Corps. It is, instead, a recognition that the heavy forces designed to fight outnumbered and win against a mechanized Soviet/Warsaw Pact army on European battlefields are not optimized for the missions that are now almost routine in the post–Cold War world. Because the Cold War Army's forces were largely forward based, standing prepared to fight on the ground they occupied, strategic mobility was not their major concern. But, as Colonel Cancian points out, the world has changed, with crises requiring military intervention arising in disparate and widely separated regions. The Army is adjusting to meet this new requirement.

Fiscal resources for national security are scarce, yet the requirement for agile and mobile military forces has not diminished concomitantly. Under these circumstances, there are plenty of missions to go around for all forces capable of getting to the fight, and the Army transformation is intended to enhance the ability of future Army forces to project land combat power. While the particulars of this transformation plan will probably evolve over time, we should support its underlying philosophy, and encourage the Army in its quest for change.

The senior leaders of the Marine Corps and the Army clearly recognize the value of dose cooperation between our two Services. In mid-May, the authors participated in the first "Army-Marine Corps Warfighting Conference" at Carlisle Barracks, Pennsylvania. Conceived by the commandant of the Marine Corps, this event vas intended as a forum for the senior leadership of both Services to discuss critical issues. Not only did it succeed in achieving that aim, but it also demonstrated the spirit of teamwork between the commandant of the Marine Corps and the chief of staff of the Army that was noted by the editor of the *Marine Corps Gazette* in "Editorial: Watching the Army" (March 2000). This collegial relationship contributed to a productive and professional exchange of ideas and has opened doors leading to further potential collaboration between the Army and the Marine Corps. As part of that process, the two Services are committed to coordinating our plans for future warfighting capabilities to avoid wasteful and unnecessary duplication, such as that described in the editor's columns cited above.

Our Role in National Security:
The Unique Contributions of Naval Forces

Colonel Cancian asks whether the Marine Corps is contributing effectively to the nation's security needs. He cites recent history, offering some critical observations, which can be summed up in his statement that ". . . Marine Corps participation in . . . contingencies has been severely limited in duration or scope." One of Colonel Cancian's concerns is that forward deployed Marine forces minimize time spent committed ashore, focusing instead on their "presence" mission, to the extent that they might disengage from a contingency, leaving it to other forces, in order to reembark for follow-on missions. This is true. It's important, however, that readers of the *Gazette* understand why this occurs.

The answer, simply put, is that the commanders in chief of the unified commands (CinCs) want and need it that way. They recognize the utility of presence as a tool for crisis response, shaping, and deterrence, and they value forward deployed naval forces as a means of implementing their respective theater engagement strategies. Forward presence is both an aid to the maintenance of a stable international environment, as well as an important symbol of U.S. commitment. While our special operations capable Marine expeditionary units, i.e., our MEU(SOC)s, are certainly capable of operating ashore for an extended period of time, this is not always the best use of an asset whose greatest value lies in its credible potential for immediate action, a capacity that can actually defuse problems before they reach crisis proportions. The CinCs wisely choose to use that potential by capitalizing upon the special characteristics of forward deployed naval forces—presence, versatility and scalability of power, flexibility, credibility, sustainability, and affordability. When an emerging crisis is addressed, defused, and reduced in scope to a constabulary mission, for example, it is wasteful to engage a MEU(SOC) for a protracted period of time in an operation in which its unique characteristics become diminished.

But if not a MEU(SOC), then why not other Marine forces based in the United States or overseas? Colonel Cancian argues that the Marine Corps is not able to deploy large combat formations with the same frequency as the Army and the Air Force, because the requirement to source rotational deployments keeps the Corps "on the ragged edge," and "with no capacity to spare for the unforeseen." We disagree. While there are certainly different levels of readiness among units, and while it is true that the exigencies of deployment schedules account for some of these differences, it is inaccurate to characterize Marine forces as either ill-prepared or lacking in the ability to deploy large, combat ready Marine air-ground task forces (MAGTFs) on short notice. The forward deployed MEU(SOC) has always been considered the "Tip of the Spear," enabling the introduction of an amphibious or maritime prepositioning force Marine expeditionary brigade (MEB), an air contingency MAGTF, an entire Marine expeditionary force (MEF), or joint and allied forces. We plan for this, and we are prepared to execute.

As Colonel Cancian points out, the Marine Corps was able to deploy over 12,000 Marines to Somalia on very short notice. Given that there has been essentially no change in operational tempo since that time, it is clear that we still retain the capability to deploy a similar force with great rapidity. Further, what might not be as well known about the Somalia operation is the fact that I MEF was prepared to deploy as many as 20,000 troops, but the initial requirement was reduced by the CinC.

Consider Operations Allied Force and Noble Anvil. Although Colonel Cancian is correct in noting that the preponderance of U.S. forces employed by USCinCEur in Kosovo were provided by the Army and the Air Force, we must set the record straight on a few of his points. First, the "late-arriving air elements" he so quickly dismisses, were, in fact, over six squadrons of aircraft—a not inconsiderable number, given the proportionately smaller size of the Corps. They arrived when the CinC wanted them, and all played a significant role in the air war. 26th MEU(SOC) went ashore after the signing of the military terms of agreement, acting as one of the first elements to enter the theater. Further, II MEF planned operations in that theater and was fully prepared to deploy and execute those plans.

Even more recently, the 3d MEB command element deployed to support peace-keeping operations in East Timor, and plans were drafted to employ all of III MEF in this operation. While the situation did not require a major commitment, the fact remains that the plan was fully developed, and the MEF was prepared to deploy on short notice to undertake the mission.

In sum, we question the accuracy of Colonel Cancian's claim that the Corps is teetering on any "ragged edge." The Operating Forces of the Marine Corps remain at a high state of readiness. We continue to maintain our scheduled deployments of MEUs, our unit deployment program rotations, and our participation in exercises, yet, when the trumpet sounds, we remain capable of deploying large, combat-ready MAGTFs of any size, on short notice, for operations of any duration. The fact that such a deployment has not taken place in a few recent contingencies is not in any way an indictment of the Corps' ability to answer the nation's call, and it is certainly not evidence of a trend.

We are most intrigued, however, by Colonel Cancian's remark about the Army's Task Force Hawk, deployed to the Balkans last year: ". . . those troops are still there, separating factions, rebuilding the society, and maintaining the peace." This type of mission, while important, is not the one for which we organize, train, and equip our Marine Corps. Marine forces committed to such an operation for the extended periods of time Colonel Cancian proposes would find their warfighting skills and capabilities decaying steadily. Should the Marine Corps seek involvement in any and every mission that comes along, simply for the sake of getting a "piece of the action"? We don't think so. Instead, we should—and do—advise the warfighting CinCs how to best employ Marines to balance available forces with overall theater requirements.

A Concluding Observation

The Marine Corps is secure in its role. We are a major force provider, fielding 20 percent of the nation's ground maneuver battalions, 20 percent of the fighter squadrons, 17 percent of the attack helicopters, and about a third of the ground combat service support capability in the active establishment. Compared with the other Services, this is, by any measure, a disproportionately large contribution to the nation's defense needs. The forces we provide are combat ready: prepared for any mission, across the well-known spectrum of operations. Claims to the contrary are without basis, and Colonel Cancian's image of a "hollow" Marine Corps is simply a chimera.

The CinCs appreciate their Marine forces. In any unified command situation briefing, the location and status of the theater's deployed MEL(SOC) is always a critical item of information. Our MEB command elements, although only recently reestablished, are already demonstrating their utility. In the recent Exercise Dynam-ic Mix, 4,300 Marines and Sailors of 2d MEB deployed to Greece, where they conducted a partial maritime prepositioning force offload. Further, our MEFs are assigned significant missions—involving large forces—in existing plans. There is no question that Marine forces are full partners in joint operations; all CinCs have voiced considerable interest in the deployment and employment of Marines within their respective areas of operations.

Having said this, there is an area that is in need of work. Often, it appears that some staff officers assigned to unified commands lack an accurate understanding of Marine forces. We must remain alert to the need to educate our counterparts in the other Services—and our allies—on subjects such as MAGTFs, maritime prepositioning forces, and the capabilities Marines bring to any operation. This is an "all hands" effort. By striving to eliminate confusion, we can help to bring clarity to joint and combined planning, and ensure that available Marine forces are assigned appropriate missions that leverage their strengths.

The Marine Corps has a richly deserved reputation for superb performance in any mission, small or large. Our role is clear, our readiness is high, and we provide a capability that is not duplicated by any other force. The Marines and Sailors of our Operating Forces have earned the confidence and respect of our CinCs, sister Services, and allies. This record of excellence is one of which we can all be justly proud. Rest assured that we will continue to uphold it as we move forward into the future.

The authors are the commanding generals, respectively, of the I, III, and II Marine Expeditionary Forces.

Parting Word

Gen. Lewis W. Walt

Leatherneck
May 1971

With the passing of years, our Marine Corps continues to add new luster to its laurels as it fulfills its dedication to strengthen our national security. Marines have always fought well and effectively. What Marines of the past fought to secure, we have inherited.

What makes the Marine a superior fighting man? Why has he never failed to successfully accomplish his mission? A man entering the Marine Corps is no better than the society from which he came. Men fight well only because of pride; pride in themselves, their service, and their traditions. This, coupled with training, ensures our continued success. The results are a fighting Marine who is disciplined and has a fervent desire never to let down his fellow Marines.

Today, however, the Marine Corps is entering one of the most critical periods in its history. Our Corps is confronted by new challenges unparalleled by any faced before.

The country reeks with a growing disenchantment with its armed forces. While this sort of event has occurred after past wars, this time it seems worse. Attacks have been directed against our oldest traditions. We are faced with a future in which the military is held in very low esteem.

We find, even without our "band of brothers," an internal disenchantment. In recent years, this unrest has been fed by a fundamental breakdown in our concept of the "team effort." Every Marine and his family has to feel a part of the team. This, then, makes our internal effort to communicate Marine-to-Marine our most critical problem. We must continually search for better ways to communicate with and understand every Marine in our Corps.

It is impossible to compress the traditions of almost two centuries into this brief article. Our Marine traditions, history, and uniform with its Globe and Anchor make the Corps what it is. For years our heritage has set us distinctly apart from other military organizations.

Clausewitz once said, "One who is seeking a profound understanding of the fundamentals of war must understand esprit de corps. This spirit is the cement which binds together all qualities which taken together give an army military value." Although "order, skill, a certain pride, and high morale are highly prized peacetime qualities, . . . they provide no spur to excellence or sacrifice." Clausewitz also said, a capable commander is required to lead such an army "with the utmost of care, until gradually, victory and exertion give it real strength, real fighting spirit."

At the very base of this fighting spirit is patriotism, or love of country . . . the cement that binds a people together and assists their fighting men. Without it, neither our country nor its Corps of Marines will have a soul. The founders of this nation gave us as Marines two great documents—The Declaration of Independence and the Constitution. In these two great works are the ideas and principles upon which patriotism in this country is built.

Every Marine starts his tour swearing to defend the Constitution against all enemies, foreign or domestic. It is time this solemn ceremony was given greater emphasis. It should be accomplished with all the pomp and circumstance possible under prevailing conditions. This act is where our young Marine meets his first tradition and starts down the road of understanding his Corps.

The accomplishments of the Marine Corps in both peace and war have been outstanding. Future Marines for years to come will gain inspiration from the record of the past. During the comparatively short span of American history, the Corps has fought brave and skilled professionals in every "Clime and Place." These operations have ranged from desperate hand-to-hand engagements with savages equipped with bows and arrows to vast island battles against modern forces.

Marines can also take great pride in the schools and roads we helped to build. Today's Marines can be proud of their pacification successes as well as their battlefield victories.

The Marine Corps has been a training ground for scholars, educators, and statesmen who have made great contributions to every phase of our national life.

A knowledge of its accomplishments can play a vital role in the strengthening of esprit de corps in our Corps.

An eminent British military historian once said, "Without knowledge of their past, soldiers are really unconscious of the existence of the most wonderful of moral forces." Certainly this applies as well to soldiers of the sea. It is something of which none of us can afford to be ignorant. Marines are informed of past heroic deeds starting in boot camp.

Accomplishments of the Quicks and Basilones are expounded in the *Guidebook for Marines*. Many of our posts and stations are named for distinguished Marines of the past. Colors and standards are decorated with streamers carrying the names of battles and campaigns in which the unit has honorably participated. From reveille to taps, our days are inspired by tradition. Such things can be turned to the commander's advantage by those who will take the trouble to weld the deeds of the past to the task of the future. If successfully accomplished, Marines will continue to function in the best traditions of the past.

For hundreds of years, mankind has had the unique ability to adapt, to change, to help civilization better survive the challenge of the times. We must as Marines continue to adapt, but we must also remain steadfast in support of fundamental principles.

Ours is not an easy time or age. Nothing has ever stood still. Even if it did, it would do no good. The thing that makes our time especially difficult is the speed and universal nature of change. We look for firm ground and find only shifting sands. The Corps will need a sense of stability and purpose.

Ships, men, and weapons change, but traditions can neither be bought, sold, nor destroyed. Tradition has always been a solid rock amidst shifting sands. Where tradition is found, you also find responsibility and purpose.

As I depart the active ranks, I challenge each of you to undergo a critical self-examination. Gauge the real temper of the Corps, identify its strengths and weaknesses, and arrive at the hard-core needs of the new professional Marine of the 1970s. You who remain face the same challenge as the Marines who went before us. Each of you, of all ranks, must continue to fulfill your responsibility to your junior Marines, your Corps, and your country. With the Marine Corps' future resting solidly on old traditions and new equipment, I am confident you will meet any challenge, any time, any place, under any circumstance. I bid you farewell and wish for your travels a following sea.

Index

fitness reports, 204

flag, 146

Flanders, 102

Fleet Marine Force (FMF): anticipation
of, 53, 64; aviation, 118–23;
description of division, 109–17; fire
support, 112–13, 118, 124–31, 228–30,
233, 234n1; Henderson with, 185;
leave, 168; organization, 26–29, 44,
229–30, 260–62; and tactical decisions,
200; and training, 140, 224; workload,
172. *See also* Advanced Base Force

Foch, Colonel 76

Foch, Marshal, 9

"Foot Cavalry," 8

Forbes, Mr. 30

Force Troops of the Atlantic, 229, 233

Forest de Retz, 33

Forrest, Nathan B., 241–48

Fort Benning, GA, 59

Fort Fisher, NC, 51

"Forward . . . From the Sea," 237

Foss, George E., 221

Fourth Armored Division, 253

Fourth Brigade, 31, 34, 59, 100, 101, 151

Fourth Marines 39

Fox, Wesley L., 162

FRAM program, 228–29

France, 1, 15, 30–35, 38, 73, 99–103

Franco-Prussian War, 73

Frederick the Great, 73, 256

Ft. Donelson, 242

Fullam, William F., 50, 52–54, 56, 58, 65n1,
214–17, 219, 220–22

Fuller, Ben H., 48

G

Gaba Tepe, 85, 91, 98

Gaieski, John, 136, 137

Gallipoli, 21, 24, 25, 27, 80, 83–85, 98

Garand rifles, 39–40

Gates, Joseph, 134

Gauls, 30

General Staff Study, 80

Generation X, 152–53

Georgia, 242–44

Germany, 30–35, 39, 68, 73, 76, 101, 193,
248

Gettysburg, 30, 189

Gibraltar, 27

Gilbert Islands, 228

Goldsborough, 27

Goodrich, 56

Gouraud, 35

Grant, Ulysses S., 8–9, 48, 194

Gray, Al, 162

Great Depression, 39

Greece, 26, 274

Greene, W. M., Jr., 224, 230

Greenwood, John E., 135–36

Grierson, Benjamin, 245

Guadalcanal, 40, 146, 185, 191, 195, 210

Guam, 146, 225

Guantanamo, 40, 146

Guidebook For Marines, 197, 198, 201, 276

Guilmartin, John F., 257

gun-barrel population, 228–29, 233

"gun gap," 224–34

H

Haas, Walter, 136, 137

Haebel, Robert E., 4

Haiti, 31, 39, 103, 107

Hale, Eugene, 59, 221, 222, 223

Halls of Montezuma, 146

Hamilton, General, 80, 83, 84

Hannibal, 12

Harbord, General, 32, 59

Hawaii, 22

Heinl, Robert D., Jr., 43, 185, 211

helicopters, 41, 111, 117, 118, 121, 129–31,
260, 261. *See also* aviation

Helles, 91

Helm, 56

Hemphill, J. N., 52

Henderson, 31

Henderson, Archibald, 46–48, 146

Henderson, F. P., 162, 184–90

About the Editor

Charles P. Neimeyer is director of the History Division, United States Marine Corps, Quantico, Virginia. Previously he was executive director of Regent University in Washington, D.C., and before that academic dean and professor of national security affairs at the Naval War College.